LET THE NUMBERS GUIDE YOU

THE SPIRITUAL SCIENCE OF NUMEROLOGY

SHIV CHARAN SINGH

BOOKS

Winchester, UK
New York, USA

Copyright © 2004 O Books
46A West Street, Alresford, Hants SO24 9AU, U.K.
Tel: +44 (0) 1962 736880 Fax: +44 (0) 1962 736881
E-mail: office@johnhunt-publishing.com
www.o-books.net

U.S. office:
240 West 35th Street, Suite 500
New York, NY10001
E-mail: obooks@aol.com

Text: © 2004 Shiv Charan Singh

Cover design: Krave Ltd., London, U.K.
Text design: Jim Weaver Design, Basingstoke, U.K.

ISBN 978 1 903816 64 6

A CIP catalogue record for this book is available
from the British Library.

Printed and bound by CPI Group (UK) Ltd, Croydon, CR0 4YY

Preface

In April 1996 I met Yogi Bhajan to discuss the numerology I had been researching since my teenage years. I described how I had been working with it and he put me to the test immediately by asking me to interpret the numbers of his date of birth. This I proceeded to do and within a few moments he interrupted me to say that what I was doing was **Karam Kriya**. He went on to describe this practice further through a discussion about time and our relation to time and space and with a drawing of a tree where each part of the tree related to a part of the date of birth. The organic image of the tree and the name Karam Kriya resonated immediately as I felt how it synthesized more then twenty years of my intensive study and contemplation of this most universal but also mysterious language of numbers. It is through his inspiration and encouragement that I have written this book.

Acknowledgments

I am grateful for this opportunity to acknowledge the chain of the teachings through the teacher. Yogi Bhajan, whose outpouring of practical, spiritual wisdom is beyond measure of value, has been a great source of inspiration for me and has consistently and unremittingly pointed the way to awakened consciousness and the discovery of God within and without.

Some of the material in this book is based on the teachings of Yogi Bhajan in reference to the ten Spiritual Bodies and a system for interpretation of the date of birth; any misrepresentations are my own responsibility. The presence of additional material is the outcome of my extended research and is not felt to be in conflict with Yogi Bhajan's teaching. My descriptions of the numbers in relation to the ten Bodies and their positions are a summary of my own experience and observations.

The material in this book has been put together thanks to the encouragement and instruction of several other teachers; the Chinese Master who will not be named but, amongst other things, helped me deepen my understanding of the numbers in relation to the elements and the different grid arrangements and the many students who continue to teach me in various ways. My thanks also to my extended family who keep me down to earth and to the mystical poet Guru Naanak whose words and sacrifice keep my spirit exalted.

Finally my appreciation to all at O Publishing, especially John Hunt, for recognizing the value of the material and taking the risk and a special thanks to Maat Barlow for dedicating endless hours to editing the material.

Contents

Section three

Section four

Section five

Appendix

Introduction

As a teenager I enjoyed the whole idea of magic but, as may be natural to a human creature of that age, it was the manifestations and the capacity to fascinate others that so attracted my attention. I set out to investigate the laws of magic and enjoyed the illusion of power that came from knowing things about my friends and enemies that they did not seem to know about themselves. Irresponsible as I may have been it was, nonetheless, clear to my investigative intelligence that there was a common language behind all systems of mystical, magical, and esoteric knowledge. That common language is the language of number.

Yet even within the world of numerology there are different systems of interpretation and use that exist. Egyptian numerology specialized in sacred geometry and divine proportion in building. Chinese numerology examined the space within the building and the numbers of time cycles. Hebrew numerology studied the link between letters and numbers and gave birth to the Kabala. Indian numerology was more abstract and metaphysical, studying the planets and astrology.

Pythagoras was one of the first teachers who had enough vision to see the all-pervasive existence of numbers as the base to every form of study. He brought the attention back to numbers and called on them to illuminate all aspects of life. Yet again and again as systems like the Kabala, Feng Shui, the Tarot, and the Eneagram came into being the focus shifted to the systems themselves and how they could be used, while the numbers that had been their foundation faded into the background.

So it was that a few years later, after a series of adventures into the darker sides of magic, coupled with the deepening insight into the gullibility of the average human being, I started to question the ethical aspect of what I was involved in. These questions led me to abandon the world of man-made magic and to explore the nature of the magic that made man; in other words a spiritual search. I saw that every religion builds up its teaching on the same backbone of numbers. I stopped being interested in the yin yang polarity, the three deities, the four truths, the five passions, the six states, the seven chakras, the eight limbs, and the nine initiations. Instead it was the numbers themselves that called me to honor them, to listen to them and to align with their innate nature without thinking what I could do with them.

It was the teachings of Guru Naanak and the humility that was the foundation of his life that touched my heart in a way that corresponded with my innermost being. Guru Naanak was the founder of the Sikh way of life and was succeeded by nine other masters or Gurus, leading to the completion of the teachings in the form of the scripture known as the Sri Guru Granth Sahib. The Sikh scripture contains a most universal, spiritual teaching in a beautiful, poetic verse written by Hindu and Muslim saints as well as the gurus from the lineage of Guru Naanak. The very first passage that Guru Naanak wrote and which sits at the beginning of the scripture starts with the number 1. It declares the unity of the entire created creation.

With some signposts from my Kundalini Yoga teacher, Yogi Bhajan, I then realized how the existence of the ten Gurus, each praising the magic that made man, showed the way for a marriage between the study of number magic and a spiritual ethic. Wishing to place this in a modern context led me to establish the Karam Kriya School of Applied Numerology.

The message is not new but needs to be renewed again and again. The greatest knowledge is not a secret that can be withheld by those wishing to manipulate it, nor is it a secret that must be withheld to prevent it from falling into the hands of potential manipulators. The true knowledge is an open secret that is available to all and does not lend itself to abuse. Only our misunderstanding that creates obstacles like pride, shame, fear, and doubt stop us from accessing this knowledge. In other words, it is a secret that we keep from ourselves.

In writing this book I have aimed to offer an introduction to the numbers, describing them through their innate properties and the way they manifest in the world. In this first section, to emphasize the ethical and truly human dimension, I describe the 10-in-1 being, the possible human. This is done through a brief account of the ten Gurus, whose life examples emulate the greatest expressions of mastery, each corresponding to one of the numbers. It includes a description of the ten Spiritual Bodies that make up the total constitution of every living person. In the second section you will be given an opportunity to verify the correspondence between number vibrations and your life experience by practicing a simple system of date of birth analysis. The third section invites you to explore some techniques to resolve the tension given through these ten facets of yourself by proposing suggestions in which you can initiate yourself towards your own mastery. You are then shown ways of applying your number awareness in the fourth section using the most basic concepts of the house, organs of the body, and stages in your life-cycles. Finally there is a concluding chapter for those who wish to research deeper into the spiritual psychology implied in the practice of Karam Kriya.

Shiv Charan Singh

Section one

Chapter 1

Numbers:
the foundation

The fulfiller of wishes

With numbers I can have
More or less
By virtue of the nine
I can be near or far
By the magic of numbers
I believe I am high
Or low
I can make a wish
And count my blessings
Numbers are the stepping stones
To cross the difference between
What we are
And what our soul aspires to be
When a wish is a command
Then numbers will direct
The genie will change shape
And the mirror of empty time
Gives you
What you want
Beware

There is no secret to knowing numbers, they are themselves the secret. Numbers are the formula of all formulas and the rule behind the rule, the spiritual ground of our very existence. Life has its problems and applied numerology is a unique solution. Numbers are seen as a problem until we understand them, then they become the means to solutions. Every problem has its numbers and when you know the numbers of the problem you are half way to solving it. Solutions are basically formulas that tell you how to put together the numbers in such a way as to find the answers to your questions.

Intuitively we can sense that there is something to numbers. They have a strong potential although we do not know what it is. Yet it is more common to be skeptical about the idea of numbers determining or even influencing the course of events or our personal nature. Given the conflict between our fear of and desire for freedom, as well as our fears of being controlled and our need to believe we are in control, this is quite understandable, but let's reflect on a few things.

There is one God and this number influences everything. If you had one eye your view of the world would be different enough to determine how you lived your life. Likewise if you had three legs, eight nostrils, or any other strange combination of limbs and sense organs, then your whole experience of reality would be modified. The numbers on the money in your pocket decide what you can and cannot buy, as do the number on your credit cards. Even in the times before money existed, exchanges required numbers – so many pigs for so many sacks of peanuts. The number on your passport may prevent you getting out of the country or it may allow entry into foreign lands. People get in touch with you by the number on your door or your telephone number. You know your age because you know the numbers of your date of birth.

If we go on listing all the areas of our life where numbers provide the base we will find that there is not much left untouched by number. Numbers are the origin of and foundation for the development of many fields of human endeavour and research. Every philosophy, every political, social and philosophical system and every culture is built on the same backbone; number is their common ingredient.

Here are some examples:

10 sephiroth of the Kabala, 10 Spiritual Bodies.
9 treasures, 9 initiations, 9 virtues.
8 limbs of yoga, 8 spokes on the wheel of dharma.
7 chakras, 7 steps to heaven or hell, 7 seals, 7 trumpets, 7 soul types.
6 sides to the dice.
5 elements, 5 senses, 5 passions, 5 types of thought.
4 boons, 4 directions, the 4th state (neutrality), the 4 noble truths of Buddha.
3 qualities of energy in the world, 3 dimensional space, the Hindu and Christian trinities and others.
2 polarities of male/female relations – yin and yang.
1 soul, 1 God, 1 spine, 1 tongue.

The numbers are like a coat hanger upon which we hang the decorative ingredients that make each one appear different. The common altar, the common language that all people bow to is number. In other words, numbers talk and in spite of all the arguments about quality, it is quantity that impresses the most since even most qualitative differences are measured in number. The truth is that we are not free until we consciously recognize, accept, and agree to the utter hopelessness and predictability of the human creature. Then on the level of the common spiritual ground of number anything is possible.

Numbers are a universal language. They cross all boundaries and have no standard expression but can be expressed in countless ways and through countless forms or symbols. Numbers are holistic in the sense that they illuminate the unity of the diversity. Furthermore, numbers are holographic in the way that, no matter the scale of our study, the same number patterns will be found in all fields of inquiry.

In order to work with numbers effectively we need to consider the nature of numbers themselves. Generally we may only know them through their material expression. The essence of number, however, is discovered by focusing on the twoness or threeness of things rather than on the content. For example, to know what is the same about five birds, five pens, and five people would be to know the fiveness. The number is the unchanging common essence amongst a world of changing appearances.

Our spiritual and material lives begin to converge when we let the world become transparent and tune into the invisible presence of the numbers. It means going beyond our normal rational way of thinking. We fear this step into abstraction, imagining it to be a complex problem. In truth it is a courageous return to break through the surface and rest again in the elementary, the simple.

Applied numerology is the activity of decoding the signs on the map of life. Then, knowing the first principles, you can transform your life and become a conscious 10-in-1 being. You can touch the central fiber of reality by the study of ordinary, everyday life through attention to the numbers. With practice you can discover these basic properties of the numbers. You will come to appreciate how they stand as the vibrational essence of all your practical, moral, and philosophical existence, both in the world around you and at the core of your being.

True numerology is not about quick fix solutions, fortune telling, winning the lottery, or finding your lucky number. Yet knowledge of number is a lifelong jewel that you can refer to again and again. By this study you will know the building blocks to a sustainable ecology of consciousness. If you try to understand them from a solely rational position then you will find it difficult to really hear what is being shared. Applied numerology asks you to make a different step so that the material in this book becomes a working manual rather than another piece of information that weighs you down. Numbers are light; it is our projections that make them seem heavy.

In our everyday use of numbers we take them for granted and view any deeper research as esoteric and obscure. The result is an almost forgotten language. It is through our intuition that we can remember the magic of numbers. Then with easy-to-use tools, such as the date of birth, we will have a window into their mystery. This book opens your awareness to the book of life and introduces the numbers as your teachers and guides.

The calendar structure of any culture is a formula of numbers that help to diagnose life's problems and to suggest new answers.

One remarkable thing is that every year on our birthday we are celebrating a number. In summary we need first to study the properties of each number and then to identify that same quality in ourselves. Then, as we come to know our self as a 10-in-1 being, we can explore the variations of our shared nature by reference to our individual date of birth. Here is a quick preview of the numbers that gives a sense of the soul's progression on its journey of awakening.

1 – The humble origin of each individual, feeling the impulse of existence and volunteering to take the first step.

2 – Immediately after the first step there is the duality, separation and hunger; the desire that becomes a spiritual longing and will empower the full circle of the journey.

3 – Development of personality and enchantment with things we meet on the way; also the capacity for positive action and the efforts to be a hero.

4 – Moments of awakening to Soul; becoming a chooser.

5 – Transformation; learning through reversals and the paradox of language.

6 – Being met by the grace of intuition; suspense, vigilance, and carefree responsiveness.

7 – The mantle of understanding enwraps you giving the elevated view from where forgiveness is natural.

8 – The healing of dying into deathlessness; not drowning but swimming in the ocean of infinity.

9 – Arriving home, the unborn essence, peace of the shore beyond – I lay me down.

10 – A natural and self-illuminating radiance; all light, all bright, glory and transcendent bliss.

11 – The communion of big I and little i (10 + 1); twins with God.

12 – The cycle repeats in its echo; you reflect it everywhere through all times.

Chapter 2

Becoming the
possible human

The human race is just emerging from a teenage phase. I say a phase because it is not the first time we have been here. Just like the seasons there is a cyclic repetition of our phases of being human.

What is it that distinguishes us as human beings? It is our possibility of free choice rather than behavior that is genetically programed, reactionary, or socialized. We are all here pretending to be choosers without knowing all the forces and laws that influence or govern our choice. The whole game of life is to practice and pretend until it becomes a reality. Then when we awaken to choice and opportunity we develop a conscious relationship to the spiritual. This might be through denial or a path of worship, but that relation exists whenever there is consciousness of choice. No one is good or bad but the seeds of all virtues and all vice are within us. These seeds are numbered.

The following chapters will take each number as if it is a seed unfolding and describe the problems that can manifest as well as give examples of the highest expression of each number. To help with your study of numbers through life and life through numbers we will approach it from the following different aspects:

- The natural magic of numbers, as introduced in the previous chapter.
- The ten Spiritual Bodies of your personal cosmos as taught by Yogi Bhajan.

- The lived example of the possible human through the Sikh Gurus.
- Sacred words to live by from the Mul Mantra of Guru Naanak.

The Ten Spiritual Bodies

My Kundalini Yoga teacher, Yogi Bhajan, first brought the insight of the ten Spiritual Bodies to my attention in 1982. Upon investigation in therapeutic environments I have found they are a most accurate method of describing the various manifestations of human behavior. The corresponding parallels between the ten Spiritual Bodies and the properties of numbers are extensive and so the study of each advances our insight about the other.

The ten Spiritual Bodies, like numbers, represent parts of our own nature. However, we are not completely in touch with all aspects of ourselves and an applied study of numbers and their expression through the ten Bodies is one way to reclaim our own spirit. In numerology it is common to think of the first four numbers, 1, 2, 3, and 4 as being related to the individual body consciousness or body-mind, whilst 6, 7, 8, and 9 are considered expressions of universal spirit consciousness or spirit-mind. 5 then is the number of communication, which connects all things to all things and particularly corresponds to the nervous system. 10 is the number of the circumference – it holds all the other parts together whilst remaining apart itself and being more than the mere sum of the parts. 10 is the light, which illuminates the whole universe and whose withdrawal would mean the withdrawal of all things. In discovering the self through these ten aspects, we realize we are a 10-in-1 being.

- SOUL, the innermost essence of being, a passenger through time and space.
- NEGATIVE MIND, an organic or vegetative vital system that is in a state of need.
- POSITIVE MIND, the creature-like body armor that works to fill the gap.

- NEUTRAL MIND, the possibility of conscious choice in relation to the world.
- PHYSICAL BODY, especially the inter-related expanse of the nervous system.
- ARCLINE, the halo of presence manifest in the world as intuition.
- AURA, the wider magnetic field for projecting ourselves into space.
- PRANIC BODY, the infinite fuel supply sustaining our temporary projection.
- SUBTLE BODY, the home of the soul's emanations.
- RADIANT BODY, when the whole ecology of our being is in dynamic harmony then not only are we transparently alight, but also we become a self-sustaining source of light and thus realize our immortality.

The Sikh Gurus

Over a period of 239 years, from 1469 to 1708, ten great beings successively incarnated in the physical form, each the carrier of the same light, the soul of Guru Naanak. Furthermore, each of these Gurus was a perfect embodiment of the numbers from 1 to 10. The eleventh and final Guru is, for the Sikhs, the scripture known as the Sri Guru Granth Sahib. The first passage of this holy text is Guru Naanak's description of the divine and is also understood to be the description of the qualities that lead us to know the divine. It is known as the Mul Mantra or root vibration of the mind. Each stage of this mantra was also a prophecy of a kind in which Guru Naanak was indicating the qualities of his successors. First there was the word and then the word became embodied in the flesh and blood of the lineage of the Gurus that followed. Then in the eleventh stage there is a return to the word.

As the eleventh Guru is the word itself we are taken back to the beginning, to the original word. It was through his words that the first Guru became recognized and known. The Word is the Guru and the Guru is the Word. Hence each of the sounds in the Mul Mantra is an embodiment of one of the Gurus and each of the Gurus, an embodiment of these words.

GURU combines two distinctions:
GU, a hidden or mysterious place, an inner cavern with buried treasure.
RU, removing the veil with a ray of light that shines into the shrouded arena of consciousness wherein lays the realization of the mystery.
An account of the lives of the Gurus will help to give a feeling for the human expression of the numbers. The descriptions of them are brief, however, for the purpose here is to illustrate their relationship to the numbers and the ten Spiritual Bodies.

The Mul Mantra, the root of the vibration of the mind

Through the sacred sounds of this mantra Guru Naanak indicated the path of human consciousness as it finds its way back to its original and divine state. When he spoke the Mul Mantra he intended that it could be recited so as to vibrate the mind as an instrument to bring one to the root of all things. The mantra is:

- EK ONG KAR – The one creator extended in all the creation.
- SAT NAM – True name.
- KARTA PURKH – The doer in all and the presence of being in all.
- NIRBHAU – Without any fear.
- NIRVAIR – No enemy or other historical complication.
- AKAAL MOORT – Timeless and undying in representation.
- AJUNI – Unborn; never takes birth through any womb.
- SAIBHANG – Self-illuminating, self-sustaining, and self-existing.
- GURPRASAD – By the miraculous grace of the mystery that is the Guru.
- JAP – Contemplatively repeat this and realize it in yourself.

This first part of the mantra relates to divine qualities and the consciousness that the soul cultivates as it journeys through life back home. Guru Naanak added a further passage that tells us how these qualities exist through four phases of time. Section Two, which focuses on the date of birth, will go into this second part of the mantra and the structures or cycles of time in more detail.

Below is a chart that summarizes the link between the numbers, the Spiritual Bodies, the ten Sikh Gurus, and the ten dimensions of consciousness as described in the Mul Mantra given by Guru Naanak.

NUMBER	SPIRITUAL BODY	SIKH GURU	MUL MANTRA	
1	Soul	Guru Naanak	Ek	1
2	Negative Mind	Guru Angad	Ong	2
3	Positive Mind	Guru Amar Das	Kar	3
4	Neutral Mind	Guru Ram Das	Sat Nam	4
5	Physical Body	Guru Arjun	Karta Purkh	5
6	Arcline	Guru Har Gobind	Nirbhau	6
7	Aura	Guru Har Rai	Nirvair	7
8	Pranic Body	Guru Har Krishan	Akaal Moort	8
9	Subtle Body	Guru Teg Bahadur	Ajuni	9
10	Radiant Body	Guru Gobind Singh	Saibhang	10
11	Radiant Soul	Guru Granth Sahib	Gurprasad	11
12	The whole is reflectively repeated in the whole creation		Jap	12

If you recognize aspects of yourself in the following descriptions of the ten dimensions of being human, do not be surprised for they are all the fundamental parts of your being. Fragments of ourselves are forever coming into being whilst others are continually falling out of being. There is no perfect middle way of becoming and unbecoming and each of us is finding our own unique path through experience and reflection of this process. However, there are some things that we all have in common since we are of the same species and on the same planet. We are all made of the same stuff and the variations are slight. Every human goes through the same natural learning process so no matter how much we aim to be different we remain always just another version of the universal blueprint. This multi-varied repetition of sameness is the JAP.

Chapter 3

Number 1

1 is alone; each 1 is unique yet its singular nature is common to all other units. As an individual it is undividable yet it is divided from all. 1 is the starting point, the origin and original, the beginning and the genesis. The birth of anything begins with 1, whether it is 1 step, 1 seed, 1 cell or 1 word. 1 is the creative cause, the primary and primal impulse, the original source. As the initial number it is a number of initiation and birth, the initial initiating initiative. It comes first before the others and is the essential essence and the very basis for everything. It is primal and primitive, the necessary foundation and the fundamentals of life.

1 is the basic building block for all other numbers. All numbers are a multiple of 1; it is the originator of all numbers. When we think of 1, its presence gives a feeling of unity; it is a unit that is united and undivided. It stands alone, by itself. It is one of a kind, dwelling in solitude, the sole soul, unique and rare. As the individual, it has an inwardness where everything is inside waiting to unfold. It is the seed carrying a potent potential and a latent impulse. 1 is in relation only to itself, never moving, always still, rigid, firm, and stable. It is the precise point, the localized location where everything is compacted and pressured into contraction and concentration. 1 multiplies to every other number, the anchor for all the numbers and the point of reference.

You have one body, one spine, one tongue, and one nose. There is one planet, one human race, and one of you. You can only go in one direction at a time, even if you try, or wish to go in many. To concentrate means to focus on one thing, to be one pointed. 1 is straight up, vertical, alert, and related to the ground. It is a totem to itself alone, lonely or solitary. 1 is the seed of individuality and the individual soul, the origin of the individual will to be and to do and the initiating source of any action of self-expression. 1 is the seed, containing the whole, waiting to unfold. It is the one road that all will ultimately travel, from the one to the One. It is the one will and the will of the One, not yet shaped into desires yet containing every desire within it.

1 is a point, a dot, and so relates to being focused and one pointed. It can be persistent and intimidating like the point of a needle that pokes and pricks, or it can be disturbing by the way it is fixed and does not move. On the other hand, the fixed nature of 1 can be a relaxed and stabilizing reference point. In its focused nature 1 is concentrated, dense, and potentially intense. It is a final point of convergence.

The first stage of the plant is the seed, which is very concentrated and contains all the potential of its multiplication without limit. The first element is earth and this refers to the solitariness of each rock, each mountain, each pebble or grain of sand.

Soul

The soul is what you are. When we say "put your soul into it," "give it soul," "soulful" or "with soul," we are implying more intensity, more real and so more of yourself. When more of yourself is gathered into focus then you have, or you are, within yourself a strong springboard for action. We need a base from which to push against as we express our existence in daily life. It is common to find this base externally or only partially internally. Part of the mysterious purpose of life is to gather up this inner focus toward the possibility of becoming a self-sustaining being. This is the individuation of the soul, a convergence of our spiritual essence. This essential aspect of our being gives rise to very particular expressions in our personality.

The soul is number 1, the seed of individuality and the individual, the origin of the individual will to be and to do and the initiating source of any action of self-expression. The law of the soul could be expressed in terms such as originality, individuality, survival, contracts, contraction, gravity, irrationality, genesis and genetics, will, intent, a drive of perfection, sabotage, and home.

The energy of the soul can be totally static, just a dormant potential waiting for the right moment or environment to unfold. Or it can be experienced as an itchy feeling that keeps us from being too lazy. It is an itch that comes from the inside that sometimes comes to the surface, just under the skin, and is so intolerable that it is impossible to stay still; it demands action to be taken.

At the potential start of any story or journey we may talk a lot about things we intend to do but never follow through with the deed. As a soul we may experience extreme loneliness or find the capacity to be at peace whilst alone. From our point of loneliness we seek co-operation and partnership in another's company. However, given the problems of relationship we may try to find solace by withdrawing back and preferring isolation. But a journey once started needs to be completed and the way back is by going through the whole circle. It is only then that the soul finds its own company is best but having completed the journey it also finds itself in all. Therefore, there is no isolation in keeping your own company.

The soul is the first (and by implication the last) point of call for consciousness. On the personal level we refer to it as soul while the impersonal level is referred to as spirit. Spirit is the quality of the Subtle Body and is discussed with number 9. The soul is the essence and the essential. Therefore, it is also the originator of everything around it, all action springing from within itself. We are referring to an inner springboard for all expressions of our existence. The action itself is a manifestation of the third body, the Positive Mind. Here, at the inner base of all action, we may get over attached to our ideas and refuse to acknowledge the value of anything other than our own impulses. When there is external pressure to act that is not congruent with the soul's own sense of its unfolding, then it is likely to put up a lot of resistance, electing to act in its own time and way, when it is ready and as if it was its own idea. This stubbornness, however, implies that great strength of will and determination is held in the seed of our being. When this strength of will is lacking it is important to develop some intensification in this first dimension to bring about awareness of Soul. However, if too much attention is spent on the personal will the seed may assume itself to be perfect before even embarking on the journey of life. Everyone else will be considered as imperfect and consequently one experiences great frustration in the flaws of others.

Being number 1 the soul likes to be in a position of spokesperson but this is only possible for itself, no one else. To express its independence and self-dependence is very important but getting the balance right is not easy. The soul may move between co-dependence at one extreme and an inability to co-operate and compromise at the other. This need may not be considered a problem, however, and it is for this reason that we have all the other Spiritual Bodies.

Incarnation is like the seed getting thrown to the wind of possibility and carried afar. The soul seed is at the mercy of the elements and may live as the virtue of humility or the virus of humiliation. Humility can become an excess of self-criticizm and in certain circumstances this leads to humiliation where the seed is crushed instead of bursting open into the next stage of development. When humble, a person with a strong soul can harmonize with and become the voice of the soul of a group (number 10) but without humility they will concentrate on themselves and disregard the interests of the group (which is called "looking after number 1"). It is worth recognizing that when someone is being very restless or obnoxious in a group they are more than likely exhibiting the first impulse of life. They may be trying to get a voice for individuality from a group that may well be ignoring the fact that it is individuals that make the community.

When we remember our soul we find great strength of will. It is the source of movement as well as the destination of all movement, the primal creative cause of the micro-cosmos of the human being. The persistence and resistance of the Subtle Body, described in detail later on, is intimately linked to the commitment of the soul to follow through in life. Self-determination and dignity of the individual's existence is based in a strong soul and it must work to explore the boundaries of its freedom and always from a principle of self-awakening. In this way humble appreciation of all other souls is embraced and maintained. The mature soul knows how to work in willing co-operation with the universal soul. It is able to take the initiative when needed, leading when necessary but without ever desiring leadership. Survival rides on a continuum that starts with individual survival. This is more dominant during the first stage of life and relates to the Soul Body as it has been described above. Species survival is at the other end, arriving at the ninth stage of life and expressing itself through the Subtle Body.

To exist in the physical world requires a contract and a contraction and the maintenance of that contraction. To exist through the changes of life and death requires the means to transfer that contract and contraction into subsequent stages of life through the different levels of consciousness. The gravitational aspect of Soul does not only refer to a downward intent. It is the pull towards a point of focus and the counter balance of the pull away into dispersion. Another way of saying this would be to refer to the "weight" of our intentions.

The soul is not a rational aspect of our being but this does not make it irrational. Yet it can manifest itself in the extremes of insanity, but also in the crazy wisdom that can only be described as revelations. This non-logical side of the soul is quite arbitrary and entirely unknown or even suspected until it reveals itself. The soul is like the lead that can become gold. Not only can it become gold but it is its single intention. Yet it needs the right guidance. When suppressed and denied the soul forces its way into surface expression in whatever way it can, regardless of public acceptability. Unfortunately in doing this it sabotages its own viability but not before it makes every effort to sabotage the forces of oppression that have denied rather than supported its natural expression.

Being the seed of our spirituality the soul must lose its original form and pass through many stages of transformation but it never loses its genetic essence, which is a spiritual genetic. The soul's genesis is not dependent on ancestral blood but instead links it to a particular group of people over many lifetimes and through many cultures. The reproductive processes involved are a relentless will to perfection, ensuring the crystallization of the most abstract concepts perceived by our consciousness. Our behavior and beliefs are all guided by the soul and its capsule, the Subtle Body, though they will be modified by the influence of the other Spiritual Bodies.

Guru Naanak

The one light of the soul that was Naanak is the same one light that passed through each of the subsequent Gurus. Each of them that wrote the poetic praise of God signed the hymns in the name of Naanak.

Guru Naanak was the founder of the Sikh dharma and started a quiet revolution, speaking out for the integrity of the innate spirit within. This was in contrast to the many superstitions that had crept into the religious life of the Middle Ages, instigating a rebirth of simplicity. This opened the door to the lowest social classes to enjoy a relationship with the Divine without a need for priestly license or permission.

If we consider the name NAANAK we find it has several meanings. It is a double negation, twice no (na na), which is what it takes for consciousness to implode. NAK also means nose and, therefore, the name means "the one without nose," a masterful expression of the humility that we feel when we contemplate the oneness of all. NA is the nameless name that exists in its own nothingness, while ANAK is the division of the one EK into countless little eks, which are you and me, all echoes of the original one.

Guru Naanak's poetry deeply expresses the extreme humility of the soul's state of consciousness. Again and again he refers to himself as the lowest of the low, the servant of the servant and the dust of the dust. He reduced himself to the smallest particle or unit. In his bodily state he had already merged his physical existence with the dust that he knew it would become at the end of its life, so establishing the vibration whilst alive that his body would be the dust under the feet of the saints. Such was the humility of Guru Naanak. He lived by his words even though many found his actions irrational and strange. They would laugh as if to humiliate him but when they questioned him they were always amazed by his resolute constancy of the way to the one God. Throughout his life and teachings he placed all the emphasis on the reality of one God; hence the root mantra of the Sikh faith with the statement that the One is extended throughout the entire creation.

Ek

The mantra begins by awakening the soul to a vague and distant sense of a One (Ek) greater than itself. The beginnings of humility and the will to aspire to that One are stirred in the sleeping soul and when the will is focused the pressure creates the seed of intent in which great potential is held. The entire expanse of time and space is a unified ecology expressed in the EK, the microcosmic and macrocosmic systems echoing from this one original source, the one word and the word of the One.

With the sound EK there is a contraction, an implosion of sound energy, which compresses itself into a stone and drops into the ocean of the void. It is an unstruck sound, a sound with nothing to strike and which becomes the point of origin for all that follows; it is the primary cause that has no cause itself. It is the laying of the foundation stone like a flagpole staked in the endless nothing that existed before time and space and only from this pointless point is time and space measured. Simultaneously the contraction is reversed and there erupts an explosion, a kind of dispersion into the soil and dust from which the seed can take root. EK is that seed, containing the whole, waiting to unfold. It is the one road that all will ultimately travel, from the one to the One. It is the one will and the will of the One, not yet shaped into desires yet containing every desire within it.

Chapter 4

Number 2

2 is not 1 for there is the absence of unity and the beginning of division and diversity. 2 is an extension of 1 and so a movement, firstly in time, which later develops into the 3, resulting in three-dimensional space and form. It is the first possible division of every number and the first number that can be divided so 2 is the first manifestation of splitting, duality, separation, and polarization. With 2 there is a difference, a gap, which also implies a vacuum and a hunger. 2 is the state of tension in the difference and that difference is our experience of relationship, the desire to meet but also the absence of the meeting.

All dualities, differences, and distances are empowered by the 2. A gap implies a chasm – between two there can seem to be an infinite abyss yet this depth is also the depth of the relation between two. Therefore, 2 is always an inseparable pair, since where there is separation there is also relation. Two 1s do not result in 2 unless they are in relationship, though when that ceases there would simply be 1 and 1 again. This bonding quality of the pair is also a number of attachments and clinging so that glue and cement, like desire, have a twoness about them. It is only in the fluidic movement of the tension that there is a sense of the 2. Without this movement there would be no sense of relationship and no number 2. 2 is, therefore, also movement. 2 always cuts in half and creates a relation of symmetry and reflection, one half reflecting the other. In this way, 2 is associated with mirrors and water.

As the relation between 1 and 3 we will find that the 2 is caught in the problem of loyalty. Where should it direct itself? It is the water for the seed of 1 but also the fuel for the vehicle of 3 that will carry the seed on toward the future. The duality of the 2 is often experienced as a suffering. The soul having apparently separated from its origin longs to know its true nature. When two individuals begin to enter into relationship each has their own needs and desires. Need pulls us into relationship just as relationship awakens us to our sense of need.

2 is not only two points but also the line between them. It suggests distance but it is not distance in space, rather it is the distance in time between two points. If 1 is the impulse and 3 is the action then 2 is the time lag between the impulse and the action. This line between two points is a kind of spider's thread or the spinner's thread that weaves the web of time differences that is used to create the veil between now and then as well as here and there. All ordinary movement happens in time and time is our experience of separation from the state of stillness, rest, and sleep consciousness. Time by itself is empty and emptiness desires to be filled. The tension of time and emptiness is the fuel, which moves us into the game of relationship.

In the duality that is number 2 our desire is innocent and naïve; there are many steps to pass through before we realize our own nature in everyone. Our need is infinite but we do not yet realize it as a need for the Infinite. We want the other person to be infinite for us and so we relate to the other as if they were number 8 (the number of infinity) and we feel their need for us as infinite. The bond of need is what makes people prepared to die for each other or feel as if they would be dead should the other person leave. To satisfy a need is to kill and what we eat kills us. This is an on-going process of refining our needs unto infinity.

You have two eyes, two ears, two nostrils, two hands, two legs, two kidneys, and two lungs, each pair having one on either side of the body, left and right.

2 is the splitting of the cell at the conception of a baby, the splitting of the seed as it opens into its roots.

The second stage of a plant is the roots; this implies the reaching out and the clinging.

The second element is water; its qualities are reflective, flowing, and bonding. Water is the life force within all vegetation and all vegetation feels the thirst for water. When it does not flow it becomes stagnant.

The Negative Mind

The body is energized by a vital system that equates with the plant kingdom. It is organic or vegetative and may be called the lower etheric body by some teachings. It can be considered as an oceanic state that may be flowing in a way that maintains good health or it may be full of problems. Our vital life force can become stuck, stagnant, filled with garbage, have many conflicting undercurrents and be full of creatures swimming around, just like the ocean. This vital energy is lost through our eyes, hands, and feet as well as through unhealthy thought processes and patterns. Our life habits can so disturb this vital life pool that we become sick and feel we have little energy available for living. When we do not learn how to sail over the ocean of life lightly then we start sinking. This is when depression and helplessness become the dominant mood of our life. With healthy thinking, right diet and regulation of sleep, sexual release and physical activity then our energy balance will be stabilized. This energy is without form but will take on whatever form our desires are. It is the hunger behind all our yearnings and is known as the Negative Mind.

Sickness begins here with the Negative Mind. When the mind does not accept to relate to the soul then the oceanic pool of the subconscious gets filled with toxic thoughts and the effects of unhealthy actions. In fact, it takes the same amount of energy to relate to the soul or to deny the soul. When we say "but I am committed" there would never be a question of turning away from the soul and its destiny. The Negative Mind is then a loyal servant to our purest desire, the urge to merge with the Divine.

The emptiness of our soul is the state that is experienced as soon as the seed opens and there is a split, a duality of being, something separate from something else. It is the gap that is the negative state. Through this extension into duality the soul experiences desire, hunger, and longing, which moves it to begin the long journey back to itself. There can be no going back except by going on through the full cycle of life and death; only by following our great yearning can we find the way back home.

This second Body is the critical faculty with which we can self-negate, as in suicide, or with which we negate the undesirable. It is the wisdom of discernment and the denouncement in discrimination. Denial is a problematic form of negation as it is really a means to ignore. On the other hand, the know-how of the "no," knowing how and when to say "no," is a healthy engagement with life through the force of death. The executive consciousness combines the discerning and critical ability of the Negative Mind with the charge of the Pranic Body where we learn who we are by discovering what we are not.

It is here in the second dimension of being that we experience separation. The process of negation begins in childhood with all the "no"s a child receives from its parents. Most of these are necessary in the sense that the boundaries of our existence are established by being told where not to go and what not to do. This may sound a bit heavy but actually it means that unless a child is about to do something that would endanger itself or others or that is unpleasantly disturbing when repeated too often, the parent leaves it to play and explore its environment. As the boundaries of the no-go area are established so our identity is also taking shape. Through the suggestions about what we are not to be or not to do, where we are not to go and when we cannot, there is a message about separation and the individual self that is an individual by virtue of living in division.

From this faculty, critical consciousness is also learnt. However, if this critical tendency is carried over into the assertive realm of the third dimension, the negation starts to shape into imposed form (rather then mere negation of form) and this can appear as slander and judgment. Slander is identifiable by the way in which it begins and ends in itself, as in certain kinds of humor, which depend upon the continuous putting down of others. The critical faculty at its best is a means towards an end, an instrument or process with which to negate the unreal. The result of this is discriminating wisdom, an essential tool for spiritual development.

When turned back on itself, the Negative Mind leads to self-negation in extreme forms such as suicide. In other words the Negative Mind must operate in harmony with the other Spiritual Bodies, especially the eighth (Pranic Body) so that the negation of the physical body does not happen before the natural day of death. If the negative self of the spirit-mind, that of the Pranic Body or the eighth dimension, has not been consciously cultivated there will not be a link to the Infinite and, therefore, a suicidal death cannot hope to find liberation. The soul will be obliged to return to physical existence to continue its work on becoming whole, uniting the material/personal and spiritual/impersonal planes. The appropriate use of the critical faculty of the negating self is best understood after considering the issues of attachments and sadness.

Being a separate individual has its good points, of course, but it also results in a feeling of loss and a yearning to be reunited with the One. This longing is not an emotional feeling but a deep, instinctual need like a hunger that nothing seems to satisfy. The depth of this instinct runs deep into the subconscious and we are driven to seek unity through relationships with other individuals. Our need for another finds confirmation in the need from another; there is a need to be needed. This deep need is eternal and infinite and only fulfilled through an eternally permanent and lasting relationship. Since worldly relationships are not permanent we concoct a dream of being together beyond this life. The only way that we might have the company of others, beyond the temporary realms of astral heavens and hells, is dependent on the achievement of immortality of each one. When we can accept the true quality and nature of our deepest need then our melancholy can transform itself to become a spiritual longing. This is not an escape from the material world but a yearning that draws the impersonal soul self into the game of life and death.

Our personal tear of sadness is a drop in the ocean of compassion and, therefore, of the same essence. The critical-self, instead of drowning in self-pity and disappointment, which misses the point, negates what is not ultimately satisfying and so arrives at the eternal. In ordinary life this simply means to learn to be critical of our attachments and to turn away from anything that no longer satisfies on a deep level. So why should anything or anyone lead us astray? Because in our need we may blindly attach ourselves to people who can take advantage of our need to be needed. When we are living through the second Body there is a kind of forgetfulness of both our source and the infinite part of ourselves, a forgetfulness that comes and goes like the waxing and waning of the moon. When the moon is in the night sky we willingly remember it and praise its beautiful and reflective light. But when it is out of sight, hidden on the other side of the earth or overwhelmed by the brightness of the solar flames, then we forget. We forget and yet instinctively we are driven by the power of its deeply subconscious mood of yearning.

A commendable quality of the Negative Mind is that of loyalty and obedience. However, the subconscious nature of the related need means that the second dimension of the self is also a bit naïve. This naivety, along with our attachment, makes it very possible for our loyalty to be used and abused and this is precisely why we need to develop the critical mind. Through the process of negation we gradually redirect our loyalty to what is more essential, more lasting, and, therefore, more true. A further development of the second dimension is the mirroring effect where we recognize that we all reflect each other. Co-operation and collaboration of both desirable and undesirable form arise from this visual echo. Reflecting people's real needs by expressing our own is the final outcome of the discriminating self.

The Negative Mind, with its feeling of emptiness, brings on an infinitely deep hunger, which can seem impossible to fill. This can lead to addictions with food, drugs, drink, and people, anything to plug the desolation of the void. This force can lead us into great attachments, often naively, and our need for the connection, however innocent it may be, can throw us into unknown dangers of bad company and abusive relationships. In the right relationship, of course, the loyalty that develops from such a bonding attachment might be thought of as a virtue. Without relationship this negative consciousness leaves us with a feeling of deep melancholy and a sense of abandonment. If, however, we can obey the pure call of our longing it will bring us to the infinite connection. Ignoring it is no good since it will creep out through the cracks in our concrete armor and we then call it a weed and try to destroy our own wellspring of power.

The need to be needed leads us into relationships of naïve loyalty where in one moment we might be abused and in the next implored "don't leave me, I need you." When we come to know the nature of our own needs and neediness we are well equipped to communicate with tact and charm that enables great powers of persuasion. This, of course, could be open to misuse and abuse and does provide some people with the means to empower their fantastic schemes and plans, which are set up by the third and seventh Bodies (these are described later on).

The second Body governs the way we meet our needs and the way we are used to meet the needs of others. It also directs the way we process our flow of energy known as vital force, prana, or chi. In its purest expression the second Body represents that part of us that needs God and that is needed by God. It is here that the law of separation operates but it is also the way to union. Our hunger confirms we are alive and we find ourselves attracted to the hunger in others, sensing that the resolution to our hunger is deep within the hunger itself. We forget, however, that others can only be a mirror to our own depth and not the resolution of it. The river of our need flows through our tears and this we find difficult to be with. Our struggle is to transform our personal suffering and from there to awaken into compassion. In this way the second Body transforms us and then surrenders its powerful grip.

Guru Angad

Guru Angad was the second Guru and the extension of the first, an extension or limb (ANG) of the primal being (AD). An extension is an attachment and sorting out the appropriate attachment is precisely the struggle of our hunger that is born with duality. Guru Angad was known for his loyalty, his attachment to the first Guru and rather than stand alone he interwove his poetry with that of Guru Naanak.

Corresponding also to the second element of water Guru Angad used to carry water for a distance of twelve miles daily to Guru Naanak.

He also devised the phonetic script known as Gurmukhi and well understood how the word was an extension of the divine thread. Guru Angad knew already that the longing of the soul in its experience of duality would find its fulfillment through the divine word. After the tenth Guru the scripture itself was appointed as Guru. These simple lines of ink on paper inscribe the words of the saints in the Sri Guru Granth Sahib. This scripture now holds the permanent position of eleventh Guru to all Sikhs (disciples of truth).

Two is the number of duality in the Guru's teaching and is one of the major causes of our suffering. The complaint that is born from our duality has two modes of expression, the two kinds of "but." The toxic one is to say "but it's so hard, so lonely, so painful." It is the "but" of complaint. The price for happiness, however, is to give up complaining. Then our lament that calls out in longing would meet any obstacle and declare "but I am committed." This is the pure loyalty that can lead us to transcend the number 2 and pass through the infinite tension of number 8 to arrive at the state of standing parallel to the Divine, which is the meaning of the number 11. In the root mantra this longing is expressed in the sound Ong.

Ong

ONG is the thread upon which the entire universe is strung like a beautifully intricate necklace. The soul having become extended from its origin is nothing more than an extension of that origin. In this apparent separation the soul longs to know its true nature. It calls out with a longing (ONG) and begins to hear the faint whispers of the inner voice (ONG), which its longing compels it to obey.

ONG is both the sound of the extending away as well as the return, the vibrational ripples from the EK that radiate outwardly and inwardly throughout the entire existence. There is a tension within us, born out of our experience of duality that we are accustomed to call the basic problem of life; ONG is the groan of this distance and difference. This duality causes all hungers and cravings, our neediness, our longings and yearnings. It is basically a sadness, which we mistakenly call the badness of life, a feeling that we want to go away but which will only do so when we go the way it leads. Babies instinctively use this sound to find their way back into deep sleep but for adults the path home is forwards not backwards, still guided, nevertheless, by the same sound.

Chapter 5
Number 3

3 is the end of duality and an unequal number. With three points or lines it is possible to make shape and, therefore, 3 is the number of patterns and closed shapes. It is in these structures and forms that many issues arise which develop into such things as habits, rules, regulations, roles, and finding the shape of things as well as our place within them. Structure gives a feeling of safety but at the same time it controls, inhibits, and traps. It supports but also reinforces dependencies, which create the habits. Structure can include and enclose or exclude and keep out and this relates to tribal and cultural thinking where likeness is embraced and difference is outcast.

There are three primary colors, red, yellow, and blue. Shades of red are linked to 1, 2, 3, and partly 4. Shades of blue connect to 9, 8, 7, and partly 6 and yellow is related to 5 and partly 4 and 6.

Your eyes are like a third leg. They give stability, as a stick or a dog might do for a blind person and are the third ingredient in the structured action of walking. In this action first we pick ourselves up, second we balance left and right, and third we go forward. This movement forward requires the eyes, the third factor, as a structure in order to see where we are going (fourth is the freedom to take risks such as dancing, jumping, twisting, and turning).

The third person in a group of three is like the witness, while the other two are caught up in the process. 3 becomes a way of keeping two points together, like a pivot for a see-saw or the point from which a pendulum swings left and right or the child in a family, without whom the couple might separate. The child could feel caught in the vice of the parents, trapped in the third part, or one parent might feel squeezed between the other two. This gives rise to issues such as control and being controlled and especially focuses on the consciousness of the victim. (Note: no one can victimize another unless there is a third factor such as a rule, a phantom figure, a dead uncle or whatever, to act as the other part of the vice.) The quality of the vice is what contributes to the symptom of the vicious circle, which is really a vicious triangle, where we keep returning to the same point as we bounce between the two walls. Yet the 3 could also be the creative expression of the tension between the two and in its structural quality can become a platform for the leap into freedom, which is a step into number 4.

2 + 1 = ? When three people converse, two tend to speak to each other whilst the other acts as witness. The inclusion of this third person would result in the exclusion of one of the others and the most difficult, but highest accomplishment of the three, would be when each one is equally included. The human attitude of equality is the greatest virtue of the third Body, the Positive Mind.

1 is the impulse of life to exist, to generate, and to reproduce its existence. 2 provides the reflective tension and charge for this and 3 is the image produced, the child of 1 and 2. Without the child there cannot be further reproduction so 3 becomes the minimum necessary structure for recreation. Just as triangles become the first possible building blocks so 3 is the machinery of reproduction, the family.

The third stage of the plant is the branching out into expansion of space. It is the fiery shapes of the leaves and the heat that allows the formation of solid shape.

The third element is fire, which also seeks to expand its range while eating everything in its path. It has the illusion that it is expanding but is not aware that where it has been there is now nothing but an empty wasteland. Fire is also the light that gives vision to the ordinary world.

The Positive Mind

The shape that we take in the world is contained within the muscular system of the body and this provides a level of armoring. According to our habits this muscular armoring is modified. It can become so strong and we tend to identify with it so much that it starts to dominate our lives. The attempt to affirm our existence so catches our attention that we lose ourselves in it and we end up with habits that we do not want but cannot stop. It is the realm known as the lower astral plane. When we must, or wish to go through changes, then these habits that are set in the body are obstacles to be crossed and are referred to as the lower guardians on the threshold of self-realization.

An indication of the wish to break out of the hypnotic state of life is the feeling of boredom. We may then go forward to the 4, take some risks, and explore new possibilities. But for this to happen we must have the contact with our basic self on which to hold. In other words, it is 3 + 1 that makes 4. Otherwise, in our state of boredom we must move back into the depression of the Negative Mind and ever deeper into the inner ocean to find the lost self/soul.

The approval from others is often taken as a substitute for the inner consolidation of self. Perhaps this is inevitable in childhood as we look to the adults in our world for assurance. Then later through a series of disappointments and broken promises we might abandon the importance we attach to our public image and the opinion of others. This is the natural progression to the fourth step when we return to explore the inner world.

When others approve of our actions they do not necessarily approve of our essence. Therefore, there is a distinction to be made between approval that helps towards an inner confidence and approval that diminishes it. The approval that contains the recognition of mutual equality supports that type of interdependent independence through which we can reciprocate the affirmation of soul in all. The conditioned approval, however, sets out to manipulate the emotional charge of others and leads to a desperate dependence where we become prepared to do anything for the sake of acceptance.

To express yourself to be known by others is very different from expressing yourself to know yourself. You have the right to self-expression; you have the right to be happy. Understand that this is not a right that you have to fight for or claim from anyone. It is given within your own navel, an inner smile that only you can permit to free. Self-expression is an expansion of your being. When it is not based in competition and control then it is an expansion that does not take up the space of others but that shows how there is room for everyone equally in the same space. Control is an illusion and you can only have control over your illusions. Everyone thinks they are on a different planet while reality just is and continues to be what it always was. Part of the difficulty is that we are not clear about the law of cause and effect. We delude ourselves into believing we might be free of the consequences of our own actions.

Through the Negative Mind we have experienced the suffering of separation and found that the only way is to go onwards. The soul must then assume something about its identity and affirm its existence as an individual. The Positive Mind is the expression of accepting life in the physical body and its interaction with the world. Strength of soul, hope for the future, and a sense of excitement to take on the obstacles of life are all given and communicated through the Positive Mind. The third Body is a vehicle or instrument, which loves to solve problems and take on the impossible and without these challenges it quickly loses its optimism and regresses into feelings of hopelessness, assuming the role of victim of circumstance.

The skill of this third dimension of our being is to translate ideas into concrete action, for by tackling practical problems and finding solutions to physical difficulties the affirming, resourceful self will find great pleasure. There is a tendency to seek out challenges and take on monumental tasks, not only to exercise resourcefulness, but more significantly, to cultivate a creative and inventive nature. It is a kind of gymnastic training ground for what will become the support structure for the soul as it evolves from a creature of habit into one of spiritual discipline. It is staying hopeful in the face of adversity that opens the way for originality and new discovery.

The third dimension is also the means to express our competitive self, which like all the Bodies has its source in the first level of Soul.

In the third we are concerned about how we look in the world, our external self-image, and sometimes we place too much importance on the success of our individual being. We are constantly looking for ways to express ourselves through our physical actions and too often we get into the habit of doing things without a purpose, even finding problems when there are none. A restless and undirected soul wants to do just for the sake of doing and this excessive drive to be busy needs to be harnessed by the disciplined self of the fourth dimension. We find value in the act of physical deeds through the Positive Mind, but if we live too much by this we get to believe that our worth is only based on physical achievements or material objects. We forget that our self-worth is affirmed simply by the fact of our continued existence and when we realize that we do not have to keep justifying our presence or measuring our success against anyone else then a whole new meaning to equality unfolds. We are born equal and we die equal.

Self-worth is a fundamental awareness established by cultivating the third dimension. A lack of self-value is usually compensated for by illusions of self-importance but it is from the position of a healthy self-respect that we develop a strong sense of fairness and the ability to judge others beyond appearances. However, we must first learn to judge ourselves and to learn to do this fairly. I have met many wonderful people who believe in equality for all except their own souls, placing themselves either above or below. The ability to judge people or things as right or wrong is of limited value by itself, although not without purpose. Our tendency as immature beings is to judge a problem and then thoroughly criticize it, forgetting that positive action would surely be of more value. The anger associated with the Positive Mind is an expression of the inability to effectively use emotions as fuel for new and useful life structures.

Judging degenerates into slander and is ultimately more painful for the one inflicting it rather than the one who receives it. In developing the third dimension we gradually come to see that the purpose of our judgmental faculty is to provide the catalyst for action, like helping and supporting those who are unfairly treated. One of the more agreeable uses of the positive self-identity is to encourage the homeless, the desolate, or the oppressed to realize their self-value and to find a life of quality and equality.

When turned in on itself the judgmental self may feel totally unsupported and hopeless and so incapable of a healthy sense of worth. It is often the case that we only learn the dynamic optimism of the positive self after first of all plummeting into a state of desperation. When we go through such an experience the third dimension allows us to discover that life is joyful no matter what the conditions are, and an unqualified and energetic enthusiasm for life is restored. Those who solely aim for success in the material world see failure as unacceptable but it does not have to mean losing self-respect or self-esteem. The skill of the positive self is to give advice but the ability to take it is something we learn as we work to bring about a balanced third dimension.

The third law of life uses the Positive Mind to instil within us a sense of care and concern for the world and the creatures in it. Depending on our mood we will either be understanding or expect to be understood, caring or expect to be cared for, we will value others or expect to be valued, supportive or expect to be supported. It is through the combined aspects of the third and seventh Bodies that we use the faculty of judgment and through this measure our world and ourselves within it. We look to judge quality, equality, value, and worth and place huge importance on our ability to do this even though we have no idea how valid our points of reference are. When our vision becomes clear, however, we will learn to judge all as equal, no one better or worse than anyone else. Such learning does not come easily so it is often through being judged by others and experiencing the unfairness of society that we can begin to re-assess our own assumptions and consequently change our behavior. But first we are likely to get angry and outraged by the injustice of such an unfair world. These feelings of anger, judgment, and slander are immature attempts to deal with emotions of sorrow and suffering on one hand and shock and fear on the other. If they did not exist there would be no anger.

When we process our sorrow and despair as described in relation to the Negative Mind and transform the emotion of fear (related to the fourth and sixth Bodies) into an empowering force, then instead of anger we would see the funny side of life. There would be a cosmic sense of humor showing the way to an effective and practical resolution. Once the assumptions upon which our anger is based begin to melt, we can receive advice as well as give it. When the Negative Mind is developed we are able to give more appropriately and receive with a healthy discrimination.

The Positive Mind's main influence is upon our actions, while the Aura (the corresponding Body) has more impact on our thought patterns. Habits and routines are still produced through this third vehicle but so too is the search for adventure. If our soul remained too long in this consciousness we would very easily get bored and look for things to do to keep busy just for the sake of it. We would try to express a self of whom we are unaware and often get into physical activities, games, and sport, which are a way to help us to achieve this. It is through the discipline of the fourth Body, the Neutral Mind, that we find our actions led to something more than just passing time. Before the soul can move on to fully fulfill its destiny through the connected fourth and sixth Bodies, we must learn to accept our failures in life. Part of this learning process is to teach us that our self-value cannot only be assessed in comparison to others or whether we win or lose.

This realm of our third dimension often seems to be governed by the law of cause and effect but it is also ruled by the law of explanations of cause and effect. Here we are caught up in a merry-go-round where we try to find causes to explain everything rather than just enjoying an unqualified experience. We set up the rules of the game, usually based on an illusion of our lack of safety, and so become imprisoned by our own protection barriers. The law of safety as presented by the Positive Mind gives us all our shoulds and shouldn'ts and provides us with the means to build a model of understanding the universe, which in turn becomes a tool for finding our personal place on the map of life. Our faculty of judgment is given with the many shades of right and wrong, success and failure, which create all the patterns of our realities.

Some people believe they can create their own reality and see it as a great gift of freedom, but since reality cannot be created they become constrained and limited by their own constructions. These fantasies are our efforts to seek and to give meaning to everything and every situation. The drawing of our personal map is often shared by a cultural group that develops a set of rituals to dictate its boundaries and in this way our management of physical and psychic space is controlled by the third and seventh Bodies.

The muscles in the body and the brain are the machinery, which organize routine sets of movements that could be called habits. When we over identify with this aspect of ourselves we cultivate a mechanistic view of the world, becoming clinical observers and placing everything behind a wall of glass. Sooner or later, however, we feel the dryness of this state and take the risk of calling upon the fourth Body.

Guru Amar Das

The third element is fire, an element of joy or anger, action, manifestation, and visibility. Guru Amar Das, the third Guru, wrote a lengthy hymn known as Anand Sahib – the Song of Bliss; it is a passage that expresses the joy of right action. He calls out to the body and its functions to know their true occupation in this world. His concern was with the effectiveness of good action and the equality of all created beings. This he demonstrated by personally bathing, feeding, and clothing those in need regularly, including the untouchable castes and lepers. He also encouraged women to be free from their position of underdog in society and challenged the social obligation that they should hide their face behind the veil or jump in the funeral pyre of their deceased husband. He is known as "the hope of the hopeless, the shelter of the shelterless, and the strength of those without strength."

AMAR means to awaken, to merge or to will and DAS represents the bearer of, the one who holds, or the wandering servant. The primal soul, branching out, wanders lost and entranced in the creation but in the midst of it all still holds the space to awaken and merge with God. MAR signifies death so AMAR DAS is the servant of that which is beyond death. AMAR also means command, AMAR DAS, the one who holds the command or the servant of the command of the deathless one.

It was Guru Amar Das who formalized the naming and the death ceremonies for the Sikhs, creating a supportive structure for the emerging identity of the true disciple. The number 3 in the Guru's teaching mostly refers to the three gunas or qualities of tama, satva, and raja. These are the formative modalities that make our ordinary three-dimensional world and the family construction of father, mother, and son. The reality lies beyond in the fourth dimension also known as the Turya state. It is said that Maya, Mother Nature, gave birth to three sons. These are Brahma, the creator or generator, Vishnu, the balancer or organizer, and Shiva, the destroyer. Like all created beings they are seen by their creator but do not see their creator.

Kar

The One expresses itself through the entire creation (KAR) and so all beings within the creation are an equal part of the One. The voice of longing resides in everything and reminds us that we are all equally an extension of the One. Those who understand this live in hope, giving strength and support to others who experience inequality and discouragement in life.

KAR is the branching out of the universal thread into three-dimensional shape and structure. It is the creation of vehicles within which the EK can sit and travel on its journey of transformation. The KAR is what gives character to the consciousness and draws us into fascination with our looks and how we appear in the world. This branching out is also expressed as a market place where Guru Naanak deals in the trade of God's name.

It is the city of the body where we search and beg for a taste of the river of nectar that is the thread linking God without to the God within. Our absorption in the hustle and bustle and bartering ways of city life is what holds us in KARmic patterns of existence; it is the drama of our lives. Realizing all as equal creates the space in which the creation becomes equal to the creator. This is the descent of the mantle of Kriste, which is the same as Krishna.

Chapter 6
Number 4

A square can be formulated with 4 points. Furthermore, with these 4 points it is easier to perceive a circle and a sense of wholeness, also indicated through the simple formula of 1 + 2 + 3 + 4 = 10. A square is more mobile and freer than a triangle as it can be moved into a diamond shape without adjusting the length of the sides. The stability that is associated with the number 4 is more from its wholeness and mobility rather than from its fixed or square nature.

There is a double duality, 2 + 2, in the number 4, which means it can hold the tension of difference. There is also the implication of choice since each choice of either this or that always has a positive or negative possibility. This amounts to four factors in all, the positive and negative of choice A and of choice B. This double duality can also be expressed in the form of the cross; to be in the center is to be at the crossroads of life and decision. When both choices have equal positive and negative elements then it requires something different to make the decision. In its instability 4 presents doubt, confusion, and uncertainty though the movement of 4 also provides the capacity for a feeling approach in making decisions (as opposed to the rational approach of 3) and this is intuition. The quality of doubt itself only exists in relation to trust. From the perspective of the neutral consciousness it is no longer a question of right or wrong action or belief but one where we take personal responsibility for our choices without being attached to the outcome. Neutral consciousness is awakened. It is to be fully present and responsive to each moment through the power of choice and continues only through continuous choosing.

With 3 there is form but also the tendency to identify with form. Going on to a fourth quality means the awareness of form and the awareness beyond or independent of form. When we are aware that "I am not the form but something that inhabits the form" then we have moved into the sense of the fourth dimension, which allows for a change of form. It is a moment of awakening and discovery. The formula $1 + 2 + 3 + 4 = 10$ teaches that 4 is a community number; it is the step from personal existence into community awareness. Each individual is a collective of different parts. These parts are reflected back to us when we take the trouble to enter into any formal or informal group dynamic. Through developing awareness of this reflective dynamic we become conscious of that aspect of us which is more than all the parts put together (10) and which can be described as our common solitude.

The shape of 4 is very revealing in the journey 1 to 2 to 3 to 4.

- 1 is the sleeping soul's initial impulse to realize itself.
- 2 is the process of separation through time and the dreamy ocean of life.
- 3 is the taking of form and the resulting enchantment of self.
- 4 is the moment of awakening and decision, which is the commitment to change the form (3) and return through the depths of longing (2) to consciously serve the soul in everyone (10).

4 is the plane of human existence and the unfolding of consciousness. The fourth stage of the plant is the flower and it starts with the bud. In the spiritual heart of every human being there matures this bud of awakening; all feel it though few listen to its inner tuition and trust its secrets.

Neutral Mind

The neutral mind is literally the mathematical movement of consciousness expressed in the equation $1 + 2 + 3 + 4 = 10$.

Mistakenly referred to as the Mental Body, the fourth level of being is the release of consciousness from its entrancement and over identification in the bodily form and its three-dimensional environment of relative reality. This happens with the spontaneous unfolding of gratitude in the heart. Gratitude is a state of presence and remembering. It is the presence of consciousness that takes the appreciation of the Positive Mind and goes beyond it, while remembering is not an effort of maintaining awareness but an effortless awareness of the sustained continuity of self. It is, however, a liberation of consciousness that comes only after the labor through the Negative and Positive Minds.

To give and receive is a decision. A decision is only real when it is conscious. We are only conscious when we breathe consciously. After mineral, plant, and animal, the human is at the fourth plane of existence and the only creature to have the capacity for conscious breath. We can change our state by changing our breath. This change of state represents making a choice, like deciding to pray or panic when you do not know what to do. It is in the way of conscious breath that we give and receive. Through the breath the world touches us most deeply. If we do not have consciousness of the breath then we do not have consciousness of the inner intimacy with the world around us. In the center of the chest there is a communal presence and it is here we can know the We-in-me. Conscious breath makes us available to the moment to meet Thou-in-all. When life is over we will be given a chance to remain conscious as spirit beings. If while alive we do not learn to live beyond our breath then at death it will be most difficult. The paradox is that we learn to live without breath by first living the breath to its fullest.

The absence of awareness is paralysis, a state of no feeling. This begins with a contraction in between the shoulder blades. Then it descends to the lower spine creating a stiffness there whilst also rising up to produce facial tension. Paralysis or non-feeling is a false type of neutrality. The mature, unconditional neutrality of love allows you to receive all the good or bad that life brings your way and transmute it into a love to return to all. The Neutral Mind does not negate, attach, or react to life. Instead it makes a poem out of it. It appreciates confusion and feels how it is closer to the truth. In these moments there is a chance to realize that there is always something else beyond our boundaries of awareness and that we need not fear it even if we cannot rationalize it.

Mathematically it is expressed in the equation of $1 + 2 + 3 + 4 = 10$, implying that from number 4 there is a direct shortcut to the number 10. The unit of the number 10 that is outside of the zero is the extra-ordinary something else, the unknown, the "x factor" also known as the "more-than" since it is the totality that is more than the parts put together. The Neutral Mind is the only means of direct intimacy with this unit that is always beyond the usual limits of our perception.

The Neutral Mind allows the soul to fully experience the emotional commotion of social living whilst maintaining a non-attached awareness of itself. The distinction between non-attached and detached might be useful since we so easily fall into the trap of unreal objectivity. This gives us an air of cold detachment, while we secretly and possibly unconsciously, hold and store our emotions hoping they will go away so that we do not have to face them. This, of course, does not work and subsequently they emerge and take us by surprise. One of the hard lessons to learn is that we are only free of our feelings when we fully experience them. We must also realize that our neutrality is not something we can set up in place once and for all and then forget about. It is an on-going process for we cannot become habitually neutral. We may habitually detach and suppress our emotions but it is not possible to be neutral by setting up any routine. This is not to say that routines are unimportant. They are an essential part of a stable existence but for this structure we have the third and seventh Bodies, fuelled by the second and eighth. Neutral consciousness is awakened consciousness. It is to be fully present and responsive to each moment through the power of choice and continues only through continuous choosing.

The neutral self of the body-mind, as it relates to the fourth chakra, is that aspect through which we are able to see all sides of the argument. Dilemmas arise when we weigh up the pros and cons and yet we fail to reach any decision. With the fourth dimension we begin to see beyond the polarities of subjective values where one person's nourishment is another's poison. We sense there is a truth beyond that of each individual and yet this perception of objective reality leads us into endless debate and no action. There is probably a greater truth but it is not accessible through the traditional means of calculated thought.

Truth in essence is a feeling and a perception rather than a conception. When we are in tune with the full context of time and space we are able to sense the balance of everything around us. The ability to make decisions from a spontaneity and clarity of our being is developed through the neutral self. Before maturing into an awareness of spontaneously knowing what to do, when to do it, as well as where and how to do it, the neutral self uses its detachment to suppress and deny its feelings. This is partly out of doubt about its own validity and a lot of frustration, pain, and emotional tension build up as a result of this cool reserve. This detachment is really a sort of sitting on the fence attitude, just patterns of avoidance. With the development of the neutral self into the spontaneous mode of being, we learn to freely express our feelings and make choices and commitments without any attachment to what happens or the consequences. When the fourth dimension, as just described, is in balance with developments in the sixth, we do not fall into the superficial forms of "going with the flow," which is, in fact, carelessness and irresponsibility or merely social conformity. The sixth dimension also allows us to go beyond the fears of what others might think when we express our real feelings and provides us with the means to communicate even the most cutting truth in a graceful and beautiful manner.

An appropriate form of neutrality and unbiased perspective in the cultivated fourth Body captivates the confidence in others. They sense their secrets can be entrusted and so confide their personal dilemmas, knowing they will not be abused or disclosed. An evolved Neutral Mind means we can easily pass through the experience of changes in fortune, financial or otherwise. Good and bad luck has little significance and other forms of superstition soon lose their importance. The possibility for genuine, selfless service becomes a reality, free of the need to be praised or the fear of blame, expecting neither reward nor punishment. In such a state of consciousness we are able to offer blessings and receive the blessings of grace. Indeed, our lives may be deeply touched by the service of such a person and never even realize where it came from.

The rules and regulations set up by the third dimension are challenged in the consciousness of the fourth by the Neutral Mind, the keeper of a law more sacred than any bound by cultural identities based in self-image. Truth no longer belongs to you or I. Instead we are invited to discover that which belongs only to itself and there is often immense pain to go through as we surrender our beliefs and meet what really is.

As with all stages of life there are many lessons to go through before this fourth quality becomes our beloved companion. Our objectivity to see all sides of an argument leaves us without any opinion of our own and no ground upon which to stand. However, this amazing ability to weigh up all the reasons for and against in each and every decision of our life can lead us on an endless journey of procrastination. This indecisiveness means we are constantly putting things off and by default we allow the world to make our decisions for us as if to be free of the responsibility. When we discover this strategy then it is time to explore the nature of our doubts and our insecurity about doing or saying the wrong thing. We must realize the quality of doubt itself exists only in relationship to trust, and freedom only by virtue of commitment to responsibility. From the perspective of the neutral consciousness it is no longer a question of right or wrong action or belief but one where we take personal responsibility for our choices without being attached to the outcome. The skills involved in deciding, committing, and following through are essential for the soul's journey and for the meeting of our destiny. They include intuition and sensitivity as well as receptivity and a future orientation.

The balance between appropriate giving and receiving is also an important teaching of the fourth dimension. If you feel you were born to labor then your Neutral Mind is awake, but any imbalance means you may not be so receptive to the generosity and gratitude of others. This lack of gratitude takes us right back to the resentments and angers of the third and seventh Bodies and can also lead to the belief that we are owed something and yet nothing is good enough. It is the unconscious attempts to manage all these feelings that can steer us into adopting the dangerous tactics of unreal emotional detachment.

Guided by the law of uncertainty, the fourth Body directs us into confusion, doubt, and indecision. It influences all our active and passive choices, whether they are based in fear and doubt or trust and faith. By an intuitive contact with the force of this archetype we can transform our life into an art where every step becomes a dance and every word a poem. There is the softness of melody but also the sharpness of decision and the precision of the moment. Our way of engaging with the world, of taking up the labor of love that is the meeting of our destiny, is dominated by the presence or absence of our sensitivity. The inspiration of all this is found through the awareness of the neutral consciousness; these are the moments when we really touch the world and let the world touch us. It is how we select what it is to be human, the way the world works on us, and so fulfills its own destiny.

Guru Ram Das

As 4 is the spiritual heart so the fourth Guru initiated the bud of the community's heart by having a great Muslim saint, Mir, lay the foundation stone of the Golden Temple and its surrounding lake known as Amritsar, the Tank of Nectar. The preceding three Gurus had worked on the more individual and personal levels, which were an important platform for the awakening of group consciousness. Guru Ram Das began to prepare the center around which a community could gather. He also began the wedding ceremony of the Sikhs and in his poems encouraged the sangat or community to come together.

Guru Ram Das is remembered for his service to the Sikhs. With no concern for his own identity he would go to meet the pilgrims who were on their way to the Guru's court. He went in disguise and served them in various ways including brushing their feet with his long beard. It was a surprise to the pilgrims when they arrived at the Guru's estate to find the same servant sitting there as guru. His life was an example of human service.

It could be said that Guru Ram Das was the embodiment of the attitude of selfless service. It is the intuitive awareness that everything has been given and the voluntary offering back without any attachment to personal gain. This is the development of the neutral consciousness. The transition from a limited personal identity to the limitless impersonal identity is mediated through the middle ground of the community. It is an environment in which to give and receive, to surrender ourselves in the divine service through God's own creation.

Guru Ram Das knew how to take people into their innermost hearts and to awaken the inspiration to serve, firstly by his example of meeting the pilgrims on the path but also in the almost paradoxical way that he would deliver his sermon. While the disciples were sitting before him waiting for teachings that would inspire them the Guru would declare, in the sweetest poetical music, how he was just an orphan without any pleasant manner of dress or gait. Then he would beg from the congregation, like a bride without a groom, to see if there was any soul there who could lead him to the beloved God and husband of all beings. This shocked the pilgrims and made them turn to their own hearts to discover the love they had come to seek was, in fact, within them already.

There are two parts to the name Ram Das. RAM is the aspect of God that permeates the entire universe; DAS is the servant of God in all places.

The number 4 is highlighted in the Guru's teaching in several ways:

- The fourth state, beyond the three gunas.
- The four ages of the universe.
- The four stages of a single life.
- The four castes or classes.

Finally Guru Ram Das in one of his best known hymns inspires us to always meditate on and speak the words of truth. He called upon the mind of the Sikh to do the jap (repetition) of SAT NAM – the true name.

Sat Nam

SAT NAM means true name, truth is the name of God, and the name of God is the truth. Our name is also our identity so where we see truthfully, hear truthfully, speak truthfully, and act in truthfulness we abandon our false identities. Then when we no longer live by a mistaken identity we realize our divine nature. As we realize that the one creator is the origin of the soul's true identity (SAT NAM), we are compelled to live in the service of this truth. Truthfulness is the way home, the way back to our original nature. It is important to realize that the divine truth is an unknown truth. This is why the fourth state is an attitude of truthfulness rather than an assumption of true content or truth as a body of knowledge.

Chapter 7

Number 5

Number 5 is half way to 10 and so it is considered as a number of the threshold, the bridge, the communicative link, relationship, and balance. 5 finds itself in the center of the circular 10 and becomes a number of integration and regulation in all respects and directions. This is also the quality of the throat, the center of balance between mind and body. Being half way, 5 indicates a point of turnaround, a point of reversals, especially those that create paradoxes. 5 is, therefore, a point of transformation. This implies sacrifice of one state for the discovery of another and the sacrifice of Christ on the crucifix on the cross of 4 and the five wounds he received suggests man's evolution beyond human to the fifth realm. This turning point also indicates the pairing of numbers that come before and after 5.

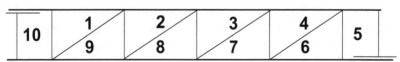

There is a natural presence of 5 in the five fingers and the five senses, which have also been related to the five elements. These correspond to five types of consciousness and thought and give rise to the five senses and the five passions that contribute to our enchantment; they are transmuted in practices such as yoga, service, prayer, meditation, and art. Similarly, the 5 is considered as the number of humanity, two legs, two arms, and the head making up the five limbs and symbolized in the sign of the pentangle.

In another sense, however, 5 is the surpassing of human nature into the angelic fifth realm.

	ELEMENT	SENSE	SPACE	REALM	STATE	
1/9	Earth —	Smell —	Physical —	Mineral —	Sleep —	1/9
2/8	Water —	Taste —	Etheric —	Plant —	Dream —	2/8
3/7	Fire —	Sight —	Astral —	Animal —	Trance —	3/7
4/6	Air —	Touch —	Sensitive —	Human —	Awake —	4/6
5/10	Ether —	Sound —	Sacred —	Angelic —	Communion —	5/10

The pyramid with a base of four and one point at the top is symbolic of the 5 as a point of common relationship. For anyone thinking about further senses other than the five mentioned, I suggest you think of each of the four at the base of the pyramid (smell, taste, sight, and touch, which are all modifications of sound) and consider how other senses might be associated with them. Examples are smell as an expression of the sense of direction, taste as discernment, sight as the sense of judgment, and touch as the sense of consciousness.

The fifth stage of a plant is the fruit. It is simultaneously a return to the seed yet also suggests something beyond that; hence we speak of the golden fruit. The fruit also brings our attention to the paradoxical question of which came first, the fruit or the seed. Paradox suggests a knot, the strange twist through which anything becomes its opposite. It cannot be resolved but we can live in the heart of the paradox. 5 is the relation of all things to all things, even those things that do not seem to have any relation. It is the threshold, the marriage at its most transformative. Through the threshold of the paradox everything sacrifices itself. It is the ever-changing center, the middle of everything, the meeting and departing of all things and beings.

The Physical Body

The body has five limbs, it is the medium for the five senses, and simply speaking it is made of the five elements. The senses act as the communicative interface between the inner and outer worlds. They could be described as the threshold for the marriage between these worlds. Through this interface we give and receive feedback, we learn and adapt.

The body speaks with five voices and when these are all present together then we would say that the voice has body. Mystically we were born from sound and it is this body that can give back the sound that created it. As with a temple, when the proportions of all things correspond to the natural proportions, then it allows the fullness of the sound.

The amazing thing about the Physical Body is that although it is merely made of matter it still contains within it the pathway beyond itself to spirit. It is the gateway or the bridge between all worlds. In some way we can consider the whole body as a magnification of the throat and the fifth chakra, responsible for communication. The throat is a threshold where things pass through in multiple directions between above/below, left/right, front/back, and inner/outer. The principal medium for this multi-dimensional communication system of the body is the nervous system; it is neither mind nor body but both. The nerves and their chemical interactions could be said to be the mind of the body and the body of the mind. They make it possible for the body to take us through and beyond time and space. The mind could not travel anywhere, even in its dreams, without the body to bring us back from one dream world and support the crossover into another. We can only learn who we really are by crossing the bridge of our human birth, said by some to be a rare and precious jewel, for it is there we meet the totality of our consciousness.

To live on the threshold of our dual consciousness is a delicate state for there is a great sensitivity, which can be so overwhelming that it sends us into one or another corner of consciousness. Furthermore, the presence it takes to remain centered in an ever-moving center requires a lot of learning. A steady adaptability and continuous flexibility that stems from an integrated consciousness is the freedom, which constantly stays a servant to the center itself. When we are under the influence of this number our Physical Body can easily be thrown off balance by even the slightest change in the way we eat or sleep, and try as we might, we can never quite pinpoint why this is so. There is a certain integrity of life experience, which is familiar to those who are predominantly under the sway of number 5, whether it be sleep or wakefulness, feasting or fasting, inertia or activity, heat or cold, one extreme to another.

The fifth dimension is the aspect through which we can finely tune our whole system and it's here that all excesses and deficiencies are regulated. The whole self is like an ecosystem that continually works to keep itself in perfect balance though it does not just recycle the natural pattern. The human system is a process of dynamic growth, and maintaining the balance in a multi-dimensional system, which is forever evolving and changing, is a complex matter. Here the equal importance of polarizing forces and their interaction is realized; black and white, male and female, yin and yang, upper and lower, inner and outer, visible and invisible, matter and spirit, generation and degeneration, life and death, divergence and convergence, and so on. Naturally, questions of good and bad are replaced by questions of balance or imbalance, harmony or disharmony, ease or disease, attention or tension, etc.

The fifth realm is the connecting link between the body-mind and the spirit-mind, each dimension experiencing itself when they meet their counterpart. It is the center of the experience of the contact between the two polarities and also the center of learning since experience is our greatest teacher. Learning is absorbed in many ways but it is by mixing the appropriate ingredients of each of our various faculties in daily life that determines what we assimilate in any situation. The right balance in our work, rest, play, diet, exercise, and social interaction is an important part of developing ourselves as a human being and through the fifth dimension we are able to reach the extremes of these natural events. We discover how to fast and feast, to sleep all day and to stay up all night. We are able to push ourselves to our physical limits, like remaining as still as a stone for long periods or being super-social or anti-social.

Developing this fifth Body involves recognizing these polarities, either entering into them consciously and accepting the consequences or learning to regulate them into a fine art. There is the chance to experience the paradox of an existing self, which becomes a not self through every attempt to locate it in time or space. Such an insight can result in a total breakdown of nervous function into the disintegration of the personality. There are dire consequences for anyone who continues to exist in this state and the fear of such a way of being makes most people work hard to maintain a strong sense of self. However, they are only setting themselves up for a bigger shock when the truth finally emerges, as its nature dictates it surely must. The mastery of number 5 is to live moment by moment with a self that is and yet is not.

The tendency to seek balance, which is a fundamental part of the fifth dimension, means becoming teachers as well as students of life. In harmony we become an example to others where they can identify the difference between such things as ease and disease and tension and attention. Our communication will also be directed toward an equilibrium where we cultivate the understanding of intuitive communication and the ability to speak to people at their own level and in their own personal dialogue. This intuitive process also means the fifth dimension allows us to mediate between people with vastly different forms or levels of knowledge. It offers the practice of synthesizing, making connections and networking, drawing together the threads of insight and putting them together in a new way. It is where the sum of all things is greater than the mere addition of the parts and this is the relation of 5 to 10.

Dominated by the question "who am I?" the number 5 leads us through the struggle with our continuously changing identity, the hovering center that we know exists but which defies any attempts to pin it down. Dialogue and relationship is everything to this aspect of our identity for only then does it know of its existence. By the influence of the number 5 some people find themselves constantly setting up and breaking down descriptions of the universe, but to accomplish anything they must inevitably first do the opposite. Life seems to be forever collapsing inside of itself and re-manifesting from nowhere. The inherent reversal in all things and events is often strikingly clear to someone who is intimately connected to the number 5 and this can make it difficult to function. However, it is not a static situation and so the urge to engage in the world is as frequent as the call to cease all activity. It is the story of the active and passive qualities in our lives coming closer and closer into relationship until they merge when the two faces become one and talk the same talk.

There is a contrast to be made between the number 10 and the number 5. The aspect, which is expressed in 10, leads us to feel on the outside of things, not necessarily as a witness but rather as a presence. Sometimes this makes us feel like an appendage, something stuck on the side and often ignored. On the other hand 5 and the whole Physical Body with its five elements and senses lets us feel that we are really at the center of things. When the radiant energy is particularly strong there will either be a charismatic appeal or, if the presence is too overwhelming, the person will be ignored and excluded. We may put ourselves on the outside because the number 5 requires us to lose our identity when we go into relationship but the energy of this number places a person at the center whether they like it or not. The most central position is the one that relates all to all and is not a stage for an actor or an object to be worshiped. With a little cultivation the experiences brought through the number 5 can be developed into masterful communicative abilities that make a good teacher. The catch is we only learn to communicate by communicating and so, too, we only learn to teach by teaching. It requires that we take a dive into the net of time and space and experience our connection to everything and everyone.

Guru Arjun

Guru Arjun engaged in the activity of turning the market place of the body and world into a Golden Temple, a Harimandir, which would house the scripture and become a place of Karta Purkh, the union of activity and presence. The poetry of the Guru weaves a link between the wandering soul and God and the word sacrifices itself again and again, available for all who turn towards it.

Following the work initiated by his predecessor Guru Arjun

completed the building of the Golden Temple at Amritsar and within it placed a compilation of the poetic words of the great saints of India. Furthermore, he put the sacred text on a higher platform than his own seat. This temple stands as a metaphor for the body, within which there is an alchemic transmutation of our inner dormant led nature towards the awakened golden radiance that is the fruit of a true spiritual practice. The word of the scripture within the temple is like the philosopher's stone, which touches one to the inner core to bring about the transmutational marriage of spirit and matter. The scripture sits in a state of passive being and only when we open it, read its words, and become those words do they become alive in our deeds. This is also the marriage of doing and being. The word is a bridge between passivity and activity, between the small personal soul and the unbound collective spirit.

Guru Arjun passed through this transformation when he sacrificed himself rather than compromise the words of the saints. After being tortured for five days and nights he made one last request to bathe in the river. A Muslim holy man asked that he reconsider as it might be quite painful, given his wounds, but the Guru asked him to look again with closed eyes. As the holy man looked to the Guru with his inner eyes he saw his radiant body and knew that the light of Naanak that passed through each of the Gurus was beyond all suffering. When they took the Guru to bathe in the river his body disappeared. The golden fruit was ripe and harvested by its divine creator.

The name ARJUN has several meanings. ARJ means petition or prayer and we realize how the whole of the Guru Granth Sahib is both God's prayer to humanity and humanity's prayer to God. ARJUN signifies a bridge, the great bridge provided by Guru Arjun when he compiled the scripture. He sacrificed his own life and body to maintain the Sikh dharma, further illustrating what it takes to become a bridge for others. This sacrifice was also to become a bridge between what had been a community with an internal orientation to one much more externalized that was required to take a strong stand for its committed faith and defend itself from attack. This represents the transition in human evolution of a person who has arrived at some basis of faith within them and then dares to speak and live by it. The world then challenges us to stand steady in our faith where many fears are brought to light but also where our courage is creatively realized. 5 is the number of transformation through which the five problems or passions, associated with the senses, are killed and resurrected as five virtues. The Gurbani (word of the Guru) also makes frequent reference to the five elements from which the body has been made.

Karta Purkh

The type of spiritual service as described above involves sacrifice to the presence of the creative being (Karta Purkh), the true creative force behind every soul. To be truly creative requires the sacrificial interaction of both our active and passive aspects. KARTA is activity whilst PURKH is the passive, but radiant being. The world is the body and market place of God and so is the physical body. Here the activity (Karta) is to trade and to trade in God's name is the highest activity. In this process there is both the activity of speaking and the presence of being (Purkh), which is receptive and listening. Karta Purkh is the living paradox.

As indicated above, the Sri Guru Granth Sahib remains always in radiant being, yet it only comes alive for us when we actively read and hear its words. Even in its activity of pouring out wisdom the Sri Guru Granth Sahib never loses its passive radiant nature of just being there (Purkh). It is the disciple who approaches the Gurbani in sacrificial readiness, to recite and listen to it, that then brings the active element of Karta into being.

Chapter 8

Number 6

There is something quite secret and unknown about the number 6. It is not a number often spoken of in teachings and, in fact, to describe it may well be to risk telling lies; better to say little or nothing. I will risk saying a little.

The form of the 6 suggests the hook of grace that is there to meet anyone who crosses the threshold of number 5, although many describe their experience as a crisis rather than a blessing. In one way 6 is the number of the cube for there are six sides or faces. A dice is used in many games of chance and often a 6 must be thrown in order to start. This relationship between 6 and luck is perhaps the most influential quality of the 6 to be explicitly found in our lives. Whether we call it fortune, chance, luck, destiny, or grace, the implication is that the 6 is the number that brings us into the relationship to the unknown.

A curious mathematical property of the 6 is that $1 + 2 + 3 = 6$ and $1 \times 2 \times 3 = 6$; it is the only number where the addition or multiplication of its components gives the same result. Addition or multiplication are the two mathematical functions which increase a number (division and subtraction decrease a number). This property of 6 implies that whichever method of increase or progress we try the first three steps will take us across the threshold of 5 to meet the unknown of the 6.

We would not be able to manage the experience of 6 without working on and preparing the Neutral Mind of number 4. This holds the quality of shock absorber without which our experience goes into crisis and throws us back upon ourselves to work on our genuine neutrality.

In nature we find the number 6 in the hexagonal shapes of the honeycomb of a bee. There is a geometrical symmetry of the 6 and the circle where six circles can fit around another circle making it twice as big. This same arrangement can be found in the game of Chinese Chequers, a great way to cultivate the Neutral Mind, where each player has ten counters that must be moved to the opposite position (remember 1 + 2 + 3 + 4 = 10).

The Arcline

The Arcline is an instrument of sensitivity to the subtleties in the outer environment. There is a constant stream of subtle vibrations flowing around us and the essence of these is simply the all-pervading godliness wishing to make contact. Since the subtle is non-rational and beyond ordinary measurement our minds then feel confronted with the question of fear or faith. Our uninspired tendency is to choose fear and then silence; in other words we decide not to speak of the subtle and hope that it might disappear. The six sides of the dice represent the six directions of our sensitivity and our insecurity. The Arcline is given to manifest the warrior but in most cases we become worriers. We talk out of fear; we keep silent out of fear. To develop the Arcline you can learn to speak to the silence and from the silence and no matter how loudly you spoke you would never break the silence.

The higher intuition and understanding is a flame kept burning by the presence of a sharp and graceful presence. This flame is known as the third eye but the wind that fans the flame is the true number 6 and the Arcline. Intuition is like the feelers of a snail reaching out and sensing the world. It is the means to predict the next moment, to know the immediate future. Through the Arcline we can sense the secret world.

It takes wind to know the wind and the Arcline is given so that we may know which way the wind is blowing. Its strength is that it is not shocked by reality, rather it expresses the awakened state that is shocking to others; it can shock others into awakening. Fear tends to close it down though in reality fear is just an honest intuition about the future. What you fear has already happened. The Arcline invites you to just wake up, awake to grace, and take the risk of faith. You exist; the dice has been thrown and now have faith enough to live the consequence.

The sensitivity of the Arcline gives the artistic awareness, the capacity to sense the subtle and to give it a voice in the world of the ordinary. Sensing the subtle implies sensing the unity and so a person with an open and strong Arcline will tend to feel a conscious responsibility to manifest the hidden harmony. This might be done through fine art, music, and dance, but can also be expressed in the art of war and the calling for natural justice.

When the Arcline is confused or weak then the opposite qualities will manifest, such as irresponsibility, carelessness, and a paralyzing fear. You would speak from a place of confusion and always be trying to cover or avoid the silence. With a weak Arcline you will feel the fear of confrontation or conflict. You will seek resolution but not fight for justice. Afraid to take responsibility for truth you become disagreeable to yourself instead of disagreeable to the illusions of others.

The Arcline corresponds to the halo and holds the balance between left and right hemispheres of the brain. Serving to keep our future projections clear, it is the projective intuition through which we steer a path of freedom into the unknown. Often termed the sixth sense, clairvoyance works through the Arcline but must be harnessed by numbers 3 and 7 to be transformed into vision. To have the sixth sense is to be graced, though some people live it as a curse, fighting against their own awakening.

Once awake to the law of the fourth state the soul is concerned with matters of justice as an expression of truth realized in the neutral consciousness. This awareness, stirred by the numbers 4 and 6, brings us closer into contact with ourselves and we consciously begin to notice the on-going dialogue that habitually runs through our minds. We notice more and more that our conversations in the world are really just conversations with ourselves where we are trying to find harmony between all our polarities. The endless debate of weighing up the two sides in every situation, the constant balancing of all the pros and cons and running through every angle of any argument serves only to create a bigger split, enlarging the chasm which must be bridged in the return to harmony. So even though our dialogue, whether internal or external, is apparently stimulated by our search for justice and harmony, we end up being increasingly afraid of taking a stand and making the leap. Just as doubt and trust are the expressions of the Neutral Mind, so fear and faith are those reflected in the Arcline.

A weakened Arcline brings great fear in meeting the tension between ourselves or any two people and rather than address this we learn to be superficially agreeable to everyone, hoping that we can bypass any conflict. This only deepens the difference and so increases our fear. It is at the moment when we become disagreeable to others, using our fear as a wind to propel us through the difference, that we are met with grace and the battle of life becomes a beautiful dance. Beauty is a quality of consciousness that comes about through the awakening of the Arcline when it receives the touch of the unknown.

An appropriate response is an intuitively guided moment, which requires that we be free of anything other than the touch of the future moment. This is not a choice to be careless but a choice to be carefree. It means being free of anything except the unknown truth of this moment as it moves into the future and the unknown truth of the future as it moves into the present. We must be responsible in how we meet this because if we let our fear of the unknown freeze us we opt for the choice of default where we surrender to convention and the social norm as our crutch and master. The proportion of responsibility can be linked to the relationship between the personal aspect of intuition (4) and the impersonal dimension (6). In all situations we have a 40% responsibility and choice while the other 60% that we are inclined to blame on others is actually the impersonal, collective, and divine choice. It represents itself to us through particular people in particular times in particular places.

The seed of truth delivered in the heart of the flower of neutral consciousness is brought out through expression of the Arcline. In this way a person may become a master of speech, knowing just what to say and when to say it. Our words spoken through the Arcline will sound like a poem written precisely for that moment and the beauty in music, poetry, fine art, and dance will be set free by the touch of this number 6 on the human halo. A mask of truth, no matter how unpleasant the pain may be, can always be portrayed with the precision, the clarity, the sharpness, and the gentleness of the finest surgeon's knife. Until we become master artists at the game of life and death, truth will continue to be a disagreeable affair. But when we do there will be an unshakeable dynamic faith and an irrational love for the irrational in the world, born out of a fear that has gone beyond fear.

An expression of an elementary awakening of this consciousness is to campaign for political and spiritual freedom for all people. Whether it is through songs of freedom or in the speeches of the advocates of justice in the courts of humankind or in the playground of world ecology, these freedom artists are prepared to fight tooth and nail, tongue and sword against any injustice. Blind though their faith may be in the early days of human enlightenment, it is only through these struggles that the archetypal warrior of grace can bless us with the touch of her breath so that we might see the beauty in all.

Fearlessness and justice are two of the main talents of the sixth dimension. Through the third we are aware of unfairness and in the fourth we make choices and decisions based on these injustices which, therefore, have soul implications. These decisions express a social part of our human nature, which is able to take a neutral look at the individualized body self of the first, second, and third dimensions. At the fourth, however, these choices are based on a feeling sense of which we are still somewhat unclear. We are more likely to be uncertain about all the implications and outcomes that arise from our choices, hence the need for neutrality. In the sixth dimension we find clarity in the consequences because of our commitment to them. These are commitments made with a degree of consciousness or made unconsciously by the fact that if we do not choose then choices are made for us. We are confronted to take the full 100% of our 40% responsibility for both our conscious and unconscious choices and it is here that we become aware of the fears, which have influenced or even dictated the decisions. When choices have been made on a foundation of truth that has been felt spontaneously (see number 4), then it is in the sixth realm that we cultivate fearlessness to carry through the task; to believe in justice is one thing but to practice it is another. If you find yourself frequently drawn into conflict and asked to take sides, then see this as an opportunity to develop this arena of consciousness.

There are times when peace can only be won by entering into the battle and the sixth dimension stands for these occasions. However, it is not where we can seek out injustices and take up the flag of some cause or other without invitation. Rather it is the ability to defend freedom when we are confronted, be it religious, political, or otherwise. If we actively seek out oppressive forces in society then we avoid working on ourselves and present ourselves as someone to be feared. The other extreme is to bow to suppression where we cannot live or speak the truth as we see it. Fear of what others may think if we speak out turns us into a passive yes type where we avoid conflict and disagreement at any cost. We fall into the silent majority, which only serves to maintain the status quo and perpetrates the prejudices of society. So to give others cause to fear us or to live in fear of others are the extremes that the sixth dimension can resolve.

For more clarity on the relationship between the fourth and sixth Bodies regarding choice making, consider the following comparison. In the fourth dimension, the Neutral Mind, internal dialogues are much more feeling orientated especially those felt in the body. They are not usually expressed unless asked for so we find it difficult to voice them. In the sixth, however, our choice making process is more geared toward the spirit-mind. Here we tend to think aloud, often talking to others but really we are just talking to ourselves. It is for this reason that we might find it hard to keep secrets, although underactivity may lead to the opposite effect where we guard secrets that should be told. We may talk a lot about everything except what needs to be said and in doing so we keep our secrets.

We direct our fears and the clarity that comes from our present commitments toward the future and in this way the sixth dimension is connected to that projected state. There are three important elements of the future to be considered. First is the known, the easily predictable where things are fairly reliable due to its cyclic nature such as the seasons, the rising and setting of the sun, and our eating and sleeping habits. The second part is less predictable but it is an unknown that is possible to determine. For example, moods fluctuate and often seem to be impulsive, erratic, and uncertain, yet with a little self-knowledge and intuition even these can be anticipated and less of a surprise when they happen. It is this intuitive skill that can be developed in this sixth state. The third element of the future is the unknown, which remains unknowable where there is always the possibility of chaos or miracles. Here we have the chance to reach the limits of our rational human understanding and to begin an irrational engagement with the unexplainable forces of the universe.

As we further work on the sixth dimension of being human, we learn to build a relationship of trust and faith to the absolute unknown. This is not to be mistaken with the half-hearted surrender of blind faith, which is irresponsible and expresses a certain lack of concern. A more appropriate form of trust is to be carefree or free of care but not careless. Potentially we have the fearlessness to face all the implications of the unknown, which lie ahead. We can leap into the void holding onto the rope of honesty fully conscious there are some things we will never know. Furthermore, we realize this unknown is perhaps the greatest significant force in our life when we really look to the magnitude of what we do not know. Here we learn to take responsibility for what we are truly responsible for and equally to let go of any attempt to control arenas where we are helpless and dependent upon the great unknown. This unknown is a force, which has been called many things such as destiny, spirit, god, death, fate, grace, luck, chance, and nothingness. Different cultures have, of course, found their own expressions and ways of responding to the absolute unknown.

The second element of the future, associated to the rise and fall of moods and emotions, gives the sixth dimension a quality of artistic sensitivity. We attempt to beautify even the ugliest of moods through art and indeed, music, painting, and dance are perhaps the most potent mediums to express the vast array of human moods.

When we communicate moods and feelings from these artistic channels then we add a touch of grace. In alignment with the fourth and fifth Bodies we find that every emotion inherently contains its opposite and is, therefore, also known by its antithesis.

We are then cautious about placing a feeling such as love as the ultimate cause or result of the universe. If love is a feeling beyond polarities then there needs to be some way of distinguishing it from the many forms of so-called love, which clearly are not what they profess to be. Just as our language carries confusion so do our actions and behavior. I would suggest that wonder is a way of being beyond polarized feelings by being absolutely present with all the feelings. A lack of wonder would indicate a lack of presence of the whole self.

Vulnerability has been associated with the fourth mode of consciousness. The term, however, indicates there may have been some kind of damage to the essential nature through exposure of undesirable feelings. It suggests that if we are open to feelings then we are also open to being hurt. But in truth it is only attachment to our own way of thinking and our self-image that causes the pain. Vulnerability is much more related to the innocence and naivety of the second dimension. By their own nature, feelings are neither good nor bad but it is essential to us as human beings to feel.

To the extent that we have a limited or unlimited capacity to move our feeling energy through our nervous system and its spiritual counterpart, we are open to wonder. To the extent that we are attached to our self-image we will protect our true identity from exposure to feelings. To the extent that we are in touch with our origin and destiny we will open ourselves to feel wonder and to flow in our true essential nature. The strength to be open and receptive to all sensitivities is developed through the fearlessness of the sixth body, represented by the Arcline and symbolized by the sword.

Guru Har Gobind

As the first Guru not to write any poetic hymns Guru Har Gobind was the embodiment of the meditative state of silence; his very life was poetry itself. His cause was justice but he never fought against anyone. In other words he was never the first to lift the sword. Accepting the responsibility to stand in defense of the community, Guru Har Gobind fought for their freedom to praise the Divine. He lived according to the principle of never being afraid of anyone or giving others cause to fear him. He is especially remembered for the occasion when he was wrongly imprisoned and then refused his personal freedom unless others, who were also imprisoned for no good reason, could be set free.

After his release Guru Har Gobind had to defend the community against the unjust attacks of others. HAR is the destructive creativity of God, whilst GOBIND means to sustain, bind, or hold together. Guru Har Gobind found himself in this paradox of conflict for the sake of harmony. His battle was for the sake of a balanced justice that was congruent in both the spiritual and worldly aspects of life; in one hand the sword of truth while in the other hand the sword of faith. This is not only an expression of carefree responsibility but also a means to go beyond duality by binding these qualities together. Doubt is always a duality and to go beyond duality is to go beyond doubt and therefore to be fearless.

By establishing the community, Guru Har Gobind had completed the second level of what Guru Naanak had foretold in the Mul Mantra. The first level was that of the individual and was expressed by the first three Gurus. The second level of community was fulfilled by the fourth, fifth, and sixth Gurus and would become the base for the third level, the universal level realized by the seventh, eighth, and ninth Gurus. Guru Har Gobind oversaw the completion of the Akaal Takht, the Immortal Throne, where political affairs of the community were discussed and decided. The most prominent reference to the number 6 in the words of the Guru is the six mansions, the six teachers, and the six teachings. It is unclear whether this relates to six schools of Indian philosophy but it is interesting to note that six of the ten Gurus have their spiritual poetry in the Guru Granth Sahib.

Nirbhau

Guru Naanak understood the development of consciousness totally and voiced it in the next aspect of the Mul Mantra. NIRBHAU means without fear and generally it can be said that what we fear is related to the future and the unknown. This stage of development is concerned with taking the risk to engage with the unknown, going beyond our fears that usually stop us. It is through the fearless consciousness that we are less self-concerned and more interested and motivated towards the well-being and freedom of others. To live in fear is to be imprisoned and it is only out of fearlessness that we maintain a balanced sense of justice, aware of both the spiritual and temporal concerns.

If our actions could be fearless (Nirbhau) we would step forward to sustain harmony and justice and we would not let our fear of the unknown keep us from entering into the conflict of life. The future is never certain and yet it is there that we are encouraged to turn. Our fears can be transformed into the warrior's power of faith from where our wandering transforms to wonder.

Chapter 9

Number 7

Many claims have been made for the power and importance of the number 7, far more than it deserves. This is like a king declaring his greatness and forgetting his advisors or a mill, proud of its machinery and stature that fails to remember the energy of the wind and the water, without which it would be useless. The seven colors of the rainbow can only be projected with the right quality of the atmosphere but nonetheless, these colors, like the number 7, have their purpose. They act as a sign in the heavens for greater, more mysterious things whilst at the same time, because they are so fascinating, they serve to distract our attention from these greater mysteries. The number 7 is a number of vision, form, and structure and colors are important in helping to distinguish them. Inner vision perceives a system of seven chakras or energy centers and the seventh may well be the gate to heaven but it is not heaven itself.

There are many systems of life and philosophy based in the law of 7. There are said to be seven steps to heaven but few realize that we mostly walk the seven steps to hell. There are seven main notes structuring our musical system (while 8 is the number of return). The week is shaped into seven days, the seventh day of creation was a day of beholding (witnessing, looking) rather than a day of rest, and the seven-year cycles are significant signposts in a person's development. It is important to note that even though cycles are sometimes related to the number 7, this does not make 7 the number of time. 7 is the number of structure and time is one of the things that gets structured by the 7 as well as by other numbers.

Although new planets have been discovered, astrology still refers to the seven planets of the ancients as if they have a peculiar importance of their own. This is just as much a statement about the number 7 as it is about those seven planets. 7 is the number of the upper astral planes (3 is the number of the lower astral planes) where there are many beings or astral bodies hanging out waiting for the opportunity to process their karma.

Several religious texts refer to the seven generations through which karmic patterns are handed down. This means that some of what we experience in this life is influenced by six generations that went before us, and how we live now will influence the six generations that will follow us. The history of seven generations is the collective karma that we inherit and pass on. In karma the past repeats itself and since our perspective can only be partial as we look back, we bring the patterns of the past into the future and live the past over and over again.

A mathematical quality of 7 is its tendency to produce static patterns, as it is not a number that has a multiple of whole numbers within it. 7 cannot be divided into any multiple of whole numbers but if we divide any number, which is not an exact multiple of 7, by 7 then it will produce a repeating set of decimal numbers in the order of 285714. This tendency to static patterns is both a quality of predictability and safety as well as one of entrapment. (You may have noticed this was also an issue related to the number 3.) There is an intimacy between the number pairs that add up to 10. Just as 4 is the bud and 6 the flower of consciousness, so 3 is the three primary colors and the three-dimensional outer space while 7 is the rainbow and the inner space where we perceive the inner centers known as chakras.

The Aura

The magnetic field known to surround your body is called the Aura. Prana is the energy that provides the electric current that can change the quality and power of your Aura. As a magnetic field your Aura stores information and can attract or repel others. It is your space where you hold the record of familiarity and family. When you meet someone you know but do not recognize them it could be that your or their Aura is weak and so the remembrance of the familiar is breaking down. This is a more common occurrence in adults after passing the seventh cycle of seven years. As we get older the Aura breaks down and the capacity of recognition is lost.

The space of familiarity can include the wider family of your race or nation. The past is also familiar and with it all your gathered friends and enemies, all contained in the Aura. Your pride and fame as well as blame and shame are the common mental constructs that give shape to your psychic space. Ultimately we must realize that the Aura is like a mirage, a play of light in the atmosphere, a projection of color with no substance. It is a sign of something but not the thing in itself.

There is a strong relation between the Aura and your sense of confidence or lack of it. When the Aura is out of balance the ego-mind creates compensatory stories and begins to believe in its inferiority or its superiority, forgetting completely the truth of equality. Both inferiority and superiority are forms of self-conceit and mistaken self-importance. The ego-mind is born to judge and must eventually make the final judgment, as God did on the seventh day of creation, that all is well. A well-balanced Aura does not mean a big projection but actually results in a kind of transparency. The harmony of the seven colors allows the usually obscured light to radiate through. It is the radiance rather than the projection that is expansive when the Aura is in harmony. A big projection of self-image demonstrates an over-identification with the image itself and an anticipatory fear of the moment when the temporary cocoon must crumble.

Too long out of touch with the light that illuminates our temporary passage on this earth leads to skepticism and cynicism. It is basically a state of self-deceit that imprisons the spirit. It is helpful to remember that the Aura is a temporary projection providing protection but also imprisonment. As your magnetic space it is like the robes of honor, the dress that marks you as accomplished like a priest or some other professional status.

The seven colors that make up the Aura and the corresponding seven chakras are symbolic of the Royal Road. It is the ladder to be climbed, the regal fashion in which to advance, but it is not the goal. A nice Aura guarantees nothing – it just means that you can travel in style. But whether you know where to go or get busier showing off your style rather than proceeding on the journey is a matter of grace that allows karma to become dharma. The difference is also an expression of, and expressed in, our relation to the past.

While the Arcline gives you a direct presence in relating to the future, the Aura is a window through which you look to the past. Formed through past patterns of thought and action, the Aura is shaped by how you view and interpret all that you have witnessed. Any attachment to our history is karmic. That means it must repeat itself and is likely to carry with it feelings such as blame, shame, guilt, remorse, regrets, revenge, and resentment. The liberation of these shadows in your Aura is through the practice of dharma. Right understanding involves the cultivation of forgiveness, mercy, and compassion, which would bring about the shining qualities of a clear Aura. Historical passions and attachments would no longer be able to bind you down and the mind becomes your servant instead of your master.

However, rather than merely denounce these qualities of attachment to the past, it would be helpful to understand how they arise for such understanding can lead us from the prison cells of our history into freedom. The myth of original sin holds a clue though it is heavily disguised and brutally abused. I am referring to the concept of the fall. Our individuality germinates like a seed that falls (or was pushed) from the tree, which is neither good nor bad, but it does create an instinctive emotion of longing once the seed has taken root. This deeply felt sentiment, which is simply the yearning for unity once more, is expressed as sadness, hunger, or emptiness. Sadness is then interpreted as unwanted and to be avoided but in making it wrong we only fuel it until it becomes depression and that in turn deepens it toward suicidal instincts. Meanwhile our emptiness has to be filled and usually this is done to excess and not with what is actually desired or needed.

Looking back to a lost paradise (of oblivion) and getting hung up on the so-called pain of separation, we obviously want to look for a scapegoat. The first one to blame would be God, but that would be blasphemous so we blame ourselves. However, self-blame is humiliating so we tend to turn it outwardly and blame others. Blame takes many shapes and is often disguised by constructed dramas of accidents and circumstances, which become our crutches. With these we deny any iota of responsibility for the present, even for those few outcomes which might actually be a genuine consequence of our own past choices.

Purifying our sense of guilt begins with a recognition of the law of karma, the law of cause and effect. This will drastically modify our view of free choice and regulate the process by which we make any apparent free choice. This purification process ends by tracing that law back to and beyond its beginning where there is no choice, no responsibility, and no subsequent blame. What remains is the pure, unqualified experience of a seed surrendering itself for the sake of its own enduring essence and the longing to move forward out into life; it is the Aura which provides the psychic form for this journey. With this understanding for all sentient beings, no matter what form they may take, comes a compassionate recognition of the labor of suffering that separation carries with it.

The brightness that glows through a well-developed Aura has a knock-on effect in the other dimensions. It contributes towards a commanding presence due to the attraction that exists between the magnetic field and the energy that feeds it. This energy, this prana can flow freely when the auric pattern is clear of any blame and shame and through this transparency the past can easily fall away as soon as it becomes the past. In this way we can be more fully present and temporarily act out the various roles required according to the occasion without adding our own scheming agendas. The actor in each of us is based on the knowledge of different realities that can be accessed through the astral realms. By tapping into this source of information we are capable of putting on some pretty convincing performances, be it for a fee, for fun, or for reasons we do not understand. In the last case we are probably semi-consciously playing out unresolved dramas of our past, each dramatic role changing the quality of the Aura, which is a bit like putting on coats of different colors and shape.

When the Positive Mind is attuned and aligned with the Aura we will be sensitive to the past of others and to any resentment they may still be carrying in their present life. When these are directed at us, even if they are done so unconsciously, we will tend to over-react, especially if we bring in our own history. To move out of this vicious triangle, which regenerates karma and prevents us from stepping into a free future, we simply need to practice forgiveness. I say simply, yet forgiveness is not to imply a concept but an action. We need to explore concrete methods whereby the idea of forgiveness becomes an experiential reality, because simple though the idea may be it is not so easy. The clue does not lie in the question "what to do?" but rather in "when will we stop doing?" When will we stop the physical and mental habits, which serve to maintain the patterns of shame or blame? When will we stop holding on to the initial judgment that acts as the cornerstone to the structure of guilt or resentment?

The stopping begins when we are touched by the fourth dimension of the Neutral Mind or the crisis of the sixth. If we do not stop, our judgment will keep us imprisoned in the glass coffin of our magnetic projection, a projection of which we are so proud and yet we complain of its tight perimeters and want out, but don't want out.

When taken in context with the other realms it becomes possible to open up our limited concepts of right and wrong. The Aura is a defense system and through this we are able to relate to friends and enemies. Those who we feel have done us right or wrong, individuals, groups, or even abstract figures such as God, come to be viewed as one or the other, friend or foe. All enemies are then avoided or engaged in battle but when our Aura becomes clear it allows us to recognize in others the same flame of life that flickers within us all. This kindles the practice of mercy and is expressed in a passive form of simply letting go though there are occasions when we may feel it is right to be cruel to be kind. If we do go into battle then it is at least appropriate to realize whether we are fighting out of anger, revenge, or hatred. Oppositional forces are understood to be part of the whole self but it is also understood that this conflict is needed to maintain the balance. In this we become greater than the

Aura; we do not identify with the coat we wear but recognize it as such and realize it can be changed.

Impotence or helplessness that may be experienced in the realm of the Positive Mind coexists with a feeling of victimization. We may regress further with this into the second dimension and engage in self-criticizm, self-punishment, and even suicide, which in psychological terms can be seen as passive aggression. Anger can only arise if there is an issue that we actually care about. If we cannot let it go, a more congruous response would be to take positive action and accept the feeling of genuine care and concern. The negative energy can then be put to good use as fuel for getting on with things and influencing change. The fuel for the Aura is prana, just as hunger and desire, felt as negative tension, is fuel for the body. This tension feeds the impulse to survive and results in positive action. Prana can also come in the form of wisdom, which stimulates right or positive understanding that is then displayed in the Aura.

Ambitious plans of revenge or self-punishment and personal schemes of selfish action can clog the channels and block the flow of the pure healing powers of prana. The positive self of the spirit-mind is the dimension in which we learn to enjoy our own company. In this seventh realm we can find a source of confidence within ourselves that empowers our own counsel, giving us the freedom to develop a unique philosophy of life. In excess, however, this tendency can produce fantasies and neurotic behavior and speech. Without the balance of the caring qualities of the Positive Mind the unstructured possibilities of self-counsel can evolve into a form of cynicism towards other people and their way of thinking rather than non-judgmental respect for other paths. Furthermore, the fascinating view of astral worlds, which is opened up in this seventh Body, can inhibit any faith in the unseen essence. There can be a skepticism and unwillingness to see or detect the one that endures through all transformations of time and space. But it is here that we can learn to be tolerant of others and to allow the view that all paths lead to the same place even if some go in the opposite direction to get there.

If there is a deficiency of consciousness in the seventh dimension there may be a lack of confidence, shyness, and feelings of inferiority.

Then we would feel lonely rather than enjoy being alone and have no courage to go out and find the company of others. Disbelief about the ability to be anything other than our history is often a cover for doubts and resentments, doubts about absolute reality and resentment for anyone who succeeds in imposing their reality on others. This may even mean we resent ourselves, secretly wishing that we could enforce our beliefs on those around. When we doubt our own doubt then it is helpful to take up some guiding principle to steer a way through the sea of chaos. Cynicism and skepticism are the deadly enemies of the self in the seventh dimension and left unchecked they lead us into a black hole from where it is difficult to return. Of course, for some this is fine but for those who are unhappy about entering the chaos alone and unguided, then it is apt to find some thread with which to trace out the pathway through the labyrinth, some signposts to that subtle home beyond the death of chaos.

Guru Har Rai

Kindness, mercy, and forgiveness were the qualities that the seventh Guru embodied. Inspired by the flower, Guru Har Rai noted that even though people break flowers with one hand and offer them with the other, the flower perfumes both hands. He was referring to the manner in which Guru Har Gobind, even though he had been imprisoned by the emperor also came to his rescue and saved his life when a tiger was about to attack him. Guru Har Rai himself also sent the medicine that cured the son of the emperor who had declared himself the enemy of the Sikhs. He studied the ways in which people could be helped and knew the solutions to many problems. His mercy extended to animals as well and he kept a sanctuary for their healing.

Guru Har Rai, the seventh Guru, was not a particularly public figure. He preferred to be a platform of elevating support for all those around him. The principle virtue that Guru Har Rai embodied was forgiveness and he taught this through example by not bearing grudges for the attacks on his predecessor Guru Har Gobind. The name HAR RAI suggests the Royal Road to God. When we lose the colors and forms of our own opinions then we come under the protection of Har/God who destroys our pride and status but allows us access to the Royal Road, RAI, which has its own color and form. In other words, when we cast of the self-constructed psychic shield then the mantle of divine protection descends to take its place. It is a robe and a crown that comes by grace rather than by self-effort. Therefore, it is not carried with the pride of ego but with the dignity of a soul that has become transparent enough to acknowledge what it truly represents. The seven steps on the ladder of attainment unfold easily and one reaches a panoramic viewpoint.

Nirvair

A true act of justice is also an act of mercy; hence the sword worn by the Guru is called the Kirpan, which means the hand of mercy. It is always a fight for and never a fight against. Fighting for justice for those who need defending is not an act of revenge, resentment, or punishment. It is one of mercy or kindness, both in the defense and liberation of the oppressed as well as for the awakening of the oppressor.

Guru Naanak understood that fearlessness itself was not enough and what was also needed was transparency where no past conflicts were carried into the future. The release of any complications arising from what went before proposes that we make no enemy of our history; this is the meaning of Nirvair. There is no profit to be had from endless regurgitation of the past, yet this is what we spend a lot of time doing. In this way we simply perpetuate the sense of animosity and revenge, digging a deeper and deeper hole from where only forgiveness can give the ladder of exit. We struggle with it hoping to find a victory but there is no real victory over the past, only an endless recycling through patterns of revenge. By abandoning the habit of making enemies of our past, through forgiveness, we immediately become free of the past (Nirvair).

Chapter 10

Number 8

8 is known as the number of the infinite, which is given as the symbol ∞. The two circles represent the relationship of finite self to infinite self and is a figure that suggests continuous movement. 8 is a number of return, the eternal return of infinity where everything comes back to itself, where everything comes and goes. The eighth note and the eight day is a return to the same starting point but one octave up or one week later so there is a return but never to the same place. It is like time flowing as a river, which implies a kind of spiralling return rather than a circular one. This twisting quality relates the number 8 to water and the organic kingdoms where the spiral force is most dominant. Chi or prana as the etheric expressions of water also move in this same winding motion. In addition the two circles of 8 suggest reflection, which is another quality of water.

The egg timer or hourglass is similar in shape to the figure 8 and is used to give a rhythm to time, which has no rhythm. It is like two worlds and while the salt or sand is displaced from one into the other, air is moved in reverse, each through the same narrow passage. 8 is, therefore, a symbol of movement and can be found in the example of extremes between power and poverty, profit and debt, a continuous, hydraulic flow of energy. It moves from full to empty and empty to full so that while one part of the 8 is full, the other is empty. As a number that links two worlds the 8 speaks of our need to be in relation to a world other than this one. In some people it manifests in a tendency to leave this world and go into the timeless world of dreams. Others access that world to bring something back here; healers are examples of this.

The three planes of three-dimensional space divide the space into eight divisions, like the eight corners of a cube, and this is one reason why many mandalas have eight parts to them (they are expressions of the three-dimensional world). The wheel with eight spokes is also a common expression of the power of 8. Other examples can be seen in the Buddhist wheel of Dharma, the octagon with the eight trigrams of the I Ching, the maypole with eight strings, the umbrella with eight branches, the deity with eight arms and the Native American healing circle. These forms of the 8, which return again and again in different cultures, may be a clue to an undying form that exists beyond time.

Also, in nature we find the spider with its eight legs and its web is like the veil of Maya.

The Pranic Body

The Pranic Body is our link to the infinite flow of energy. It is a link and the power that it brings with it is not a possession. Abundance is about access to the flow of life and energy, not the gathering of it in any static form. Misunderstanding leads to battles of power where people struggle for a little bit more from each other's limited energy supply instead of working on making the infinite link. Imbalance in relation to prana can lead to things like water retention, forced and abused authority, refusal to acknowledge natural authority or a tendency to live life in dream time instead of here on earth.

A balanced flow of prana expresses itself in cleanliness and purity of mind, body, and the world around, otherwise there could be obsessions with cleanliness or an abandoned chaos.

Prana is the infinite vital force of the organic world. As plants breathe out oxygen we inhale it and through this dimension we experience cleansing and recharging. Prana is the same as chi or qi, the energy that runs through the meridian channels of the body. It is infinite and through its flow we can experience the relationship of our finite consciousness to the infinite one. This, however, could result in a very dreamy and spaced out state and transcendent and ascensionizt thinking might be used as a way to ignore the shadow and fly too high (though this is not a reason to never fly). Dreaming of high and mighty ideals without the know-how or practical wisdom will turn the imagination into another means of escapism. Step by step and breath by breath, keeping the feet on the ground with the head looking both below and above the clouds is the balance between the Pranic Body and the other dimensions. But when the pranic force dominates our consciousness so that we only see above the clouds, sensing the infinite, then we develop a very serious approach to life. Our outlook may become fatalistic since we perceive the inevitable death of all finite things.

Asthmatic breathing is one of the difficulties that can result from bad experiences with power and the abuse of power. Prana is power and in itself it is pure and unqualified until it enters into relationship with other forces. Power possesses though we like to think we are in control but it has its own existence and runs through us like water. We can swim in it if its immensity and chaos does not drown us and of itself it is neither good nor bad; it is only our manipulations that make it otherwise. It can be used either way and is like the fuel in a petrol tank of a vehicle, which may take someone to hospital or carry stolen goods. Obviously, people in authority are often involved in the use and abuse of power but, in fact, we all are in some way. Depending on how we experience our own Pranic Body, we will enter into confrontational or co-operative relationships with those who hold positions of authority whether they are real or superficial.

Pranic power has a lot to do with healing and dying and when we realize that we begin to respect it more. It is a force for purification and cleansing so where there is a lack sickness will follow and an absolute deprivation would result in death by sickness. An increase of pranic flow would bring about the death of whatever was causing the illness but too much makes us very serious, which in turn could leave us obsessed with cleanliness and purification. It is, therefore, important to learn how to regulate this vital force, just as we might turn a tap to control the flow of water.

In this eighth dimension we can experience how patterns,

rhythms, and structures take form from emptiness and fall away again into the void. The imagination is infinite in space and eternal in time so that a lifetime can be felt in a moment and space crossed in a flash. This is the realm that allows us to daydream and if it were not for the right alignment of the other dimensions we could well daydream our life away. We would spend all our time with our head in the clouds, never enjoying the experience of bringing our ideas down to the ground. Ideas can only be realized step by step, breath by breath, which means starting from the beginning.

Sometimes we prefer to keep our ideas as ideals or fantasies, only to be accessed in the world of dreams rather than bringing them into actuality. It is like a traveler, who loves to travel but does not want to arrive anywhere, for to arrive is to be finished, to have done all we were born to do, and to count the days without purpose. Ideals belong to the past or future. We either want to bring back a lost period of supposed perfection or we hold some fantastic projection of what could be. To arrive at these ideals is to stop the flow of life and death in their interaction. The alternative offered by the eighth dimension is to abandon them and focus on the moment of now; that is to feel and experience the present as a moving process of order and chaos negotiating each step as it is taken.

To fully enter into the eighth domain is to be timelessly beyond time, not by transcending time but by inviting all time into the ever-present moment of now. It is the perpetual remembrance of the present, which is also perpetual forgetfulness of the past and future, but whilst still in the physical body of human existence this can only be experienced to a degree in rare moments of meditation. Out-of-body experiences move on the stream of prana and re-entering the Physical Body could be difficult if it were not for the other Bodies. It is, therefore, a dangerous practice unless we know how to maintain a connection and how to re-enter. We only partly disengage from these other dimensions when we are asleep and if we do fully separate, then the body is vulnerable to possession by other forces, which is one of the ways people become spaced out and psychotic. If you plan to astral travel be sure you know a safe practice for leaving and entering the body such as the continuous linking of the breath with a mantra. However, it is more important to ask yourself why you feel it is necessary to have these experiences, since the search for God is only concluded by finding the Divine within yourself.

Death and dying are essential to life and the natural healing processes and the eighth dimension of the self is an inherent aspect of this. Our encounters with the forces of death inevitably draw us into this realm even if we make no attempt to consciously take part in it. Death gives us a serious outlook to life and makes us more careful though by being too active in the negative self of the spirit-mind we can become over solemn and cautious, regarding everything as fatalistic. At the other extreme we run the risk of growing flippant and resignational, which is a form of psychological suicide.

Amongst other things healing involves letting the causes of our ailments undergo a death process and sometimes dying itself is very healing. The source of illness may be in the body-mind or the spirit-mind and just expresses the dance of the battle of life and death where a certain aspect is clearly having the upper hand. Undoubtedly, there is a time and place for everything as the pendulum of time swings in its eternal return. Natural death may sound appealing and easy, whilst many illnesses seem to be complicated by painful patterns of resistance, which paradoxically are efforts to avoid pain. Energy in the form of prana flows and moves like water and if it cannot go one way it will go another. This ability to allow things to flow is the not self of the Pranic Body, the negative self of the spirit-mind, where we can merge into the flow of life and death rather than remove ourselves from it. There is no side-stepping here and when we go into unconscious oblivion it is more than likely an attempt to split the self apart in order to avoid the unavoidable experience of death.

The potential to merge with the energy of another, as we offer ourselves as an alternative route for obstructed energies, is also given in this realm. The self itself is not the healer but part of the process and when unobstructed in its own flow automatically becomes a channel for healing. This sharing of suffering as well as purification and cleansing are, therefore, significant experiences of the eighth dimension.

When energy flows then power manifests. If we ignore or fail to recognize the natural and appropriate directions of energy flow by not living in the balance of the moment, then power will force us to give it attention. When power is denied it will impose itself upon us in ways which truly make death a gruesome affair. The uses and abuses of power by people in authority are how they deal with this part of being human. When they are fully in balance with all the dimensions they have a commanding presence that needs no status of authority to be recognized and will challenge anyone who does not deal with power in their own lives. When power is taken by one from another it becomes corruptive and can be extremely abusive and such misuse of power will certainly find resistance.

Generally speaking, expressions of power and authority, which demand to be heard and taken notice of, indicate a weak self-identity that also fears the loss of the self. On the other hand, someone with a strong sense of their origin through the ninth dimension of spirit consciousness will try to avoid any positions of authority. Yet if they do find themselves in that situation, it is usually in response to a widespread request of the community. These people command great respect for they are both master and servant at one and the same time.

(Note: an interesting contrast can be made between the tendency that allows ourselves to be abused, which arises in the second dimension, and the inclination to abuse others, which might surface in the eighth.)

The important thing to realize is that power, prana, or energy is not personal but rather an infinite storehouse, a common pasture to which all beings have equal rights of access.

Guru Har Krishan

As a young boy, an embodiment of living purity, Guru Har Krishan knew that all things and all people must die but that purity itself does not die. Rather purity is what remains; it kills all that is not pure. Guru Har Krishan offered his mind, body, and soul over to live this reality. Upon hearing of the suffering of the people of Delhi when he was only eight years old he went intentionally to that city and drunk of the waters that were spreading disease amongst all. Overnight Guru Har Krishan left his body, that died of the sickness, but by morning the whole of the city was free of this plague. Thus the eighth Guru took on the suffering of many and sacrificed his life for the healing of others. He sacrificed without discrimination for all who needed it, not just the Sikh community. His name means the action (KAR) of cleansing or bathing (ISHAN). The deeds of this young Guru were a pure act of purification.

Akaal Moort

To exist in the ever-flowing moment of now is to be free of fear of the future where there is no motivation to revenge the past. The soul identifies itself with the pure form or representation (Moort) of the infinite energy, which is undying and timeless (Akaal). KAL translates as time and death whilst AKAAL is beyond time and death. To exist in time is to exist in a form that will die but to exist in the form of the formless is to be a form that will never die and which knows no limitation of time. The time, which is beyond time, timeless time is like the deep ocean into which all our wastes accumulate. This infinite sea of prana cleanses and transforms all into a basic life force, which can again nourish everyone indiscriminately.

Chapter 11

Number 9

As the last number before starting the sequence again on a new level, 9 suggests completion and the arrival home. Considered as a number of perfection it stands at the end of the journey giving the traveler a sense of where to go, a bit like the hermit, the ninth tarot card. To progress as far as 9 requires calmness, patience, endurance, and perseverance and there is a sense of peace and finally being able to relax. However, the impulse to get to 9 can also show itself as impatience, restlessness, and frustration because too much attention is set on the target and not on the journey with each of its steps.

If there is no awareness of 9 at the end of the line then our energy is lost and dispersed in all the eight directions. 1 has a quality of focus and concentration and 9, as its opposite, is more scattered and diffused, giving a feeling of aimlessness, vagueness, and ambiguity. As the least concentrated and most spread out, 9 is hard to discern and comprehend and in this respect has been termed the number of mystery. It is this mystery that is veiled by the glamorous qualities of the 7, which is why some traditions speak of 9 initiations.

As the biggest number, 9 could be the number of the giants, yet in its multiplicity is also the number of small beings that live together as one greater body; ants, bees, wasps, and termites are some obvious examples. The multiplication of bacteria (healthy and unhealthy) and viruses is another example of how the 9 contributes to the microscopic foundations of concrete life.

There are nine numbers and as the end number, 9 is again the foundation for the beginning, a stepping stone for the new. By looking at your life in nine-year cycles you can discover this – you will see how things are completed and begin in the ninth year. The full cycle is eighteen years and this is made up of a nine-year high wave and a nine-year low wave.

9 is the last step of the 1 when it has become the many through multiplying itself in order to reproduce itself. Before 1 can recreate itself in the 10 it must be scattered like seeds sown in the soil where each seed may produce many. The subtleness of 9 never loses itself in this process, just as every number which is multiplied by 9 will reduce to 9 again; for example:

$9 \times 9 = 81$, $8 + 1 = 9$.

Yet in the intermediate functions of addition and subtraction the 9 seems to lose itself in an altruistic sacrifice for the other number; for example:

$9 + 5 = 14$, $1 + 4 = 5$

$23 - 9 = 14$, $1 + 4 = 5$ $(23 = 2 + 3 = 5)$

In division any number which is not a whole multiple of 9 will, when divided, give an endless decimal run of the same number that is obtained by addition of the original number; for example:

$10 \div 9 = 1.11111111$ $(1 + 0 = 1)$

$11 \div 9 = 1.22222222$ $(1 + 1 = 2)$

$12 \div 9 = 1.33333333$ $(1 + 2 = 3)$

9 expresses an excessive generosity born from its altruistic nature as in the above divisions. Through division it adds the parts of a number and makes it whole again and then repeats it to infinity and beyond. In spite of this surrender, the 9, which is the subtle essence of the seed of life, never loses its integrity. It may seem to get lost or even disappear altogether but in the last step of the journey it is 9 that is present.

Patterns of 9 are often shown in the magic square or grid of 3×3. When we understand the whole combination of the various sets of three numbers, which exist in this grid, then we master the number 9. You will find more about this in Chapter 28 in Section Four.

9 is the many seeds that have come from the multiplication of the one seed. It is the essence of the plant that has traveled through

all the stages of transformation yet remained ever the same. Having traveled so far the 9 brings with it tiredness – exhausted, fed up, and impatient, like a child at the end of the day, the restless irritable mind state wants to sleep yet it is not able to relax. But the 9 also offers the resilience and persevering endurance that it takes to journey to the end. Until reaching its completion 9 seems to be a shore impossible to reach, always infinitely in the distance. Even when we imagine we have it in hand it slips through the fingers like sand. We have to become the sand to realize the 9; it is not a state to be possessed. "I am at peace" is a state that can be realized but peace can never be something won, gained, or had. It is when we finish with wanting more that we cross the infinity. When we rest content with what we have then we are more than these things – we are the contentment. This is mastery, otherwise the state of calmness will remain an elusive mystery.

Perfect peace is a state that is immutable; it is steadfast, unshakeable, unbreakable, and unyielding. The shocking truth is that to arrive at this state we must first go through all the changes, yield until we can bend no more, and be broken until there is nothing left to break. By humility to the tyranny of the essential we are spared the oppression of the non-essential. And there is nothing to wait for, the 9 awaits your homecoming.

The perfectionizm of 9 can lead to intolerance. Being naturally in touch with certain non-visible principles it finds itself bewildered that everyone else is not. Perhaps it forgets the long journey it has made and so cannot understand why everyone else does not think as they do.

The Subtle Body

The Subtle Body is the collective will rather than the individual will; it is "Thy will" rather than "my will." This is the crystalline form where the soul's entry and departure in the world is recorded; it's also known as the akashic record. It is the capsule in which we pass from death to rebirth. The Subtle Body could be thought of as the soul's survival bubble, which becomes more and more transparent as we move from issues of personal survival to those of species survival. This primary or essential quality of the Subtle Body implies that it is a willful cause of much of what we experience in life and, therefore, it has also been referred to as the Causal Body.

Dispersion is a major issue of this Body, which also relates to the number 9 as a number of diversification. The lack of focus (number 1) results in tiredness and a desire for stimulants like sugar and coffee, or cocaine in a more extreme form. As the last number before a new level of beginning in 10, the 9 influences the Subtle Body to be complete and perfect. Perfectionizm is a very demanding state, often seen in those who eat too much or too little; a quality that is very close to the all or nothing state of the number 10. It is important to accept our mistakes and even appreciate the perfection within them. Remember, a cat has nine lives.

The first (1) and last (9) relation in life is to the mother in the sense of birth and death, a birth into another state. The mother considers her child to be perfect even with every default, each mistake a perfect expression of her offspring, and she will continue to feel like this until she is free of the Mother State and finds herself back to the Woman State.

The Subtle Body is the great vehicle, which transports the soul through its many transformations and transmutations. It carries it through births, deaths, and more births providing access to its spiritual genetics as well as all the skills and insights acquired through its long history. Spiritual genetics implies past life recall but more significantly, an awakening of our connection to any spiritual community that has been our other family over the centuries. Rich though it is in wisdom, we have great difficulty in retrieving such a primal memory and even more so in transferring that wisdom into our present environment. It is this far distant knowing that makes us want to walk before we can crawl and to run before we can walk.

If we pass consciously through the gates of death and birth we develop a calm endurance, which will bring us to a state of mastery. If not, everything remains a mystery and we stay gullible to the false masters of the world. Soul and Subtle Body exist side by side, complementing each other by marking our beginnings and giving a sense of the end of all things, including ourselves. The Subtle Body allows us to take things to completion though we often fail to see the value in what we are doing and so lose the intensity of our initial drive. We run out of motivation and leave things unfinished but through this ninth dimension we can learn that the only purpose is to go beyond any personal purpose to a universal one. Indeed, some things will only reveal themselves at the very end.

The intensity of a sense of purpose without a specific goal can be very frustrating, leading us to jump aimlessly from one thing to another, be it in our tasks, conversations, or our way of thinking. It is as though we are trying to locate the perfect job or the very best word but this merely disperses our energy, leaving us tired and exhausted yet wondering why we have nothing to show for it. Our own lack of calm focus creates a pressure where there always seems to be too much to do. We will then compensate for this by being demanding and abrupt towards those around us in an attempt to get focused through their focus. This might develop further by insisting that everything should have been finished yesterday so that we become quite tyrannical and very insensitive in our communication to others and even to ourselves. Alternatively we could cultivate refinement and subtlety through this domain of the Subtle Body.

Here we find ourselves thinking that we have been around a long time. As it is the original self of the spirit-mind it is in this realm that we feel as if we have lived before and may yet live on indefinitely. Feelings of having been here before and the familiarity it brings are very characteristic of this ninth dimension. In some respects this can be frustrating as we start trying to figure out why we are here again and whether it is because we are failing to grasp something. We feel a sense of purpose driving us on in life yet whatever we try to do turns out to be meaningless and pointless.

This is a realm in which we can display many skills and turn our hands to many crafts, yet we become masters of none until we learn what this ninth dimension is really about. When we are present as the original self of the spirit-mind we abandon questions about what we should be doing and concentrate more completely on the matter in hand. There is a sense that we owe it to the essence of our own nature to complete what we have begun by bringing it into existence. The endless drive that stems from the sense of purpose can lead us to disperse our energies in too many directions, spreading ourselves out too thinly so that we accomplish nothing. This may express itself in our daily behavior and communication as well as through the whole extent of our life. The qualities of peace, calmness, patience, and endurance, cultivated in this dimension, allow us to apply our skills to the detail of the present. We come to realize that it is not the task that matters but the journey to completion, enduring every project to the bitter or sweet end. To become a master requires going deep into the essence of our craft and to go deep into the essence of that requires calm attention, peaceful wakefulness, unyielding presence, and a very great endurance beyond measure.

Once we go deep into the essence of our craft we master the essence of the greatest craft but if that remains a mystery then all else is a mystery. When things are too mysterious we shy away from looking deep because it seems to demand too much effort, so we shut down the original self of the spirit-mind. This closure, however, makes us shallow, confused, and gullible and much more susceptible to deception where we can easily be persuaded against our better interests. It is, therefore, advantageous to go to the core of things, which is only achieved by enduring unto completion. Then it is possible to transfer this skill of going deep within into every realm of being human. If you are not there yet, be patient, in time, all things in time. Since time is without end, our endurance must also be endless for only in the dissolution of the self is there an end to time for the self.

From another angle, going into the essence means staying where you are and going deep into the core of where you are. It is for this reason that in the ninth domain things come to us, we do not go to them, our karma meets us, we do not meet our karma, the universe comes to our door, we do not seek the universe. When we stay where we are we have the opportunity to cultivate refinement both in our speech as well as in our work; thus the ninth dimension is the refined self. By cultivating refinement, our speech and work become crystal clear and within this transparency we become the essence itself. We do not know it but we reveal it.

We gain insight into the laws of cause and effect when we stay where we are and learn that things are propelled along by what went before and pulled forward by what has yet to be. As a seed unfolds it is pushed out from the inside as well as being drawn out from the outside. Every action gives birth to further events, events which are themselves already waiting to be met, and yet that seed can only ever reproduce itself as its death guarantees its rebirth. In doing what it is perfectly designed for, it remains in essence what it truly is, illustrating how the quality of integrity is secured through altruism.

The ninth dimension is that realm in which we become the essence of who we are, an essence that remains as it is through all apparent changes. In certain situations this condition reveals very noble deeds of an altruistic nature though it can be displayed in extreme forms of self-effacement in a quite inappropriate manner. This means that for most of us we need to develop this quality in balance with the other dimensions of our tenfold self. Awareness of appropriateness is a significant skill acquired through the Subtle Body.

Guru Teg Bahadur

Guru Teg Bahadur's name perfectly expresses this enduring quality, which results in the state of Ajuni (see below). TEG is the sword and primal will of God, BAHA means "very much" or "great" and DUR is found in the words duration, durable, and enduring. DUR also signifies "door," implying that patience and calm endurance or enduring calm is the great door to the sword. This is the sword that endures all struggles without impatience to strike. It endures all blows, sacrificing first and striking only with that quality of consciousness that survives after all else has died.

The ninth Guru displayed remarkable endurance both in his life and in his death. He spent twenty-seven years in meditation without knowing this was to prepare him for a great and altruistic sacrifice. He was to offer his life so that everyone, regardless of their religion, could worship freely according to their own practice. In a written message, given to his executioner as he was beheaded, he wrote "though the body could be destroyed, faith could not." It was through this faith that Guru Teg Bahadur realized the undying and, therefore, unborn essence.

The Gurbani frequently refers to the nine treasures that can be found in the body. These nine treasures are also nine virtues, which take the soul back to a state of peace, its true home. They are brought into being by truthful action while meditating upon God's name. The virtuous treasures are humility, loyalty, equality, service, sacrifice, justice, forgiveness, compassion, and peace.

Ajuni

The soul lives in perpetual memory of the pure form, experiencing neither death nor the pains of rebirth and in this respect it is unborn (Ajuni). The cycle is broken yet calmness and peace remain. A great test of endurance is needed to pass through life and rebirth and it is an experience so overwhelming that we lose consciousness and so have to be woken up by another round of existence. But when we come to realize that our essential nature is unchanging and endures through all transformations, then it is possible to stay conscious. We recognize we do not die and so will never experience birth or rebirth ever again, but will remain forever awake in the subtle realm of Soul.

Chapter 12

Number 10

Many of the qualities of the 10 are similar to that of the number 1. The zero brings two possibilities to the 1. It might enhance and intensify all these qualities, bringing a brightness or illumination, or the zero will nullify the qualities of the 1, not only to zero them out but actually giving a presence to their absence.

10 is known as a number of all or nothing but it is also the possibility of being all or nothing so that we are nothing in such a way as to be all. The number 10 is 1 qualified by 0 or 0 qualified by 1, the whole one or the one whole. When 1 finds its way through the journey to 9 it completes a circle (0) and becomes 1 again and this reunification is expressed by 10. 10 says all (0) is 1 without highlighting the differences. 10 is more than 9 so it is more than just the steps that it takes to go from 1 to 9. To be more than all the parts put together is also to be the part that holds the whole, the part that wills all the other parts to unite. Take away the transcendent aspect and all the other parts will fall apart, each fighting for its existence. 10 is, therefore, the measure of the radius of any being who realizes the self as the one that is more than all the parts just thrown together. As a measure of the radius, 10 is also a measure of the radiance and our radiance is the extent of our radius.

In the tithing tradition of giving 1/10th of the day to meditation and 1/10th of earnings to charitable causes there is the aspect of setting apart as well as the concept of sowing a seed and letting it return. 10 is this apartness or standing out quality. It takes courage to stand out and to be outstanding. Another way to say this is to speak of the appendix; the unit that is more than the whole is an extra quality and that is actually its extra-ordinariness. However, we are quick to think of it as superfluous and attempt to eliminate it at the first chance, or at least to ignore it as much as possible. Therefore, the 10 might wonder if it really exists.

The Radiant Body

The Radiant Body is like millions of suns that have no center but where everywhere is its center. It is you when you realize that you are the glory of God, your grandeur, your light body and in some respects what you could call your guardian angel. When we are in connection with our radiance it gives us great courage but when there is none we feel nothing can be accomplished in life. When it is strongly manifested through us we either feel everything is possible or nothing is possible.

The unity of 10 is represented as a 1 outside of a 0 and we sense its presence as a transcendent quality in our environment rather than within us. When our personal plans go wrong we often direct our anger, fear, and confusion onto this presence, blaming it for thwarting our schemes and demanding to know why. In fact, it is our greatest ally, which is trying to give us clues as to our true nature in life. However, we tend to forget to listen to it and set about our own programs.

We can tune into our radiance by listening with every hair on our body and head and by developing a sense of the interconnection between people and events, recognizing they are not so much the accidents and coincidences of life. The cosmos is a well designed, self-regulating whole with microcosmic echoes of the universal hologram. In the microcosmic sense our radiance is the unity of our individual consciousness, the total which is more than the sum of its parts. The holistic nature of the tenth dimension means that when we tune into it we are trying to get the whole picture. To face up to the full story with all its known and unknown implications takes a lot of courage and so it is in this tenth self that we find the courageous self.

In ordinary life this tendency shows itself in the way we complete whatever we do. Our leaning toward extremes is influenced by the fifth and tenth dimension, extremes of doing and not doing. In the fifth dimension these will be in the physical world whilst in the tenth we tend to take matters of principle to their ultimate limit. Such a tendency is either viewed as courageous, as in the case of certain martyrs, or it may be considered obsessive and fanatical. The wisdom to hold back before starting a task until we are sure we can finish it stems from the tenth dimension, though when taken too far, we may never get started on anything. It can help to think of each moment as a completion in itself and where the finished product is the beginning of something new. In this way we are not limited by a static image of what ought to be, which frees us to engage totally in the movement or stillness of whatever we are doing.

The tenth dimension of being human demands that we respect the many parts which go to make up the whole and this must be understood in two ways. Firstly, that we are what we are by virtue of the interaction and balance of our various dimensions. Secondly, that we ourselves are just a part of a greater whole whose greatness depends on the quality of its parts. The forest is great because of its seeds yet no seed can claim superiority over the forest and without this recognition we are unaccomplished and we accomplish nothing. Excessive effacement through self-torture and asceticism is one extreme in our encounter with the tenth dimension of ourselves. Here the sea of life becomes a desolate desert through absolute renunciation where the seed will crack but will not grow and is reduced to dust instead. While we are still in the Physical Body we need to learn the difference between a sacrifice that produces no fruit and one that will flourish.

The tenth Body is the all-encompassing realm within which the one becomes the many and the many become the one. This is a space where every direction is a mirror image of yourself and where there is no center because everywhere is identical to the center and the center is everywhere. It is a space to be multiplied and amplified unto infinity whilst at the same time reduced to the tiniest speck in the midst of endlessness. This is the experience of the absolute self of the tenth dimension of being human. In this domain personal power is absolutely abandoned yet paradoxically never lost. It gains a thousand fold by surrendering all. This is the dignity of the royal self, the regal self, wherein we may be totally awake and yet totally asleep.

Guru Gobind Singh

The tenth Guru completed the cycle. He had the courage to relinquish the power of his position while still alive. He did this in a manner that expresses well the relation between the numbers 5 and 10. He made this profound move from all to nothing by inviting five Sikhs to give their heads. After the initiation of these five Sikhs, known as the five beloved (Panj Piare), through a new form of baptism he bowed before them as their disciple (chela) and asked to receive the same baptism from them. He considered himself as the zero or nothing and the baptized community known as the Khalsa (the pure unalloyed ones), to be the one, the greater unity. Remembering that the 1 is humility we can understand that the zero with the 1, as in the 10, gives an extraordinary humility. He also gave the newly baptized Sikhs the instruction to keep five items on their body at all times (Kara, a bangle, Kanga, a comb, Kachha, a pair of shorts, Kirpan, a sword, and Kesh, uncut hair) and to recite five prayers every morning. Amongst other things this was to aid the Sikhs in the struggle to transform the five inner passions or enemies (lust, anger, greed, pride, and attachment). Guru Gobind Singh further brought the dharma of the Sikhs to a state of self-supporting existence by appointing the scripture as the permanent Guru so that the word, which is number 5, sits in the center of the 10 – the Khalsa community.

GOBIND means "sustainer" (binding together), which is precisely what Guru Gobind Singh achieved when he gave the Sikhs a sustainable Guru with a sustainable message and a sustainable code of conduct by which to live. By adding the surname SINGH he was reminding us of the qualities of a lion, those of courage and nobility, for that is what is required to maintain commitment and discipline of a true disciple of truth. Sikh women were similarly given a surname that would help them to live as self-sustaining, regal and dignified individuals and that was KAUR, which means "princess."

For those Sikhs who take the baptism there is another dimension added to their identity, that of KHALSA, signifying "unalloyed" or "pure." Unalloyed defines that we are what we are by virtue of our own qualities and not because of any other factor. We do not need the importance we place on the approval of others or our medicine, our money, our status, our car, and countless other support systems that we set up in the world. We can take none of these beyond the gates of death. Thus, Saibhang, which means self-illuminating or illuminated by virtue of its own nature, is another way of referring to the unalloyed quality of the Khalsa.

The Guru makes reference to the door to God's court as the Tenth Gate. The body has nine external holes but there is a hidden tenth gate that is the inner portal to the Divine. Some teachers suggest this gate is at the top of the head where the soul departs at death; others say it is in the heart. The nature of the number 10 suggests it is nowhere in particular but exists everywhere. However, only one who knows the divine radiance and hears the divine sound can really say where this gate is.

Saibhang

There is great courage when the soul is willing to merge into the essence of all things, unattached to all that is transient. This is the meeting with the self-illuminating and self-supporting existence (SAIBHANG). The number 10 signifies a return to unity but with a greater whole that it began with. It also indicates the qualities of an EKOsystem to be self-supporting, which contains everything within itself.

This humble courage paves the way for Guru's grace (Gurprasad) and the final mystery is removed. The soul is once again side by side with the radiant light that is SAIBHANG; more powerful than millions of suns that have no particular source but which is all pervading.

Chapter 13

Number 11

Eleven is 10 + 1, which is the relationship between Soul and the Radiant Body. It implies a permanent parallel relationship between the small I and the big I. If this is not being realized then the 11 will become a number 2 and the desire for a permanent parallel relation is sought for in this world where it is not realizable.

In its highest expression the 11 is to be a twin of God, the individual unit in parallel with the universal unit, a relationship that no longer bears any tension. It is the end of all desiring, testing, competing, doubting, fearing, judging, rejecting, or demanding. Neither possesses the other and both want the same thing. You can imagine the flight of two birds so in tune with each other that it is impossible to imagine that one is leading or following the other.

Gurprasad – Siri Guru Granth Sahib

GURPRASAD relates to the eleventh Guru, which is the scripture known as the Guru Granth Sahib. GRANTH means a large book as well as a knot and SAHIB, a master. It is the words in the book and the message they convey that acts as the eleventh Guru. These words have the capacity to untie the knots in our lives and tie us instead to God. The state of grace is to have gone beyond all (PAR) and yet still to exist as an individual in relation to the whole. This is expressed in the qualities of the number 11, which is 10 + 1, God and me, me and

God, the state of a saint (SADHU).

The relation between 1 and 10 is like the relation between a sword and its splendor. The vertical convergence of the number 1 is the sword and once it has been put through the fire and passed through the various stages of the alchemic transmutation then the radiant splendor starts to emanate from the perfected metal.

Chapter 14
Number 12

In the number 12 the process of the universe continues. 10 + 2 imply a perpetual extending of the same formula in endless repetition, but always in conscious relation to the whole. 12 (1 + 2) adds up to 3, which is the number of repeating patterns. Given that it is constructed from the 10 and the 2 then the nature of the repetition is through reflection.

Jap

JAP consists of JA, meaning "go" and PA which stands for "realize" or "obtain." When these are combined, JAP is usually translated as "repeat" or "meditate." This indicates an instruction to the reader to realize a consciousness in the stages set out in the Mul Mantra and expressed in the lives of the ten Gurus. The Gurbani says "when the nine tanks are fully fulfilled then the tenth is spontaneously realized." This confirms the importance of clearly understanding the qualities of the first nine Gurus and the treasures and virtues as they manifest and are expressed in the Mul Mantra. Only then is it possible to arrive at the tenth state, that of Saibhang. This message was further reinforced by the tenth Guru when he recited the opening lines of the Ardas prayer, which remembers the sword and the names of the first nine Gurus in their successive order. By doing this it was as though he was concluding all that Guru Naanak had predicted when he delivered the Mul Mantra two hundred and fifty years earlier.

The word is a navigator and the way we use words and the choice of words we use directs our course across uncharted territory. The words of others that have gone before us through these states of consciousness will help to guide us on our way.

10 + 2 = 12. In this twelfth phase the radiance is now a mirror and reflects to all the hidden light that waits for the chance to initiate itself into the alchemic journey, which is the path of the soul through the stages implied in the ten Spiritual Bodies.

Finding it everywhere

Jap implies that the whole cosmos is a repeat of some very basic patterns and formulas. We do live in a holographic universe. Whether we zoom out to take a bigger view or zoom in to take a closer look we will find the same thing everywhere. The numbers are the essential keys that allow us this ability to cross-reference. Through them we can transfer our inquiry between different levels of study and different issues in life. Numbers are also a tool that makes it possible to store a lot of information in short form. In other words, once you have made your own direct association between various factors that correspond to a number it then becomes possible to forget all these factors and just remember the number. The number then becomes a key with which to unlock the necessary details at will. For example, each number between 1 and 10 will be found to correspond to a part of each of the following themes or topics:

- The date of birth
- The different types of problems – in energy and in people
- The classification of cures/tools
- The eight trigrams of the I Ching
- Rooms in a house
- Family members
- Life stages and phases of time
- Body organs
- Different sections of conscious perception

- Stages of any sequential operation
- Planets
- Colors
- Axial dimensions of space
- Elements
- Ten Spiritual Bodies
- Animals
- Generals or ministers in charge of different sections of the country and its affairs
- Strategic arenas in the battleground
- Eight directions of the compass
- And so many other fields of study

Some examples will be given in later sections of this book. Our first diagnostic application of numbers will be the date of birth.

Section two

Chapter 15

Getting to know yourself through time cycles and the date of birth

The date of birth: how to use it as a transformational tool

Time rolls like a river alongside us; sometimes close by and at other times we may feel quite out of touch with it. Visualize it as waves of the ocean as we walk along the beach on the edge of life and death; perhaps it is on our left or maybe it is on the right. It would be impossible to go forward if it were in front, except to be absorbed into its infinity. Indeed sometimes we feel ourselves drowning in its chaotic undercurrents. To walk away from this ocean of time is impossible for no matter how far you walk it is still right behind you. You may feel it as a hungry monster that wants to eat you up and maybe you are afraid to turn your back on it. If you do try to walk away from time you'll probably find yourself looking over your shoulder to see how close it is. Time is like death; it will outlive us all and we do not know whether to value it highly or not at all.

Mathematically, we try to multiply time to have more of it and we try to divide it in order to be economical. We mask it with additional factors to hide the void and we take it away or have it subtracted from us, like when a deadline expires and everything then falls from beneath us. This on-going and ever-changing relationship to time, endlessly flowing from an unknown past to an unknown future, and from the future into the past, is a two-way movement that can bring us to a different present.

Time is organic; it belongs primarily to the biological or vegetative state of existence. And like the vegetable kingdom, it has its seasonal phases. The only difference is that the deeper seasons of time overlap into each other, like the days turning around within the months, the months within the year and the years within a century.

In this chapter you will find out about the organic basis for interpreting your relationship with time using the calendar structure and your date of birth. It offers a means of diagnosis that allows you to see the date of birth as a window into new opportunities in your own or other's life stories.

The organic body experiences cycles of time in various ways – the heartbeat, respiration, patterns of sleeping and waking as well as the shifts between hunger and satisfaction. The breath also changes every two and a half hours from one dominant nostril to the other. This same rhythm expresses the movement of vital energy through the inner organs of the body. While all these cycles are important signs of life they are also unique to each individual and so we find that they are not marked by the common ground of number. It is the outer cycles, which are shared with others, that get recorded and numbered to establish a common reference.

The time cycles that we number, the days, months, years, and century, and our relationship to them are all represented in our date of birth. The practice of Karam Kriya acknowledges these rhythms as well as the vibrational influences of the numbers with which we label them. This combination is so strong that it provides a very important basis from which the negotiation of meaningful insight and change can begin. Our date of birth provides a window into our life patterns, which is also our karma. It is, therefore, a scientific tool for transformation and when applied with integrity becomes the art of self-realization.

The tree of life

Calling on the natural world we will explore the calendar through the model of a tree. Nature is an excellent mirror for all those who wish to become fully conscious. There is one seed of the physical tree and it is concretely focused. Its purpose is to disperse itself throughout the whole tree in order to reproduce itself and in this way it becomes the soul of the tree, without which it would have no meaning. The seed of spirit is quite the opposite, subtle and refined as an essential essence that exists everywhere and nowhere in particular. Its goal is to intensify itself toward a specific point of focus; this is individualization of the soul.

The roots of the body are limited just as those of a physical tree but the roots of the soul are embedded into infinity, the drawing downwards reflecting an endless urge upwards. Similarly, our body structure is also limited, each part different just like the trunk and branches of a tree. For the universal spirit there is only one tree, one perfect blueprint. Each individual person is a temporary manifested expression of this perfection through which the crystallization of spirit into individual soul can happen. The trunk and branches of a tree store the fire energy whilst the leaves have a more external and releasing expression of the flames. From the material point of view each nation, race, or type of people is like a different type of tree or forest, whilst from the view of the universal spirit each variation is merely one branch from the same tree.

As the plant flowers it opens into softness and vulnerability, expressing the urge for life to continue and from where the new seed will be delivered. The flowering of the human body unfolds as a sensation, an opening, and an expansion of awareness within which a new strength is found. The new seed is like a gathering up of the soul as it individualizes itself. In our human existence it is possible to flower perpetually and to experience a sense of the soul's perpetual renewal. Human life is the chance to become truly immortal. This does not mean physical immortality, but immortality of spirit as the fruit of how we live the human experience. It is not a guarantee but an opportunity given by the fact of being a consciously breathing creature. This organic approach has informed oriental medicine for thousands of years and is very relevant in current times where many of our problems arise from a disrespect for or ignorance of the organic life processes in our self and on the planet.

Heavenly influences

No matter which cultural reference system is used the calendar structure represents the earth's relation with its wider environment. In the daily cycle we record each day as the earth turns on its axis. The twelve months or zodiac cycle records our movement through different sections of the solar system while the annual cycle records the full cycle around the sun. Centuries or dynasties could be said to represent a greater movement of the solar system within the galaxy as a whole. Clearly there exists a range of influences that do not arise simply from the forces of this planet (earth) alone, since it is not in isolation from the rest of the universe. The planet could not exist except in relation to all that is beyond it. These other influences are worthy of our consideration. In fact, we would be foolish to practice any true art without taking such influences into account. We have tried through the ages to know and to engage with these influences in various ways including:

- The study of the planets – as in astrology, closely linked to the worship of animal spirits.
- Various forms of channeling and mediumship such as talking to angels, entities, and beings from other planes or planets.
- The practice of referring to oracles – such as the I Ching and tarot.
- Metaphysical research and its models of the universe; examples are the Kabala and Eneagram.
- In relation to mythology, through understanding the stories of the different pantheons of gods and archetypal forces and identifying their manifestations in our lives. This would involve reading the impersonal and abstracted elements of these into the personal events of our daily existence, a kind of archetypal psychology.

All these and other practices are attempts to find a relationship between heavenly, divine, or otherwise esoteric influences and whatever can be interpreted as their signs here on earth. Humans have studied the layout of the ground around us, interpreted climatic changes, analyzed how our living style reflects our inner space, diagnosed the emotional anatomy as it is reflected in a person's constitution, and studied the relation between a person's life experience and their date and time of birth. In other words, people have always tried to get some kind of an intuitive feel for the overall evolution of the planet and the beings that inhabit it.

The unseen and unworldly forces move through everything that takes place here on earth and it is not necessary to look up to the sky to realize that but simply to look through the world that is in front of us. This is not to refuse the specialist insight that practices like astrology offer, but to encourage the non-specialist to learn to read the deeper sense of the ordinary world and the mysteries that move through it. This is partly done through the intuition, which is the readiness to receive and act on (not analyze) revelation, not particularly from above but from everywhere, inwards and outwards, anytime, whether awake or asleep. Intuition is an on-going negotiation with the unknown at the frontiers of the known. Too much rational or structural understanding can act as a barrier and heavy veil rather than act as a platform, a window, or signpost toward the revelation of mystery. It is hoped that the description of the date of birth given here can serve as an anchor for bringing precision to the intuitive awareness.

For an intuitive interpretation of the date of birth we need to understand the calendar structure itself as well as some understanding of each number. Only then can we consider the possible meanings of the different numbers in each position of the calendar structure. The calendar records the most influential time cycles and is a combined record of the day, month, and year. Each of these cycles is divided into smaller cycles whilst also being part of a greater cycle. We will consider each of these recorded cycles and try to understand a little more about their characteristics.

There are several different ways in which we can deepen our understanding of the time cycles. For example, Guru Naanak described the phases of time following the first part of the Mul Mantra that was described in chapter 2. The sacred sounds he spoke were:

AD SUCH

JUGAD SUCH

HAI BHEE SUCH

NAANAK HOSEE BHEE SUCH

This refers to the four phases of time through which the reality (SUCH) of the formula of the Mul Mantra manifests and sustains itself while the fifth phase is the all-encompassing reality of total time. Briefly these phases are:

AD is the primal beginning and suggests a time when all that exists now was nothing more than a potential. It relates to the primal and essential substance from which all things emerge and to which all things return; a time before there was time. The beginning is also an end and so we can relate them to the numbers 1 and 9 as well as the earth element.

JUGAD is the process of the ages (jug jug) running like a river from the beginning of time. It would be natural to think of the water element as representing the current of time pouring out from some mysterious source. The duality of this time-flow links with the number 2 whilst the infinity of time relates to the number 8.

HAI BHEE is the present state of affairs and the shape of time in the present. This term suggests that no matter what cultural form we have found to fill the emptiness of time and to veil the reality, the underlying essence still persists. The numbers of form are 3 and 7 and relate to the element of fire. These are the numbers that we find most fascinating and distracting and which, therefore, deflect our attention away from the divine presence in the present, leaving us instead with a photographic or screen view of the current moment.

NAANAK HOSEE BHEE is the inevitable becoming of what will be in the future and the on-going presence of the reality. It is the wind that transports us to the future, like falling seeds from the cultural trees, blown onto their destiny. The wind not only propels us into the future but also bears news of the future in the intuitive breeze that caresses our forehead or stirs the breast. This aspect of time is connected to the air element and the numbers of intuition, 4 and 6.

SUCH is the reality of the basic sutra or formula as it exists unchanging through all the changes of the qualities of time. Related to the ether element, SUCH is like the backcloth to the theater of life in all its phases. It is the sound of time being born and the sound of everything else born through time.

Now let's take another look at these phases of time through the qualities of the seasons as if they were five great acts in the world drama.

Act 1. Winter – the great sleep

Time is a potential coiled up like a spring but it's also fully uncoiled. It is the beginning and the end, the origin of time to the end of previous time and on to the beginning of time after previous time. This moment is when the fruit falls to the ground and the great sleep commences. The coming down, or earthing, is in natural harmony with gravity and becomes concrete as an event. Then there is the long wait through winter. The seed rests in its own potential in a place from where it can grow. It is a time before time, grounded but also stuck, immovable and heavy. Every story ends where it begins and begins where it ends. It is the story before it is told and the mystery that remains after it has been told.

Act 2. Spring – the dream river

As a time stream it flows through the ages, in time, through time, as time. It emerges from its fixed position as the seed splits and enters into the problems of duality and relationship. It begins to root and spiral through the darkness, a chaotic but powerful force. This spring-like river of energy is full and outpouring yet it is also empty and drawing in, clinging and attaching to the earth. It is the time that creates the distance between two planes and becomes the time that we measure and the time to which we become enslaved. It can take us to infinity or keep us bonded in the cycle of endless return. This is the time to waste, time to pass, time to use or lose and the problem of how?

Act 3. Summer – the fascinating show

The past is in the present, the present becomes the past and the past is repeated in future projections. We try to capture the present in our souvenirs and photographs but they immediately become the past, a static illusion of a here and now that lacks any movement. It is not the time that is measured but the measure of time, which then becomes historical. Time branches out and takes shape and habits are formed so losing flexibility but it does allow us to develop skills, organize time, and give time an order. Historical time is the time that we try to understand and which we believe we can explain. The historic present soon becomes the false past while our search into the past offers clues to the present.

Act 4. Autumn – the reality check

This is the truth that we sense must come. It is the future, the present becoming the future, and the future that becomes the present, which awakens us to the truth. It's a surprise! Time is unknown but anticipated, full of moments that might be and that will be, all unfolding and flowering into opportunities. To open is to risk, yet the invitation to intimacy is a state of being. Intuition and a sense of awe culminate in the delivery of the fruit/seed. It's the wind that turns the mill of man-made time and strips the static present from its decorative leaves of illusion.

Act 5. Harvest – the turning

This is the summary of the whole story, the lessons learnt, the moral, and the marriage that goes beyond a mere completion by turning the end into a new beginning for the audience. It is the fruit before it falls but ripe and ready to pick. The fruit is the sum totality of the whole where it is more than the parts. This phase of time is total time, all time, multi-directional and multi-dimensional time, and beyond time as the paradox of time. It is a time of which no one can know the speed nor its beginning or end, the wheel of time when the fruit is ripe and ready. It seems that nothing is happening. The fruit is self-enclosed and in relation only to itself yet it is also aware and open, centered and holding the seed in its center while radiating its readiness.

Life may begin in any season but then follow the normal sequence from then onwards. Biologically we start life in the transition from winter to spring. The period to go through one season may vary from person to person but each season will be about the same length. Each age is present in every age but the emphasis is on particular qualities indicating the predominant stage. Confusion about the stages and their qualities arise in relation to the transition from winter to spring and from summer to autumn. This is because in the center of these transitions all the elements are present.

Within the patterns woven through time are the shared seasons within which we each live the seasons of our own lives. The patterns of time that give us a sense of the stages of progression and regression, of evolution and devolution are definite tendencies that predominate the specific stages of our lives. The seven-year cycle is quite widely known but there are others. Nine, ten, eleven, twelve, and eighteen year cycles all play a different role, each cycle influencing a different aspect of our overall experience. These influences can be determined simply by listening openly to a person's story and identifying key events and the ages they happened. Variations exist but the main patterns are not difficult to discover. The subject of life cycles is a large study and a fuller account would distract from the main purpose of this publication.

Different calendars

With some minor changes calendars have been around for thousands of years, mostly taking the form of days, months, and years, with centuries or dynasties as the larger cycle. This institution, which was designed to serve us, also becomes our master and has considerable influence on the way we run our lives. For interpretation the date of birth is best taken from the calendar that predominates our life at the time of birth and that is stamped in our official birth documents. Secondary influences can be determined if the date of birth has been translated into another calendar for other official reasons, or if we live our daily lives dictated by a different calendar.

The window of the date of birth

The table that follows indicates some of the key qualities that relate to each portion of any date, in any calendar. It is a window through which to see yourself or another person in a new light. This window will further take on specific dimension according to the actual numbers of any individual's date of birth.

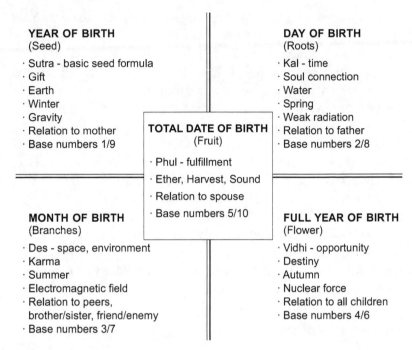

YEAR OF BIRTH
(Seed)

· Sutra - basic seed formula
· Gift
· Earth
· Winter
· Gravity
· Relation to mother
· Base numbers 1/9

DAY OF BIRTH
(Roots)

· Kal - time
· Soul connection
· Water
· Spring
· Weak radiation
· Relation to father
· Base numbers 2/8

TOTAL DATE OF BIRTH
(Fruit)

· Phul - fulfillment
· Ether, Harvest, Sound
· Relation to spouse
· Base numbers 5/10

MONTH OF BIRTH
(Branches)

· Des - space, environment
· Karma
· Summer
· Electromagnetic field
· Relation to peers,
  brother/sister, friend/enemy
· Base numbers 3/7

FULL YEAR OF BIRTH
(Flower)

· Vidhi - opportunity
· Destiny
· Autumn
· Nuclear force
· Relation to all children
· Base numbers 4/6

Author's Note. The following chapters give examples of the numbers in each position of the date of birth and are to be taken as elementary samples and are not conclusive. I have been reluctant to present a description of each number in each position of the date of birth since it absolutely lacks the quality that is present in a negotiating conversation with a person about their life. The important thing is to develop a basic feel for each number and the time cycles. From this firm basis the idea is to listen carefully to the individual and to yourself and find the unique expression of the combination that is being lived as well as the development that is being negotiated. Then you can move onto the advanced sections and begin to deepen your understanding of the numbers themselves through a wide variety of their expressions in life.

In the next five chapters I have tried to present some common features in a way that each individual can recognize as their own particular expression of the ten dimensions. The descriptions invite you to take a bold look at some of the problematic sides of the human character. By accepting a difficulty it becomes the first step in the process of getting through it and similarly, to accept a problem turns it into a friend and a tool for our self-development. It is not easy to move beyond where we are if we do not know where we are. If we deny a problem then we only feed it, for we cannot deny something that does not exist. If who we are is who we really want to be, then we have also to know who we are not. It is the process of negation, the know-how of the no, that clears the way for self-illumination (eliminate to illuminate). If I am not accepting myself as I am then I am accepting myself as I am not. You see?!

It seems easy when you contemplate just any one of the above statements, but when you take them together you cannot be sure if you are coming or going. The point is that whoever you are, or are not, and whoever you may be or may not want to be, the process is happening and in some way or another you are involved in it. Reading the material that follows will help you to make the most use of the earlier descriptions of the ten dimensions, bringing them into alignment and taking an active part in your not-being as well as your being. Once you are tuned into your own experience of them you will be able to take a co-operative and co-creative part in their harmonious alignment and interaction. When you reach Section Three of this book you will see that it offers definite ways, which make it possible to work on cultivating the qualities that you feel are the most needed.

Chapter 16

Yearly cycle: the seed

The last two digits in the date of birth correspond to the seed of our being and the element of earth. It is our essence that contains the whole information within, the primary formula and latent potential. Within this cycle many other factors of life become apparent. There is growth and decay through seasonal changes, hibernation and a real sense of things beginning and ending. Each calendar from any part of the world began only once with its year number 1.

The annual cycle expresses something of the collective unconscious and is marked by various festivals, celebrations, and other special occasions of remembrance, which are deeply rooted into our ancient origins. The monthly cycle only makes sense in the context of the yearly cycle, which is often divided into four quarters to give a definition of seasonal themes, also marked by the solstice and equinox days. The annual cycle lends itself to a number of other longer cycles such as seven, eleven, twelve, and eighteen years. The decades also appear to have their own patterns where each ten-yearly cycle is dominated with a different social theme.

Given that the annual cycle is a natural one it can be considered as bearing primary information. It is a cycle honored through the magical dimension, for example, as expressed in earth-based religions. This cycle is the ground upon which we build the constructions of our life plans; we even plan our life subconsciously according to the sense of the number of years we might live. Each year that we celebrate our birthday it can be noted that it is a number that we celebrate, each number of years bearing a message to yourself and to others who inquire as to the numbers of years of your life so far.

Every year we grind the grain for bread to feed the general population, we press the seeds for oil, we store some seeds to plant in the coming year, and of course when the time comes we plant the new seed. It is about survival and the magic of the life impulse that does survive.

Time

Time is the beginning and ending of all things, the explosion of a seed as it multiplies itself and the contraction into a tiny point in the self-renewal. Beginnings are the origination and birth moments of people, events, communities, projects, and so on, and there are two dimensions of a beginning. In the physical, the first step of the journey is the seed that begins the plant, the first word of a conversation, the source of a spring that starts to flow down the mountain, and a spark that ignites a fire. Then there are the beginnings from the mental realm; an idea or a concept taking shape, a dream arising or an anticipatory thought that could lead on to fear, excitement, or conflict. In their completion entities may disperse totally or continue to exist but with transparency, like a crystal immersed in water whose existence is solid and enduring through time but which cannot be detected because of its transparent nature. Dispersion would be like dust to dust and ashes to ashes.

There are cases where the ending never seems to end; for instance when someone dies and their tyrannical or guiding influence seems to linger on indefinitely. All these possibilities will be dictated by the presence of a primal law that has been here since at least the beginning of time. Beginnings and endings may be abrupt or gradual, sudden or smooth, intense or gentle, in fact, quite like the diversification of birth and death. Then there is the mystery of "I" as the beginning of time for the individual.

Gift as earth and earth as gift

Earth is like the beginning of time, which cannot know itself, for to do so would have been to exist before it existed. The earth element does not know itself and we are not aware of the gifts we have. The emotions of the earth are usually fast asleep like rocks and are only released slowly over a long time of being worn away or by a sudden crush or break.

The GIFT will normally be a helpful tool and provides a basis of strength, which can be relied upon. It is something that usually comes naturally and should be easy to access. When deliberately suppressed it becomes limiting and self-destructive and if ignored or not consciously acknowledged it will still operate but only minimally and at times of emergency. It is, therefore, your basic survival strategy and when cultivated can be the means to your spiritual flourishing. How you use your gifts can be directly traced to your relationship with your mother and how she used or abused those qualities. This is not about blaming the mother but about the choice you made for the mother who would give you the gift of life. It is about how you subsequently chose to imitate, reject, or learn from her, even her mistakes. However, relationships are mutual and so you can offer something of your gift to your mother, be it on the human, absolute, or divine level. Your mother's womb was your first home when you came to this planet so issues relating to home and other places of rest and nourishment will be presented by the number of the year of your birth.

Particular locations on the earth become centers of convergence and divergence for energy, ideas, and people. The force of gravity is relevant to the earth and so locations may have a feeling of pressure or dispersion, heaviness or lightness, as well as high or low. There may be a need to ground and sedate or a need to stimulate and lift up.

The numbers of your year of birth

By adding together the last two digits of your year of birth you can reduce it down to a number of 11 or lower. In the example of 1957 it would be as follows: 57 = 5 + 7 = 12 = 1 + 2 = 3. The gift is number 3.

With experience you will learn to also consider the influence of the numbers 5 and 7 in the example but as a starting point we shall take the addition of the last two digits.

Now read below to find which spiritual body is your gift. There you will discover its function and purpose as well as the qualities, which are your possible survival kit, and some of the problems to work through in order to realize your full potential.

1. SOUL: This is the seed of individuality, the consciousness of a self, which survives through all apparent changes. It is the original will to exist, the initiator of the action of self-expression and a center of being.

Issues will be related to individuality, originality, strength of will, independence, self-determination, autonomy, conflicts of will, impatience and intolerance, stability and firmness, initiative and humility, and a need for nourishment and nurturing. The life impulse may be too static and you could feel frustrated.

Home is a place of rest so sleep in your bones; everything begins at home.

2. NEGATIVE MIND: Through this second body the soul expresses its feminine nature. It is the first tool of self-reflection and the means to operate discriminative wisdom. It arises out of the initial experience of separation, which is the price to pay for individuality so that you know what you are by knowing what you are not.

Here there are matters of attachments, yearnings, relationships, co-operation, tactfulness, loyalties, needing to be needed, naivety, enslavement, critical abilities, discriminative wisdom, discretion, and melancholy. All these come into play through the negative mind, the gift of innocence.

You may sense a lack of connection to your origin and a kind of emptiness of memory. This can also feel like a lack of direction and a tendency to negate offers of direction from others. It may seem as though there is no anchor in your life but, in fact, the negative or the nothing is your point of reference. The same applies to the apparent lack of motivating impulse for the negative state is itself a source of motivation. It can even feel like you have not been born but at the same time there is a wish to be born.

Home is an attachment to home or feeling homeless, possibly through the abandonment by the mother and followed by a sense of rejection from women in general. You want to be needed by your mother and have a need to be needed at home. There may be homesickness and a yearning to go home, yet at the same time you are constantly critical of the home. Separation comes with your loyalty to the home and your feeling of rejection by the home, yet that abandonment can be realized as the great infinite and the bright emptiness, which is your true home.

3. POSITIVE MIND: The Positive Mind is the masculine or active and outer expression of our individuality. It is the tool for relating to the physical environment and arises out of a positive acceptance of existence as a separate being.

Some of the issues which influence the behavioral manifestation of the third body are self-value, self-worth, self-respect, hope, fairness, equality, quality, resourcefulness, enthusiasm, encouragement, challenge, optimism, boredom, expansion, expressiveness, vanity, and right judgment.

As a gift the number 3 provides a survival kit of positivity, a hidden and primal laugh, involuntary joy in spite of everything, and the capacity to laugh at the worst scenarios of life. You want to be seen especially by your mother as this provokes you to exist. You may feel victimized by her and angry for having been born.

Home is a place to experience quality and equality, a place to be seen and valued. You may feel that your mother did not really see you and this can give you a feeling like it was a mistake to be born. You may feel ashamed of your origins, your home, or your mother.

4. NEUTRAL MIND: Realizing there are a lot of individuals leads us to look beyond ourselves for sources of knowing. This detachment from our individual needs to those of the group is both the cause and the outcome of the Neutral Mind. It is the search for truth beyond the individual's truth and a transformation of sensitivity from instinct into feeling or intuition.

Truth, detachment, selflessness, service, discipline, overworking, trust, doubt, neutrality, commitment, memory, and choosing are the products and causes of the fourth body.

As a gift the number 4 gives you decisiveness but you may need to work through the state of doubt to really cultivate this gift. In this position the ability to choose is applied in relation to choosing what and when to begin and end in your life.

There is doubt in your origin and existence, which connects to confusion about life direction and origin. It is possible that doubt was the cause of your decision to take birth, but doubt reveals a hidden and primal sensitivity, which may still be sleepy and dormant, waiting for the right touch to wake it up.

You want to trust your mother but you may experience broken trust as part of learning to trust yourself.

Home is a place of service, a place to invite people and to serve them, but also a place to be receptive. There is a commitment to home but also feeling at home in your bones.

5. PHYSICAL BODY: This is our temple of residence whilst on the planet and vibrates according to whatever we make our god or gods. It is the essential vehicle for all spiritual growth, the unique and rare precious jewel that is not easily obtained. For any process of life to be of significance, it must be transmitted through the physical body and its five elements. The most important of these are the nervous system and the chemical exchanges and communications that take place in the brain and throughout the entire body.

Some areas of interest that arise here are communication, synthesis, knowledge, uncertainty, teaching, learning, experience, experimentation, balance, wholeness, health, nervous energy, social skills, sacrifice, the paradox of freedom and constraint, exchange, meeting, and exile.

The gift of 5 is related to learning and teaching, particularly learning from your frustration and educating it, and learning in your sleep or maybe even learning to sleep.

Communication is an issue of survival and these concerns are expressed very verbally. There is especially a need to be heard by the mother. Your own voice is an important point of reference as it has the capacity to be consistently present yet always changing in the form and content of what it gives out. There will be a kind of persistence in your voice, which will irritate others until you learn to refine it. This is the education of your frustration.

Home is a place of constant change or a constant change of homes. It is where you learn to feel at home with change, which means stability through change.

6. ARCLINE: Traditionally represented by the halo, the Arcline is the final outcome of seeking the truth outside ourselves, which began with the Neutral Mind. Through its development we gain a degree of clarity about our social ideals that is both caused by and the cause of our ability to fulfill our social commitments in action. Our way of being will manifest through the Arcline as harmony, beauty, grace, introspection, secrecy, justice, responsibility, fear and fearlessness, carelessness or carefreeness, group awareness, and social convention.

Your gift of number 6 is provoked into life when the world wants you to take responsibility and again this would begin with your sense of responsibility toward your mother. The best thing to take responsibility for is your own state of rest and peace.

6 is connected to shock – the gift of life, your birth, may have been a shock for you. To go beyond this surprise is to realize that your gift is to be a surprise to the world. It is to take responsibility only for your own life and for the nature of your surprise that you want to share with the world. 6 also relates to the sense of urgency; there may have been a fear of being born but at the same time an urgency to take birth.

Home is found in music or art and is a place of beauty and artistic expression. Sing at home and let your song make you feel at home. Home is a secret home or a home with secrets where peace is justice and justice is peace. There may be a fear of home and a fear of resting yet somehow you find yourself resting in fear, which can also feel like a fear of gravity. There is an urgency to go home.

7. AURA: Finding only a certain amount of fulfillment in the social, emotional world, the individual turns back to itself seeking its

higher self or its source. The Aura will start to develop beyond its family heritage when we begin to understand the possibility of an all-pervading and absolute being, a cosmic consciousness of which we are a small but definite part. The Aura is, therefore, the means to extend our perception of the complexities of universal intelligence and the many possible realms of existence, which can become real just as easily as they can be imagined.

Protectiveness, mercy, forgiveness, blame, resentment, guilt, confidence, inferiority, wisdom, loneliness, aloneness, sensitivity, over reacting, imagination, pride, intellectual conceit, skepticism, and cynicism are some of the manifestations of the auric body.

With the gift of number 7 there is a tendency to play an archetypal role in life, which can either be an imposing or admirable model for others. This relates to the power of your inner vision as well as impersonal vision.

You want to be able to see the mother and to protect her and there may be a long search for origins through explanations.

Home is prison or protection. You want to be a king at home or at home when a king. Home is a psychic construction.

8. PRANIC BODY: Prana is the life force mainly carried through our breath and is the connecting link between our finite self and infinity. As we tune into infinity we expand our pranic breath and its manifestations and as we tune into our Pranic Body we consciously connect to infinity without having to leave our physical body.

The activity of the Pranic Body creates issues such as purity, seriousness, carefulness, dreaminess, healing, cleansing, executive skills, authority, wisdom, leadership, the use and abuse of power, fatalism, and compassion.

You may have been a mother to your mother and involuntarily find yourself being a mother to others. Your identification with eternity can make you quite dreamy or think you are just a dream and it is important to remember that physically you are not infinite even though you are spiritually.

The gift of 8 includes a latent capacity to channel prana for the healing of others; to heal is also to kill the sickness. Life events will often remind you that the final direction of all beings is beyond the gates of death and by some mystery your integrity lies through the channel of life and death. When you realize this it will help you to recognize that your integrity cannot die and is, in fact, the one thing that survives.

Home is a dream, dreaming at home and of the ideal home and you feel homesick for your spiritual home. Home is healing and to be healed is to go home. You clean the home and feel at home with cleanliness or purity.

9. SUBTLE BODY: This is the vehicle that carries the individual being through the evolving process of lives and deaths. The soul has no access to any of the other bodies beyond this physical world and remains in the Subtle Body, which contains the karmic record of the individual's growth. The other bodies are recreated each lifetime when we take physical birth but it is the Subtle Body that extends out into a tunnel when we leave our present existence. The walls of this tunnel hold the vibrational essence, which records our life of what has been and is to be.

Endurance, calmness, patience, dispersion, transference, mastery, mystery, gullibility, lack of purpose, completion, altruism, and refinement are the issues related to the Subtle Body.

The gift of 9 includes the gift of tenacity but such stubborn intent needs to develop an awareness of the appropriate direction that presses it to go on. Without a sense of direction the foundation of your calm perseverance will disperse without fruit. The wonderful paradox you may experience is your frustrated efforts to find calm, which, of course, cannot be fulfilled until you calm down.

Home is essential and the essence is home. You sacrifice all for the home or you sacrifice home for all and there is dispersion of home and home is dispersion. Home should be perfect and perfection is home; you are impatient to go home and home is impatience. Home is a place of comfort and comfort is home. Everything ends at home.

10. RADIANT BODY: The Radiant Body is like millions of minute suns that are everywhere. It is to this realm that we return when our individuality, be it our ego, soul, higher self, or any other fancy

name, dissolves and becomes food for the infinite unknown. When the Radiant Body is shining to its full extent in the mundane planes of existence we may feel our life is completely out of our hands or we may go to the other extreme by being too obsessive and control every event that happens. The Radiant Body is like an infinite magnification of the soul where so many similar qualities are at play, the only difference being the Radiant Body is expressed by virtue of the absolute and not by the individual. If it were not for the Radiant Body, nothing would be accomplished and nothing would exist.

Dignity, regality, nobility, and courage are all related to this dimension.

The gift of number 10 is to listen totally and unconditionally, which is immediately transforming for both the listener and the one who is talking.

Home is everything or home is nothing. You may only feel at home when you are away from home and want a home just to be on the outside of it.

11. Although number 11 is not a body as such, it is often claimed to have special significance. The explanation is simply that it indicates a relationship between the Radiant Body (10, the personality of the infinite) and the individual soul (1). When this relationship is in total harmony there will be a co-creative dance between them and the individual will display a profound degree of spiritual common sense. However, when there is no conscious involvement in this partnership, the 11 will most likely reduce to a 2 resulting in the experience of separation, which is the negative mind state.

The whole journey of life is to realize your innocence and to recognize that scarcity is your greatest resource.

There is an experience of being alone yet dependent and this dependence can mature into a loyalty to the qualities of number 10, the radiance, which is you as more than the sum of all the parts. This is the part of you that is apart from you, just like an angel by your side, usually your left side.

Home is a partner in a spiritually creative relationship. Home is your alliance.

Chapter 17

Daily cycle: the roots

The duality of day and night is the roots of our experience of time. Day and night is like life and death, existence and non-existence, brightness and darkness, and connects to the element of water.

The daily cycle is one of duality expressed in the alternating of day/night, light/dark, full/empty, and seeing/not seeing. The day is also a part of weekly, monthly, and yearly cycles and in this context time is a flux and flow within a bigger expanse, like the tides of the ocean and the rise and fall of the waves. This flow is the wisdom of the ages charging the present and displacing the future like the sand in the egg timer that displaces the air as it falls into the lower chamber. Time as a process flows up and down, becoming full and empty like the rivers of time passing by and rolling along. It is time upon which we can float or in which we drown. We can dive into it and swim around or we can drink it, for time is fluid time, which cleanses, heals, and creates suffering; it is time that purifies. One day is finite but the endless repetition of days brings our attention to the infiniteness of time, the never-ending flow of time and the ocean of time. We sense the timeless moment that grows bigger rather than smaller by the process of self-dividing and that makes the moment more and more empty till we feel the full emptiness of time, the black hole of time, the void.

Time

Time in itself is infinite and infinity is the roots of the soul; the roots of the soul are infinite and the soul is rooted to infinity. However, we do not experience our link to the infinite and this is our greatest weakness that creates a sense of a big (infinite) gap or emptiness in our lives. We try to fill it in every kind of mechanical, medicinal, emotional, psychological, and intellectual way possible but none of these solutions ever lasts. If we could discover that the emptiness itself is the connection and relationship to the soul, then we would hail it as our greatest strength. Even death, which is given the lowest value in most societies, would take on the highest worth when experienced consciously.

In time, life is living itself and death is in its process of dying; there is loss and gain, fast and slow, more and less. Take time away and there would be nothing to measure, even though time in itself is nothing; it is empty and endless. Time and space are just the mediums through which we take birth, live, die, and take birth again and although we are not these things we tend to lose our identity in them. Time is like many personal rivers that flow toward the same universal ocean and we create space (and the mind) as the vessel to move along these waters of time. This saves us temporarily from drowning but our apparent creations have consequences, otherwise known as karmas.

As a child the daily cycle is our first experience of a natural time cycle that is given by our environment and is an experience shared by everyone on the planet, no matter what calendar system is used. This cycle may be divided by regular feeding and sleeping habits or other routine, everyday tasks, by the ticking and chiming of clocks, and so on. Officially in many parts of the world it is divided into hours and minutes, which are sectioned into work, rest, and play with interruptions for meals. It is a cycle marked by the need for daily bread.

Time is the basic problem of existence where we question what to do with time, how to pass the time, how to fill the day, how to fulfill our need of today, and how to know what we need. These are the basic dilemmas that face us each morning as we enter again into a semi-conscious relationship with time. Sometimes we fight it, other times we wish we had more or less of it but probably most of the time we dream it away.

Water as soul link

Water is the element that nourishes the roots and corresponds with the daily cycle. We can live for months without food but only a few days without water. The energy that is the water element relates to life force, libido, wealth, health, power, chi, and prana. It is known through the tension or charge that exists between the opposites of, for example, yin and yang, night and day, female and male, rich and poor, full and empty. It is the organic power or force that is toxic and stuck in sickness or pure and flowing in health. The right relation to the daily cycle is the best self-medicine.

Water is a particular kind of feminine energy related to instinct, flowing, channeling, and healing. The flow of the energetic stream empowers the structures of our life. It is an energy supply to be tapped into and its flow can be managed/regulated, controlled/ blocked, or left to the wisdom of its own inherent chaos. The emotions of water flow in all the variations of streams, rivers, and waterfalls found around the world. They can be stored in the form of lakes, dams, bottles, clouds, ice cubes, and snow and the release of watery emotions may also take on many qualities.

Water is a conductor that allows a connection between the ego of our everyday personality and the primal impulse of our soul and, therefore, we can think of water as our daily bread that represents soul food and the link to the infinite. In mystical terms this daily soul food is known as amrita or ambrosia (heavenly nectar) and drunk through daily recitation of prayers and mantras in every religion. It is through this that we feel alive and real, where we connect to our soul essence and all our past experiences of this life and other recent past lives. There is not so much the detailed content but the vibrational essence, just like a homeopathic solution that contains no trace of the substance but which holds the memory in the same manner.

Each individualizing soul chooses a certain way of experiencing its connection with the world and uses the daily flow of energy as the means. The soul connection is also the medium through which other energies come to us, therefore being a source both of strength but also a potential weak link in the chain. At the same time, however, it is the power that, like water, can divide or be divided. Through the channel of time and water our nature is empathetic so that we can tune into the soul essence of others and know the essence of their past sufferings.

By way of the SOUL LINK comes an indication of the relationship to our father or men in general. It is through the soul link that we learn to discern the difference between the primary male, the original patriarch that is vertical, and the secondary male that is horizontal, which has masqueraded as the patriarch during the era that is passing, an era that would be better termed as the male ego era.

Psychoanalysis works on understanding and resolving ourselves as a historically produced being and such knowledge is interesting and useful. However, it does not guarantee that we go further and distil the lessons of the past into their purest form. This distillation requires attending to the moisture that is to be distilled. A weakness can become a great strength when it is played out masterfully and our soul link should increase in power as life goes on, just as a river does as it gathers force in its flow toward the ocean. This, of course, depends on whether we understand the essence of the tradition that flows into our evolution rather than the rules of tradition, which belong to the element of fire and its association with karma (see the monthly cycle).

So whilst water itself is a feminine principle, mirrored by the lunar influence on water, its relation is to the male in two different ways. Firstly to the primary male, the seed that she receives and nourishes, then to the secondary male as in the son that she creates from the seed.

Note: The earth element (not the planet earth) displays properties usually associated with the masculine principle but the earthy seed is carried by the feminine mother. Similarly, the water element, exhibiting qualities of the feminine principle is carried by the masculine father. This is the yin yang philosophy, which is related to the soul link and the cycle of day and night, where each quality of the polarity has the opposite deep within its center.

The numbers of your day of birth

Reduce your day of birth to a digit of 11 or less and read the descriptions below to get a few ideas of the more specific aspects related to your soul link.

For example, if you were born on the 14th of the month: 1 + 4 = 5. Your soul link number is 5.

Remember, these are just very general guidelines, which will give you ideas of what you experience in relation to the flow of time, energy, needs, weaknesses, and power.

1. This expresses the need for stability and focus. You need to be an individual and the originator and if no one needs you to get things started you may wonder if you exist at all. You might spend a lot of time and energy trying to initiate all sorts of things that never actually get started or you may be the one who gets an event off the ground but then you do not turn up yourself. If you are with people too much you may find yourself put on the spot all the time and feel a strong urge to be alone. To be in touch with power you need to learn to focus and do one thing at a time. There is a need for solitude but sometimes you may lack any sense of motivation or impulse. You could feel a lack of stimulus or provocation and have a need for it from someone else. This lack can be interpreted as tiredness and a need for rest but, in fact, you need to concentrate your resources. One of the ways you may try to do this is to sleep a lot or somehow turn your home into a cave of retreat. This is fine if it works.

2. Through this number there is danger of naivety and yet your power comes from being in touch with your innocence. The need to be needed is felt most strongly through this number in this position and the sad energy that results must be worked out in meditation, calling out rather than seeking to take in. There is a need to be loyal to someone or something and this can be expressed in the way you reflect the emotions of others. You have a need for vital energy yet there is a hidden vitality within the need itself. You may feel split, especially in relation to the left and right sides of your being. It is very important that you realize the feeling of separation is itself the relationship and learn to find its richness and not to dwell on the feeling of lack.

3. Here the weak link expresses itself in shame, self-negation, and other problems around self-value. There is a need to be seen and reassured and a need to be understood, especially by the father or some other male, and without this empathy you feel the unfairness of life. There is a need for fun and activity as well as for protection and safety but sometimes you refuse to ask for help when you need it. You can connect to your power through laughter though sometimes it is first useful to get in touch with the anger that is beneath the shame. There is a strong need for practical and physical self-expression, which includes showing your tears or your sadness. There is also the need to prove something, which is basically that you deserve attention and that you are capable of many things. You must find out that you are OK and independent of the things to which you are attached. Physical activity is important to you but it needs to be directed towards something meaningful and not merely become a drug in itself.

4. The need to make decisions is highlighted by the difficulty in choosing. There is a need to receive though you may often deny it and a need to be thanked, yet you may reject thanks when given. One way to become receptive and respectful of your own needs is to learn to thank others. You may well feel betrayed and wounded from an experience of trusting, especially the father, and so you do not trust the possibility of the next human contact to be sensitive enough. However, your power lies in the heart of the wound though there can be a conflict between the need to be open and the need to be protected. The need of love and touch appears to go along with the need of pain and your needs may seem too painful for you to be fully in touch with them. This results in the absence of certain feelings, like reflecting back the feelings of others so as not to feel. There can be a lot of doubt about your needs but also a need to doubt. There is a need to work and yet also the rejection of work or the way in which you cut yourself off from work. Your experience of separation is like one long drawn out moment yet at the same time it is a lasting memory of a sudden moment, an inner shock. You may feel strongly the absence of love but this is not a reason to complain; rather it is the force that must empower you to give love in a world where you are aware of its absence.

5. Through this number you feel a need to do and yet not to do as well as a need to be and not to be. You will experience a need for paradox as you try to relate the active and passive parts of yourself and work through the confusion as to how you can be dynamic and yet still. This is your need for balance, especially in the physical things of life like sleep, diet, and exercise. Here you feel that the world needs you and that you need the world, just as the fruits need to be eaten or as the birds need to be heard. The need to be heard is also very strong as it helps with the need to feel your center and it is through communication that the soul link is engaged and the infinite power tapped. Communication of your longing and yearning is important yet there will be a tendency to deny or negate your deepest hunger. You can either recharge or drain yourself through the use of the voice but you must learn to listen to yourself. In spite of the need to speak there may often be no words and the loss of voice.

6. Here there is the feeling that you are needed to take responsibility for others yet equally there is a yearning for freedom as well as romance and beauty. There is, of course, the sense of their absence, which can be due to your refusal to have these qualities in your life. The 6 in this position can give you an awareness of the beauty of need itself if you choose to realize it. There is a fear of need and yet a need of fear, a fear of loss and separation but with the possibility to lose fear, to split from your fear. Passionate fear can become a fear of passion. Power is gained when you take responsibility for yourself, which is done through faith, and in this context faith would be the manifestation of the power of the soul. There is a connection between number 6 and the hands in a spiritual sense as in the idea of a spiritual midwife. Water is the flow of the birth channel for the soul as well as for the physical body and a spiritual midwife may not take people into this world but beyond it, through the gates of death.

7. The need to know and to understand is the main expression of the 7 in this position. There is also the need to see and the absence of seeing as well as seeing into the emptiness. A lack of control determines the need to be in control and to control what cannot be controlled, which is the void. You may try to control your needs

because you feel controlled by them and as you have a need for plans you make them up regardless of whether they are needed or not. Need is a difficult thing to come to terms with and so you find strategies to cover them up. You may use the approach of blame, which is a projection of a picture upon someone and hides the truth of your need to really see. You need to forgive and forgiveness needs you. Here there is the danger of too many shoulds and shouldn'ts and an endless search for the reason why. The power is found when you can ask that question without qualifying it in any way. Enjoying the pleasure of sorrow you also feel the sorrow of pleasure that makes for a contemplative nature, a need to rescue others and a tendency to be protective (possibly having begun with your father) which can become a need to imprison. There is a need to judge but also to judge needs and, therefore, to inhibit their expression.

8. With this number your soul link becomes more transparent and brings the need for power as well as the power of need, which is sometimes expressed in the hunger for money or prana. It is very important to recall the infinite nature of need here otherwise it will devour you. Negating its power will not help either; rather you can use the need for purity to ensure the pureness of your relationship to power so that power can be your purity and purity your power. Dreaminess can be a weakness in this area but access to the dizzy heights also means you can work as a channel for the healing energy, which is all the more reason for purity. There is a compassionate need and a need for compassion but only when you give what you need does it come back to you. Be careful in your negation of authority and the authority with which you do that.

9. This ninth number leaves you with the need for peace and to make peace and to pacify your needs, especially in relation to the father energy, whether personal or universal. Your need for peace can be so powerful that you become very impatient and unpeaceful and yet there is a kind of peace in the steadiness of your persistence. This is your enduring need and the need to endure, which is also the enduring emptiness and the need to endure the emptiness. The need for perfection implies that you feel someone needs you to be perfect for them and so you feel your need to be perfect and that your needs

are perfect. There comes a need for completion, which also creates a need for direction, the direction home. Here you find the need for a guarantee, moved by an absence of any guarantee and yet within the center of the emptiness is the very thing that seems to be lost. If you could fall into the center of this absence and your deepest desire you would find it right there. The demanding nature of number 9 might be expressed as the constant wearing away of someone's resistance, a steady insistence like a stream of water that never ceases.

10. The need for extremes and intense experiences are the main aspect of this number in this position. There is also the need for courage and a need to be needed by courage and the need to listen as well as to listen to your needs. Listening attunes you to the presence of power in every fiber of your being and because number 10 provides a link to the collective soul rather than the individual, it is possible to feel quite overwhelmed and yet a desire to be overwhelmed. There can be a need to explode along with an explosive need and these needs may explode out surprising both you and those around you. The power is not in the fighting against the flow but in handing over that power where you discover that your own needs are met within the collective.

11. 11 is the combination of 10 + 1 and gives you the feeling that I need God and God needs me. However, the intimacy and power of such a relationship is often too much and the situation is usually turned into one of number 2. There is a need to feel that you are in company because the quality of 11 allows you to sense that 1 is always walking beside you. You are forever in company so choose it to be the Divine and it will be. Be in partnership with the courage of number 10 and assume it to be a being and not just a concept that stands to your left and a little behind. If you have balanced all needs to equate with God's needs then this results in a spiritually instinctive common sense that can empower others. Otherwise refer to number 2 to know the problems of the 11.

Chapter 18

Monthly cycle: the branches

The calendar month represents the trunk and branches of our life. It is the landscape of our being, our shape and form, making us visible to the world. This visibility corresponds also to the element of fire.

The monthly cycle is a man-made construct even if it may have been an attempt to harmonize with the lunar cycle. Since it is impossible to manipulate the daily or yearly cycles we only have the months (and hours and minutes) to play with and this we have done in different ways through different cultures over the history of calendar keeping. The dominant pattern tends to be a twelve-monthly cycle where each month is divided into a number of days of between 28 and 31. The cycle of four weeks is another approximate expression of a lunar month. The month is part of the yearly cycle with three months considered as a season. The period of gestation from conception to birth is approximately nine months, which is, in fact, a lunar cycle of ten lunar months.

Time

The experience of time as structured comes from the past, which, by the law of repetition, infers or implies a future. History is the retelling of the story through the mechanical reproduction of ideas and actions that result from social training. Time is captured in photographs or video movies and locked into the machinery of time, the clock, where it is imprisoned and becomes stretched and compressed. We compartmentalize time into manageable fragments – broken time, dead time, the killing of time, time of boredom, busy time, time for fun, time with friends, and time wasting. All this we set up into the vicious circle of habitual time and time gets hot (the heat of the moment) and flows into karmic time.

We think that time is a problem to solve but actually the real problem is the mind that tries to do the solving. Mind is itself a construction and it is designed as an instrument for measurement and perception. The mind is given to perceive the natural divine order and support its expression according to various contexts. Like a teenage child, however, it prefers to rebel against the given order and construct its own ideologies. It develops its own illusion of autonomy and tries to break away from the holistic universe, attempting to outwit the creator who made all things to come and go, live and die. Nonetheless it remains merely a temporary machine and it uses time as its fuel.

Time and its endless flow to and from infinity cannot be changed but the shape we make of it can. How we try to use it can be re-negotiated, how we try to stretch, squeeze, burn up, save, buy and sell, and compete for time can all be transformed. We can free ourselves from the karmic wheel of action and reaction in the way we use or are used by time, and Karam Kriya is exactly this practice to use positive action in our limited time.

Karma

Man-made time is then a karmic construct of secondary information manipulated through the strategies of science and technology whether psychological and ideological or material and concrete. Karma is the mill driven by the waters of desire to grind the grain of the soul. Science, whether spiritual or mundane, maintains our schemes and structures, upgrades them from time to time, and uses the influence of the cultural mood to reinforce them. Like a teenager with a car there is the tendency to become over identified with and fascinated by the machine rather then utilize the machine for any more meaningful purpose other than to boost the illusion of self-importance. Karma is the physical and mental space we inhabit. It is the secondary effects of multiple secondary causes. It is our self-reproducing cosmetic identity, a decoration that gives the mask of our social status and image.

Karma as fire and fire as karma

Karma is linked to the element of fire; the heat of the moment is the catalytic energy that ripens the soul seed. It can be sparked by friction and most of our karmic reactions are due to being rubbed a certain way. The emotion of fire can be stored and released by various methods and the ego manifestation, our personality, can be compared to a flame that needs fuel to keep burning. Fire is visible and karma is created by our concern for all things visual, our self-image and projection. If karma is something to be burnt up then it also means burning our self-image and self-importance.

Karma is our social conflicts of life – how we as individuals encounter other individuals and so characterise them in our inner conversations. Karma is a habitual reaction to the world and when we notice our habits of thinking and behaving then we are in a position to resolve the karmic consequences of past action. It should not only be viewed as the result of something that has been done in the past but also as the present generation of further experiences. In other words it is the direct result of the continuous existence as an individual. This is just a law, neither good nor bad, and from which few, if any, can be free.

Going beyond good or bad, the way we express the karmic form in our personal lives is an indication of the social character we are cultivating in this life. Our social character or persona of this life is a result of past deeds and the selected ray upon which to travel this part of the journey. Whilst we are developing as holistic human beings there is also a need to focus on particular areas or specialties and each life is a chance to perfect a different facet. By working on the whole we reach the one, by working on the one we reach the whole; it is a two-way traffic.

Karma is an indication of our limited identity, its structure and behavior, whilst the pathway (discussed later on in relation to the total date of birth) is more a mark of our holistic approach. Karma is not to be seen as a way of explaining the ultimate cause of our dilemma. This is one of the traps of the karmic personality, which is always looking to find the cause; final causes are beyond the realms of rational understanding. It is best to consider your number in this section as a clue to the quality of your karma and to the laws governing your present experience of karmic processes, especially patterns of defense and self-imprisonment. Finally, do not forget that a coat is put on at the start of a journey and at the end it needs to be taken off. This is the moment when you reach your destiny and strip off the karmic uniform.

Our personal characterizations both influence and express themselves in the formation of cultural traditions. For example, collective karmic identities can be recognized in the construction of buildings. They are expressed in the cultural impact and effects indicated by the internal and external arrangements and decorations. The shape of a building as well as the types of signs and symbolizm expressed gives a kind of animated quality to the environment. So animal life may also be relevant at this level, like the pets of the house and animals that relate to the cultural identity. Examples of these are dragons (but note the difference in European dragons), turtles, the phoenix, blue or white tigers in China, lions in some parts of Africa, cats, dogs, eagles, and the sphinx in Egypt, the racoon, snake, and the wolf or buffalo for some Native Americans. A building may even have a creature-like quality that has significant influence over the activities that take place within and around it. This is also true of our machines of transportation and how they represent our animal nature.

The building or certain rooms may be shaped like boots, swords, or other recognizable objects. The purpose of a building extends beyond the basic needs that it is to serve. For example, why do we build a yacht instead of a raft to sail the seas, why do we need over a hundred different models of cars just to get from one place to another? It is a cultural preference according to local customs and value systems that contributes to the forming of particular characteristics in particular places. These characteristics are not only an expression of the people who created them but they also have a power in themselves, which then creates an influence over the people. Such cultural forms offer both protection but also imprisonment.

Likewise our inner psychological space is inhabited by various animations, some highly individualized and others inherited from our culture. It is an inner astral space, a zodiac of creatures and animated machinery.

The numbers of your month of birth

The number of the month is the number of your karmic shape. If you were born in January your number would be 1. The numbers of November (11) and December (12) can be explored in their subtle depth as combinations of 10 + 1, and 10 + 2, but for ease of interpretation the first level of analysis is found by reducing all numbers to one single digit. Hence:

November = 11 = 1 + 1 = 2

December = 12 = 1 + 2 = 3

With practice you will learn the more subtle influences of the combinations of numbers such as 11 and 12.

You can begin to have quite a different relationship to numbers when you realize they are representations of your own states of existence. It can be quite challenging to acknowledge and own the qualities associated with them, as you can no longer blame them for your condition but must instead start to accept yourself as you are. This section uses the example of the planets as a way of representing or referring to the numbers and certain aspects of their properties. The idea is not to excuse yourself for how you are because of a planet or a number but to encourage you to be more active in finding the best expression of who you are in this life.

The connection of the planets as described below is not exclusive to the numbers of the month but it is one of the most obvious correspondences. Your karmic shape is like a planetary costume, bringing color to your life. Your karmic and social conflicts and patterns will be mostly linked to the astral energy of the planet expressed in the number of the month in which you were born. These planetary associations are just reflections of your inner personal universe. You can explore the connection between the planets and numbers in other positions of the date of birth but it is most strong when in relation to the karmic number as indicated in the month of birth.

The karmic numbers have a particular connection to the past and also to our eyes – our ways of showing and hiding ourselves, our ways of seeing and being seen, the way we shape our world around us, both psychically and the physical environment of our living space, as well as to the animal kingdom and the colors. Now remember all that you have just read about the monthly cycle and the relation of time and karma and enjoy relating it to the particular month of your birth as outlined here.

1. SOUL = SUN: power, vitality, the will to exist, seeking self-expression, that which everything revolves around, unmoving, stable, a source and a resource.

House area: the cornerstone, anchor, buried treasure, altar, narrow passage, entrance, underground, hidden.

People with karma of number 1 often find they act as a reference point for how others place themselves socially and physically in space. They are solitary figures, their own best friend. They like to live alone or to have their own private space.

Past: the fall, original sin, shame of primary guilt (guilt of existing), which may be expressed as natural shyness, primal beginnings, something stuck in the past.

Your karma is to learn to see all as one, see the one in all, be seen in your solitude, lonely eyes, sleepy eyes, closed eyes, searching for one answer to all, showing and hiding through humility and solitude, eyes of shame or shyness. The challenge is to validate yourself in a non-egotistical manner and not to be trapped by the false and temporary approval that other give you.

Color: dark red, deep browns, stone grays, the dark color seen when you look into the center of the sun, the gold of the sun.

Symbol: altar, column, stone, earth, ash, feet, seed, serpent, elephant, the sun, needle, magic wand, infant.

2. NEGATIVE MIND = MOON: only known because it reflects the sun, periodic moments of darkness and apparent non-existence, mirror

and reflector, feminine, nurturing or needing to be nurtured.

House area: of water, washing, drainage, losses, difficulties, separation, suffering, needs, hunger.

With the karma of number 2 you may feel you have no sense of place or role in social settings unless there is someone to reflect. You reflect others in action and this is related to an absence of structure. There is a need to help and to be helped; a need for joy and joy needs you to realize its value. Therefore, you seek a social space where you feel needed but through naivety you might end up being an entertainer to others who do not respect you.

Past: sins of the flesh, desire/hunger, guilty of wanting, being needy, guilty of attachment and attachment to guilt.

Sad eyes, showing and hiding through the tears, innocent eyes.

Color: dark/black for loss and mourning, dark yellows.

Symbol: water, reptiles, fish, mirror, plants, moon, yin/yang.

3. POSITIVE MIND = JUPITER: also known as Jove, joyous, success, good luck, action, practical ideas, resourcefulness.

House area: family space, fun, entertainment, helpfulness, optimism, recognition (equality), sometimes fame, acquisitions (and stores), rituals or rites of passage.

Past: feeling like a victim, blaming others, angry but not able to take revenge, guilty of success/failure, feeling undeserving, lots of questions; you cannot accept that you are able or deserving and you use the past to prove it.

Angry eyes, smiling eyes, eyes that say "see me." You seek a place to be seen and to realize your equality with others. At other times you feel your shame and you might seek to hide or to look in the eyes of others for verification of your shame.

Color: orange, bright red.

Symbol: trident, triangle, cat, lion, sphinx, dragon, fire, candle.

4. NEUTRAL MIND = URANUS: spontaneous, detached clarity, gratefulness, the unexpected quiet revolution.

House area: inspiration, reception, guests (hosting), community, risk, injury, pain, gentleness, generosity, charity, service.

A person with karma number 4 has a sensitive inner space about which they might be quite protective. There can be doubt about your self-image and you doubt structure but in a very structured way.

Past: guilty of taking too much and so giving too much to compensate for all the taking, guilty of skepticism or skeptic to cover the guilt, taking blame and saying sorry.

True eyes, eyes of doubt seeking to prove that you do not know. Seeking a place to allow your softness to be visible.

Symbol: flowers, small birds, swan, deer, cross, square, flutes, cushion, ribbon, hand.

5. PHYSICAL BODY = MERCURY: communication, nervous system, sensing experiences, synthesis, and processing information.

House area: often not specified but could be considered as the area of communication, relationships, exchange, marriage. Corridors and hallways should be considered.

If you have a karma number of 5 it means that there is a struggle with communication. If you speak you will feel like you are really exposing yourself, becoming very visible, but then also if you do not speak you are not noticed. For you communication is an important means to understand the world around you and a way to be understood. Speaking is an action in itself through which you can transform beliefs into action and interpret action as expressions of belief. You can use your voice to create your learning space but if you are not confident you will not ask and be left feeling that you have no space.

Past: guilty of speaking, speaking of guilt and of forgiveness. The past catches up with you in the way your words are like a boomerang and return.

Eyes that speak as well as seeing and being seen in your words but also showing and hiding your words and yourself through your words. You seek a place where you can be heard.

Color: turquoise green, medium blues, bright yellows.

Symbol: fruit, harvest, angels, caduceus, embroidery, words, bridges, pentangle, chameleon.

6. ARCLINE = VENUS: love, devotion, beauty, gracefulness.

House area: of fortune, surprise, ambush, battle, beauty,

opportunity, justice, grace, silence. This could be the garden or an area of quiet within the house.

The karma of number 6 accepts silence and is challenged to be silently accepting but this does not mean non-action that is based in fear. Rather the challenge is to act from the silence. It may be that you have to silently accept in order to enter the battlefield of life and death and take action. There may be a fear of joy but to laugh would be very liberating.

Past: guilty for being beautiful, feeling embarrassment, guilty of fear and fear of guilt, a tendency to take on responsibilities out of a sense of guilt, fear of the past reoccurring in the future, fear of judgment, which can prevent you from entering into conflict and fighting for justice.

Beauty in the eyes, fearful eyes, showing and hiding your fear and your beauty. The visible silence, silent visibility. You struggle between seeking a place to have a fight and seeking to avoid all conflicts.

Color: shocking, sharp and striking colors, warrior blue.

Symbol: flag, sword, arrow, cube, dice, magic box, musical box, bell, hunting birds.

7. AURA = NEPTUNE: a king but not the king, unique unstructuredness, creating your own structure, unlimited imagination and so fantasy, ideals and illusions, inferiority/superiority complexes, forgetfulness.

House area: of knowledge, status, profession, temptation, fantasy, order, tradition or ceremony, the office and center of administration.

The karma of 7 can influence you to act as a king who has all the answers to every question and to make rules for everything to give a sense of your kingdom. You like to be in control but must learn to see the work of the creator who is the only real controler. You have a strong visual sense, unless blinded by resentment, and could work in any field asking for graphic skills.

Past: capacity for revenge or forgiveness, pride as cover for guilt or guilt of pride, past images replayed in the mind's eye.

Eyes of judgment or mercy, phantom in the eyes, inner vision, see the seer. You look for a place where you can see the whole show, you want to understand but do not realize that you are the answer to the question.

Color: mauve, violets, pale purples, electric colors.

Symbol: rainbow, Christ, king, judge, crown, throne, cage, prison, mask, veil.

8. PRANIC BODY = SATURN: father time, rhythm, need for structure and organization, death, fate, power, leadership, authority.

House area: of economics, wealth, riches, vitality, health (welfare), time, imagination, wisdom, compassion, and also of death.

A karmic number of 8 gives you a challenge to accept the power of your existence and not abuse it. You will find it hard to respect any authority that others claim to have unless it is an expression of their inner being. You may prefer to live in your dreams and find the ordinary world lacking in depth. The challenge, however, is for you to bring this depth.

Eyes of purity, power, infinite and flowing compassion, showing and hiding your energy, infinite eyes are eyes to see the infinite. You search in your dreams for a place of purity but it is your work to bring purity to this world.

Color: deep and dark blues, flowing white, pure and healing.

Symbol: mandala, wheel of eight spokes, egg timer, the trigrams of the I Ching, octagon, ocean, mother, whale, dolphin, fountain.

9. SUBTLE BODY = MARS: self-identity, purpose, desire (impersonal life impulse as the cause of all karma), beginnings and endings. The warlike quality of Mars is an expression of the relentless and impersonal impulse of life to survive; it is not related to fire and anger.

House area: of ancestors (physical or spiritual bloodline, not tradition, which is 7), the master's area, rest, recuperation, magic, oracle, madness/genius, sabotage, completion, perfection, the bedroom, and the burial or cremation ground.

Karmic patterns of number 9 include sabotaging your own structure as well as other systems, which relates to impatience and a drive for perfection. The challenge is to give yourself permission to be perfect because you are and, therefore, you can make mistakes and consider these as perfect too.

Calm eyes, restless eyes, mysterious eyes, eyes to see the mystery. The demands you make are psychic and projected through the eyes or you express your demands very physically like banging on the table. You are, of course, searching for the perfect place when it is you that has to bring the perfection by seeing it in every apparent mistake.

Color: wedding crimson, blood red, dark of the soil, gray of the rock.

Symbol: crystal, treasure, mountain, hermit, father, confetti, incense, desert.

10. RADIANT BODY = PLUTO: death and rebirth, disintegration and change, charisma, firmness, extremes.

With a karmic number of 10 your appearance in the world is intense or non-existent. You are a bit of an outsider and like to socialize too much or not at all.

House area: the 10 represents the spirit of the whole house.

Radiant eyes or blank eyes.

Color: radiant white light.

Note: many of the qualities from number 1 are present with the number 10 but they will be more intense or extreme.

11. November, the eleventh month is expressed both through the lunar qualities of 2 (11 = 1 + 1 = 2) and the planet Chiron. See number 2 for the general details. However, we can add that the number 11 brings a karmic challenge to see yourself reflected in the whole world and to see the unity of all. Your karma is to represent the relation of the individual soul to the universal soul.

12. December, the twelfth month (12 = 1 + 2 = 3) continues to find itself as the image of Jupiter, the same planet as March, number 3.

Chapter 19

Century cycle:
the flower

The full year of birth represents the flower of life, opening into opportunities for our destiny. This unfolding is linked to the element of air, the breath we have yet to live and all its future possibilities.

The 100-year cycle is one that is marked by the coming and going of whole communities and generations, a cycle where human destiny delivers itself to and through its children. The centuries have been marked by their own particular themes. In the 1600s there was crisis, colonization, and conquering. The 1700s saw science, technology, and industry. In the 1800s wealth and imagination flowed and in the 1900s we scattered ourselves into dispersion, madness, peace, homelessness, acceleration, and predictions about the end. The 2000s bring us into the chasm of duality; the division of those who realize the universal unity and those who refuse it will grow deeper. It is also a time to return to our innocence, the end of shame and blame and, therefore, to enjoy the connection to infinity by transforming our emotions of longing into devotion and a sense of belonging.

Time

Time here is the future that we anticipate but also the memory of those inspired moments of insight into our destiny. There are the wounds that eventually make us pull back from the untruth until we actively touch truth and where the future is the present. Here lies anticipated time, the time of choice and choosing, the moment and time that is our destiny. Future time is unknown time, the winds of time, and the time that we fear, for we do not know what it may carry on its wings. Time can be frozen in a projection where we make a future from the past to numb our encounter with time or the unconditioned time where we invest our faith.

Air as destiny

Wind power is what inspires the artist to intuitive priorities in communication. Wind is consciousness, awakening, and presence. The winds of fortune are a feminine energy, linked to justice, luck, grace, beauty, and intuition. The wind can also be caught in the sails of a ship or the propellers of a mill. But the regulation of the power of wind requires more than mechanical control. We are very much dependent on its grace to blow steadily but not so hard that it will blow the mill over. Our prayers may manifest in the mill through the songs we sing, the dances we dance, and the offerings we place at the altar. These are the inner winds that awaken from the sense of We-in-me and Thou-in-all, our sense of humanity and the possibilities of community awareness. The emotions of the air can be like the wind: unpredictable, soft, and enveloping or sharp and penetrating. It can also be stored in containers like gas bottles or balloons and released slowly through a valve or suddenly and explosively.

Our DESTINY indicates where we are going in our process of awakening and is often perceived by others more so than by ourselves. It is the flowering of our labors that we hope to fulfill in the peak years of our lives.

It is important to distinguish between fate and destiny. Fate is what we meet without trying; it is just the past catching up with our karmic interaction with the world. Destiny, on the other hand, is something we work towards and which requires our constant investment. As soon as we become lazy about our destiny we are drawn into the karmic structure that uses our fears to empower itself and then we find ourselves back in the machine of fate. To ensure our moment by moment investment into our destiny we need to remember that it is always in the future and always just in front of us so that we somehow never quite arrive. This sense of never quite accomplishing our destiny does not mean we do not access it, but rather this highlights its dynamic nature. Choosing our destiny is not something we do once and for all and that's it; choosing is only alive when it is sustained.

Aspirations are achieved by bringing them down to earth and investing them with inspiration and this is helped in a practical way by using our gift (as in the description of the annual cycle). The wrong kind of relationship to our destiny can leave us with dreams which are in the past, a frustrated will that lacks inspiration, or an angry or victimized consciousness that distracts from the frightening uncertainty of the future. With our destiny we hope to express our new self or our self-to-be, our anticipated self. It is our way to go beyond the present into new freedoms.

Human community is about the presence of the people in the place, the breath we bring to the spaces we inhabit, both in our bodies as well as our houses and other buildings. Our attention goes to who is who in the building, what are the relationships, the ages of the people, their family roles and vocations, and astrological or numerological data of the person. It is from this level that we sometimes have to find the capacity to make the most out of a worst situation. When little can be done to improve the surroundings, such as in a prison, it is the quality of the presence of the human spirit that transforms the place from a dungeon to a temple.

Attitude or energy

Corresponding with the two kinds of power, wind/presence and water/energy, we can say that different difficulties will arise in relation to each of these. The first is a question of attitude while the latter is a question of energy. With regard to the wind power, its expression is most important in the presence of the person and the reciprocating winds of grace or fortune. The interesting thing about attitude is that we can change it even if we cannot change our environmental circumstances. This can be done through the development of such things as prayerfullness, intuitive awareness, honesty, unconditional love, the consciousness of the "We in me" (Thou), human service, and divine praise. In the practice of Karam Kriya the focus for presence is less on the space and more on the people that inhabit the space. When working with someone in regards to their destiny it is important to bring their attention away from questions like "will I get rich, will I get married, should I be a priest or a politician?" and to explore the attitude with which they could approach their life so as to experience with a sense of destiny.

Generally speaking it is harder, or just more challenging since it calls for more consciousness and responsibility, to negotiate a change of a person's attitude as opposed to changing the energy flow, whether within the person or in their environment. Therefore, water power or energy flow has tended to become the more popular concern of practices such as Feng Shui since it does not call upon the responsibility of the people to influence their environment and their own lives. Rather it places all the emphasis on external factors in the naïve hope that the people will gain benefit from this without their own contribution of presence. (Note: This is contrary to the original spirit of Feng Shui, which concerns itself with both the movement of the wind and the water powers.)

The numbers of your full year of birth

The full year of birth will influence us in moments of truth in our lives, moments when we feel we really meet our destiny, and moments when we decide to do something as an expression of our love and gratitude. These moments are all touched by the grace of manifesting the best we can do in life but they also lay us open to many fears and doubts.

The archetypal forms described here just give a few ways in which we are touched by the numbers of our destiny, indicated by our year of birth. Add all the numbers together until you obtain a number between 1 and 11.

In our example of 1957:

1957 = 1 + 9 + 5 + 7 = 22 = 2 + 2 = 4. The number of destiny is 4.

Notice the paradoxes that fear brings and the state of indecision that leaves us at the mercy of fate. Destiny is met by decision not by waiting. Grace comes to the one who surrenders in prayer, not to the one who simply gives up, freezes in shock, or gets angry and thinks s/he knows better.

The emphasis in these descriptions on fear is meant to show the depth at which the diagnosis can go into one area of concern. Other issues related to destiny and its opportunities could be explored with equal profundity such as trust, discovery, love, the sense of touch, and the air element. I encourage you to contemplate these and other themes for it is of little value if this book does all the work for you.

1. For a very long time there has not been a year that has given a total of 1, not since the year 1 AD in the western calendar. The years 10, 100, and 1000 are counted as 10 but it would be true to consider an intimacy between the numbers 1 and 10. This first archetype is, therefore, very dormant whilst the tenth is an abundance of energy. Hard though it is to encounter something that has been latent for so long, we can at least say this area would produce a fear of being alone and yet with the possibility of a single moment of great destiny. Hence, the person who founds a religion or revolution has a destiny linked to the number 1.

The virtues of human awakening will connect to the qualities of Guru Naanak, which have already been discussed. There is a fear of humiliation or a destiny of humility.

2. There might be an interesting paradox here where the individual could feel a lot of fear of abandonment yet equally yearn for the freedom of the unknown. There is a fear of water or the anticipation of a drowning feeling should the destiny be met. Choosing your destiny would be expressed by an active negation of untruth and anyone influenced by this number would be wise to cast off things or people before being cast off by them.

Destiny is met by creating opportunities in order to attach to truth and justice. There is a need to be touched by grace, perhaps a need for a miracle and the greatest miracle could be to discover the beauty of saying no to all your doubts. You long for freedom, which is expressed in the freedom to yearn.

There is a fear of naivety or naivety through fear, a fear of attachment, attachment through fear, and a longing for the future as well as a loss of the future. You might also fear the loss in the future, which can turn into a loss of fear and fear the emptiness, fear not being needed or fear depression.

Guru Angad embodied the human awakening by becoming an extension of the founding principle where he stayed loyal to the origin and original essence but took the risk to extend himself into life.

3. The paradox of this mode of expression is found in the fear of both success and failure, which results in stagnation from where the law of fate takes over. Choosing to see the truth in life brings the realization that even in our worldly failures there lies a deeper success. By spontaneously acknowledging your role as an actor on the stage of the world you go beyond the identification of failure or success, recognizing these are merely parts of the drama.

Here there are related fears of competition, anger, unfairness, asserting the self, and of not being accepted. Your destiny is to help others by encouraging and inspiring a sense of quality. Choose to be seen and be seen to choose and though you may feel fear to be seen you show yourself through the fear. Visibility comes through the hands and their actions.

You have a fear of being judged though you judge through fear and maybe you are afraid to accept your self-worth or to accept that you deserve freedom. The wind of fear is like a wind that strips you of your worthiness and your self-value but all that can be stripped are the decorations and this leaves space for your true worth to be seen.

Positive action is perceived to be something to accomplish in the future and hope is always in the future rather than in the present.

Guru Amar Das overcame all his fears about what people thought of him, which brought his future destiny into the present, and from then on committed himself to serve those that had been outcast from society. The virtue of seeing all as equal is important to create opportunities for the human awakening.

4. The fear of giving and of receiving, the fear of the sensitivity of love and of the cold sensitivity of detached consciousness are the paradoxes of this fourth arena. If you chose to trust the "I don't know" rather than just doubt the "I know" state of consciousness, you would have a perpetual meeting of your destiny. Normally "I don't know" suggests a state of confusion and doubt. It could, however, be an expression of a deeper trust from where we feel stable enough to risk the truth that we really do not know.

There is a fear of choosing, of trusting and committing, but your destiny is to serve the truth and to speak for the beauty of the soul, though you doubt the future and your own awakening.

Guru Ram Das became the servant of his servants and in this way acted as a shock absorber for the wounds of the souls of his disciples. Instead of being afraid to receive he received their fears, digested them, and then eliminated them and so made it possible for many to face their own destiny of becoming truly human.

5. Aspects that contribute to the paradoxical threshold of this fifth archetype are the fear of existing and of sacrificing existence and a fear of communication and relationship along with a fear of no relationship. Choosing exactly the paradox instead of finding a resolution to it is the way to your destiny. The course of the teacher is to be yet not be, to relate yet not relate, and to not communicate yet communicate. The paradox is to face the world yet not face it.

You have a fear of balance and of imbalance but your destiny is to be the balance in the imbalance and the unstable in the stable. You are asked to be still whilst in motion and in motion whilst still, illustrating this destiny's great marriage between being and doing.

Victory is in the word, naked and raw but sensitive and firm, sharp yet graceful and clear and true. This is the word of the teacher.

Guru Arjun is known for bringing together the holy word of his predecessors and other contemporary saints of India. He produced one volume, known as the Adi Granth, and placed this scriptural text higher than his own to demonstrate the superiority of the word over the person. Indeed, it was for the integrity of the revealed word that he accepted to be tortured and ultimately sacrificed his life.

6. The experience here is of conflict when we state an opinion but there is also the fear of having no opinion on anything. This can lead to an endless dialogue, searching for the best opinion even if we fear having one so your destiny is to take a stand in life and live by it. The transformation of fear is when it becomes the wind that plays the instrument of the soul as it sings the songs of the battlefield of life. The destiny of 6 is to transform fear from a wind that stops you to one that propels and empowers you to live what you know you must. Fear of freedom can become freedom from fear so why turn away from the freedom of flight when you could take the flight of freedom?

You have a fear of responsibility of injustice and of speaking out for injustice and a fear of deviance and yet you fear conformity. There is fear of silence, of beauty, a fear of fear and of the future, the unknown, and of destiny itself. But you also sense the beauty of fear, the silence that is fear and the true silencing of fear, so you have the possible destiny to become completely fearless.

Singing and other forms of art do not exist solely for the entertainment of people but are also the mediums of warriors of justice. At times the sword in concrete or symbolic form seem to be the way of justice but a sword without a song and a song without a sword has little effect in bringing justice to the world.

Stillness and silence are the means to open up the opportunity of the number 6. The sword that strikes from the stillness and the song that is sung from the silence touch the stillness and silence in others. This requires that we stop all efforts to discover the quality of effortless effort and to free the divine impulse inside where we can be and do everything. Such freedom is only meaningful when others experience the same freedom.

The greatest song is a freedom song and it is a fighter's song. Liberty comes through the appropriate labor and that is a labor for the collective freedom rather than for the personal. This is not about taking responsibility for the freedom of others but about realizing the consciousness of community or the "we" inside and letting that awareness govern our actions.

Guru Har Gobind was the first Sikh Guru to wear the sword and to take a stand for the freedom of his community to practice their faith. Whilst in captivity he refused to be released from prison unless others were also freed.

7. The seventh destiny has to face the fear of not understanding, which is also felt in the fear of being wrong. However, sometimes there is also the fear of knowing and through that the fear of being right. Destiny comes from the understanding that it is born out of faith and when fulfilled it lifts all others above itself. So there comes a fear that the unknown is in control but which could then become an understanding that it is so and you accept to be crowned by the unknown rather than be ruled by your fears. The fear of not being understood may well hide a fear of actually being understood.

You may try to be in control of fear but all your efforts result in being controlled by that fear and this paralyzes your capacity for control. This is very like the fear of imprisonment, which is itself an imprisonment by your fears of your fears.

The fear of taking permission means you do not take permission to feel fear. The way to liberate the fear is not by asking why and looking for explanations, but rather to allow it and experience it. The question of permission also relates to permission to touch and to be touched.

Here there is also the fear of the past returning but you have a possible destiny that releases you from all conditions of the past. This fear of repetition can develop into a fear of forgiving and of being forgiven because if the whole thing is being repeated, then why not stay in the persecution of your fear? Why not stay in your fear of judgment (which is a persecution by your own fear of judgment)? It is as if rather than being found guilty by anyone else, you have decided upon your own guilt and punishment without giving yourself a fair hearing. In this same way you may not allow others a fair trial when, in fact, it is your destiny to show absolute mercy and kindness and to grant yourself permission to receive the same.

7 is a very visual number that presents the opportunity to see the beauty of life and to offer the world visions of beauty whether written, spoken, danced, or painted.

Guru Har Rai became known for his kindness and learnt to see an angel in every star and in every flower.

8. In this mode there is fear of death and the death of fear. The transformation of fear gives the opportunity to liberate the fear of others through letting fears die. There is also the fear of power and the power of fear as well as fearing the abuse of power. This could come from yourself or another and is best met by taking responsibility for your own relationship to power. You have a destiny to heal yourself and others through dying (not necessarily a physical death but by allowing the death process, out of which life is rediscovered).

There is a fear of authority and the authority of fear, which is your sensitivity to intuition. When you allow your intuition to be a real experience you realize its reality and, therefore, give it the authority it merits. Your fear of dreams and a dreamy fear mean your intuition works in a dreamy sort of way.

Power is money and money is power and so there can be a fear of money as well as opportunities for giving and receiving wealth. To be a healer is to be spiritually wealthy in the sense that your spiritual bank account overflows with prana or chi, which can wash away the diseases and sicknesses of others. Your destiny is related to the hands and it is here that you feel this power.

Guru Har Krishan is known for his death where he took on the sickness of many and healed a whole city by his own dying.

9. You probably like to demand to have your own way and go your own direction but also when you have all the freedom you do not know which direction to go. There is confusion between freedom of direction and freedom from direction. In the end you have to take responsibility for your direction.

A fear of completion mixed with a fear of never arriving at the end leaves you in an intense state of double frustration, yet your destiny is to complete. When you complete the little things in life your destiny takes one step closer to you. There is a fear of not being able to endure life's labors and yet you realize how you endure your fears.

There is the fear of mistakes or imperfection and a fear of imperfection offset by a fear of accepting the perfection of the imperfection. This must include the discovery of the perfection of fear. Then there is the fear of mystery and mystery of fear (its ambiguity and the ambiguous nature of your fear) and the fear of mastery and the mastery of fear. You also have a serene calmness wonderfully complemented by a fear of tyrannical impatience. With such a work before you how could you have any destiny other than to become a master? This, however, will not be achieved without devoted intention to breathe each breath one at a time.

You fear abstraction, which reveals that abstractions touch you for you are intuitively receptive to them. They are the essential but mysterious essences that form the basis for everything and are also the subtle qualities of life, which may scare you yet also inspire you. Your destiny offers an opportunity to give and receive the subtle touch that brings peace.

You may fear the experience of your own subtle nature that endures beyond death but this is indicative of the realization that such a quality exists. It is only a matter of when you will meet your destiny and become that which you most fear and yet that which you choose, and that is to arrive home and rest in perfect, enduring calm.

Guru Teg Bahadur realized this state of enduring calm that lay in his essence was the essence of all. From this most subtle yet solid base he was able to sacrifice his head for the freedom of all people to worship in their own way. He knew he was losing nothing because his basic nature could not be taken from him and nor can it be taken from anyone.

10. Here lies the fear of nothing and the fear of everything, the fear of the possibility of the impossible and the impossibility of the possible. There is the fear of starting from nothing and arriving at everything or starting with everything and arriving at nothing. You may have the fear of experience and the absence of experience or the fear of being overwhelmed and yet you sense there is no victory without being overwhelmed. You fear going all the way, going all the way through fear but great is the destiny of being beaten by the greatest.

There is fear of courage and the courage born of fear and the fear of listening and the importance of listening to your fear as your teacher. There can be fear to stand on the outside or a tendency to go there because of fear, but, in fact, you only stand on the outside of your fear as your fear sometimes stands outside of you. There must be a relationship between the outside and the edge of the circle for the number 10 to manifest.

Guru Gobind Singh lost all his four children, many of his disciples, and at one moment found himself utterly alone, yet he was able to listen to the will of God and establish a new beginning for the Sikh community. In order to do this he had to stand on the fine edge of the circle of his community so that he was totally part of that circle, which ran like a thread through the whole community. At the same time he had to stand on the outside, apart from the circle, to discover the opportunity for a new beginning on a different level and scale.

11. If the total year adds up to 11, then along with considering the issues of the second archetype, there will also be a fear of relationship with God and of the infinite longing which powers that relationship. However, your destiny is to be graced with such an opportunity so instead of being eaten by your fear, learn to eat your fear as fuel for an immovable faith.

Sri Guru Granth Sahib, the eleventh guru in the form of the word, mentions fear as the bellows, which stoke the fire of spiritual discipline. Furthermore, it invites us to realize that fear of the world is in proportion to the absence of fear and love of God. Loyalty to a great master transforms fear and loyalty to the greatest master transforms all fear into the master's touch of grace.

Chapter 20

The whole year
of birth: the fruit

The total date of birth is the realization of our wholeness; it is the fruit, the fruition, and the fulfillment. It corresponds with the element of ether.

Time

Total time is in each moment as in a hologram. It is undivided, unspecific, and includes all time both empty and full. It cannot be measured, going neither forwards nor backwards with no beginning and no end. At the same time it is time that does go forward and backwards, constantly beginning and ending. It is a circle of time; the time it takes to go and come full circle and the synthesis of the past, present, and future. The word "time" stands beyond time giving it an identity, a name, and it cannot be separated from the word, as when we say "no sooner said than done." The word "time" becomes a command and the word is a command to time, a command to time to empower the moment.

The fifth act of time is the moment of marriage, the coming together for communion. It is the moment that we learn the moral of the story. Learning is the integration of all the phases of time for the experience of a dynamic and contextual harmony. When we have learnt how to learn then our consciousness is present as an unchangeable influence in any and every situation.

Ether as path

The life PATH, shown by the total number of the date of birth, is an indication of the qualities and consciousness that we bring to every part of our life, both inwardly and outwardly. It is the natural outcome of learning our lessons in life and marks the way in which spiritual light is being transmitted to and from us. It is the sum total of our experience at any given moment. It is a light, which inevitably shines through the filters of our past and is regulated by how we allow it to shine through our fear or faith onto the future. It is the self-regulating expression of all that we live and the very principle of self-regulation. In its own way the path has no beginning or end, it is timeless time.

The path is always everywhere yet never somewhere and, in fact, the all-pervading yet imperceptible nature of its light is its strength. Our path is that which we hold as most important and what we make as the supreme God in our lives. It becomes the peak of the pyramid and our fulfillment. Like the ether element it is the quality that holds everything else in relationship, the bridge between the other four elements and the vibration, which moves all things and upon which all things move.

Threshold

The heavens also have their earth, water, fire, and air elements and it is in the ether that they meet. It is the dynamic of interaction and exchange. Therefore, it is the level of communication. It is sometimes considered the level of angels since they represent the messengers to or from heaven. It is at this level that consideration is given to the whole and to the integration of the other four aspects. The overall sense of harmony and the totality that is more than the sum of the various parts are what we listen out for on this level of the practice. The thresholds between different parts of the whole space, between people in the building, between the minds of the people and their bodies are examples of areas of communicative exchange and where the balances and imbalances are ultimately to be addressed.

The total number of your date of birth

The number of the fifth element is found by adding the day, month, and the full year together and reducing it to a digit of 11 or lower.

The date of birth 14. 1. 1957 adds up as:

$1 + 4 + 1 + 1 + 9 + 5 + 7 = 28 = 2 + 8 = 10$.

10 is the number of the path.

The descriptions below suggest the qualities that you can work with to integrate your identity. The totality is also the peak point of your pyramid of life and so has an effect on all the other aspects, which have been described in the previous four time cycles. It is the key number in relation to your partner but cannot be worked with consciously if the karmic patterns are dominating.

Please remember that this section, like the others, just gives some elementary examples and is not to be read as a limitation in your life. In the same way if you are exploring other people's date of birth, be wary of projecting these qualities onto them. Rather, just notice their date of birth and let each individual teach you their own unique expression.

Here then are the total numbers through which we find our radiance and the totality of our consciousness. Further understanding of these aspects will be found by reviewing the other four time cycles and imagining them to be more extreme and pervasive when expressed through the fifth element.

1. See 10 since the total number will never add up to 1.

2. Here there is innocence, longing, the need to relate to what is lasting, devotion, loyalty, and being a mirror to your partner. It is the mode to obey your inner voice and to learn to cry and regulate your tears. You may criticize tactfully and have the ability and courage to say no or to hear no. It is where you are not being heard or not hearing others and where you have the need for exchange with the other. Your speech might be like an on-going complaint but through this you experience yourself.

3. This third arena is where we find active body language, hope or hopelessness, a feeling of victimization by your partner or being

appropriately cared for, and also a need to learn to give care. It is where you like to change the shape of things like moving the furniture around, and the place of equality, quality, and wanting equality in relationship and giving it. You want your partner to be a fun-loving friend and to learn to laugh and express and regulate anger. There is the ability and courage to say and hear yes. You may speak to be seen or rescued and your words can become a static repetition or may be used to change the patterns. It is important to you how your partner looks because of how you think you will look with this partner at your side.

4. This is the expression of trust, doubt, indifference, indecision, being a workaholic, sensitivity, or numbness where you learn to express love and to open up and to uncover old wounds so that they may heal. Here the words touch you and you touch others with your words and there is the ability and courage to make decisions and to speak and hear the truth.

5. There is a lot of nervous energy with concerns for health. 5 is a synthesis and where you can be too much of a martyr for your partner. You may be unwilling to sacrifice anything and feel like marrying yourself. You enjoy cooking but it is hard to get started and you also have the ability and courage to change and to speak and your words are transforming. You find the floating center in the continuity of change.

6. You are romantic and expressive though often you speak to hear yourself. It is where you love beauty, art, and music but you feel fear and avoid conflict yet you are concerned about justice. You may try too hard to please others and keep inner pain a secret, fearing to speak but your fears need to be spoken. Secrets may slip out even if you try to keep them hidden but it is the area to learn to speak for truth and you have the ability and courage to speak from and listen to the silence.

7. Uplifting and protection belong to this seventh expression. It is where you make enemies and forgive them, where you speak to know or as if you know. You may have superior or inferior feelings toward your partner and you learn to speak with mercy though you

still speak what you see. You speak through the written word; you speak to control and are controlled by the word. There is the ability and courage to know and be known and to forgive.

8. Here you are concerned about cleanliness, purity, and wisdom. Your thoughts can be experiences and sometimes you may be too serious. Your words can heal, you are dreamy, and you have power and authority in your relationship with your partner. You need to learn compassion yet there may be purity and pure exchange with the other. You perceive the word as a river and you listen to the river. There is the ability and courage to die to the word, through the word, in the word, and as the word and to speak and hear the sound of death.

9. In this ninth expression resides endurance, mastery, subtlety, impatience, learning refinement, and integrity in your relationships. You speak to find a point of focus in order to complete. You can be abrupt and direct in your manner of speaking but will benefit from learning to be more refined and calm. Change is something you endure but it is to teach you that there an aspect of self that does endure through all changes so that you can find out what your permanent unchanging nature is. You are able to change direction and know that change is the essence of all things, while the essence never changes. There is the ability and courage to speak and hear the essence, which is there in the beginning, the middle, and the end. In relating to others you will sometimes feel that you lose the motivation and will to speak. Other times you will find yourself really insisting that you are heard and you will persist until you are.

10. This position indicates courage, intimacy, overwhelming, and learning to listen in relationship. You may be intense in communication or lack any and some may see you as a challenging presence with the courage to speak and hear all or nothing.

11. If undeveloped this aspect will be working with the qualities of the second expression, number 2, but otherwise you will learn to speak with a spiritual common sense. You may feel no need for a partner but have an intense relation with God in the mystical sense. You can be obsessive, possessive, and fanatical or have a spiritual balance and consistency.

Section three

Chapter 21

Achieving the balance: things to do and ways to think

This section gives constructive examples of things to do and ways to think which can help us to achieve the balance of a healthy 10-in-1 person. Remember that every problem has its numbers so numbers can also guide us in facing our problems.

In the rest of this section we will look at the connections between the pairs of numbers 1/9, 2/8, 3/7, 4/6, and 5/10. These relationships are five different versions of the totality. The lower numbers relate to the more personal and physical worlds, also known as the body-mind or body-consciousness, whilst the higher ones are linked to the universal and spiritual worlds, the spirit-mind or spirit-consciousness.

The pairing of the numbers and, therefore, of the Spiritual Bodies, suggests a short cut to complete the spiritual journey of self-knowledge. This is because whenever we work on one particular number we will automatically work with the other half of the pair. We may recall the equation $1 + 2 + 3 + 4 = 10$ and see in it the answer to all our quests; it is the quick route to self and God realization. The mantra EK ONG KAR SAT GURPRASAD is based on this equation. After the first four steps (described in Section One under the Mul Mantra) there is the possibility of going directly to the eleventh stage of grace.

Ways of working

A simple process to help identify things to do for each pair of numbers is to find systems that fit into the expression "as above, so below." This is to look at natural and physical expressions of the number 5. We can then read into them the five pairs of numbers.

Fortunately, we do not have to look far since most systems of ancient and esoteric healing were established on such a basis. For example, the oriental, eastern, and hermetic understanding of the body follows the insights of the four elements – earth, water, fire, and air, all connected by the fifth, ether. These elements were associated with four pairs of body organs – spleen and pancreas, kidneys and bladder, heart and small intestines, lungs and large intestines, and linked by the fifth pair, the liver and gall bladder. The anthroposophical teachings of Rudolph Steiner expanded the four humors of Greek medicine. Both Steiner and the theosophical teachings in general cast light on the four planes of being, mineral, plant, animal, and human, which find a more spirit-mind expression as physical, etheric, astral, and mental. It would appear that the teachers of some of these systems did not grasp the fifth dimension or perhaps, realizing its significance as a central point of transformation, decided it was best kept secret. Likewise, in the Orient, the earth element was given a more central place than either ether or wood. Again following the natural world, as has been mentioned before, we can also observe the five stages of a plant. Firstly there is the seed, secondly the shoot, third comes the branches, fourthly the flower, and then the fifth step, the fruit that contains the new seed.

Each of these different expressions of the five pairs of numbers tell us something more. As we go on exploring the world we find many mirrors to our own processes and clues to how we can help ourselves. We can then develop ways of working on our ten Spiritual Bodies that are natural and non-mysterious.

Natural magic

The inner inspiration to change our lives may come from direct or indirect meetings with great beings. It is when we are ready to hear the message in the stories of their lives or the words of their teachings that we manage to go beyond our rational thinking and move into a subtle and intuitive mode of being. The simplest yet often most challenging way to make this shift is through the magic of not-doing. Many of the great spirits that have walked this earth brought about meaningful change by living the four aspects or stages to the practice of not-doing. These are precise and mathematical conditions with which the true disciple is confronted. Each chapter in this section is written in the spirit of the natural magic of not-doing. As you read on you are invited to attune yourself to a different kind of listening.

The four magical practices are the journey to liberation. Going through the first three states we arrive at the fourth to open the consciousness and realize what is known as the tenth gate, the gate to liberation. Even the very word "liberty" is constructed from the same stages. LA BA RA suggests the laborious struggle of not-doing, the three stages of labor. These lead us to the moment when we really stop doing and say Thou. TA is the attitude of gratitude to Thou and realization that "Thy will be done."

The mathematics

Your life is built in a totally numerical and mathematical order starting from multiplying, through division, then addition, and onto subtraction and repetition until the absolute dissolution from extreme multiplication, unless, of course, you find the secret to reverse this process!

These four mathematical functions, which govern the entire universe, hold the clues to the four stages of natural magic. These are the four steps to becoming the possible human. Only upon fulfilling the destiny of the possible human can we reach the transcendent state of the divine communion.

From the start of our bodily existence as one cell we have the impulsive intention to multiply, which we do through a process of division. Following these first two stages we add layers of form that then must subsequently be subtracted to allow the expansion into a fully existing human being. What happens here on earth will be reflected in the heavens, as above, so below. Growing through these stages, the cosmic self comes to meet us through the same mathematical functions but in reverse. The next chapters are designed to guide you on the way to this divine meeting.

Chapter 22

1/9 – Soul and Subtle Body: one and many

The first magic is multiplication. It is especially the mathematical function of numbers 1 and 9, to multiply from one seed to many and to bring the diffused essence to concentrate in one seed (reverse multiply). Every species and idea wants to reproduce itself and survive and so it engages in the activity of multiplying. The way to know this magic is to consciously cease all activities that attempt personal multiplication as well as all activities that attempt to reverse multiplication. The natural situation will be the magic of coming to one-pointedness or coming into focus while the unreal naturally disperses. It is related to the force of gravity and anti-gravity. The soul gravitates down from its fragmented self and breaks through deceptive screens as it arrives more fully in the body. Nothing is multiplied and there is the magic of the world as it is, both in the concrete/material and the abstract.

In the struggle of this impulse to multiply we experience two corresponding dimensions of our individuality. On the one hand our identity is felt as the soul within the sphere of the body and on the other we can encounter ourselves as a greater sphere of existence with the body in the center. In contrast the number 9 gives us an experience of being outside of the body and dispersed into all the fragments of our outer existence, especially mentally. 1 is the individual seed, which does not know it exists until it opens up into creation and then it is no longer 1. 9 is the essence of the seed, which will endure through the many seeds that are created and, therefore, it is a collective sense of self, which is not individualized until it reaches the number 10.

Going back

Certain people either need or want to get back to the beginning and relive the very first moment, the birth of individuality. For some this can be healing whilst for others it may be a way of staying stuck. Certainly, it can help to go back and reclaim some of our fragmented essence that has been scattered amongst our historical dramas. We tend to attach ourselves to significant events of our past and in order to retrieve those fragments there are methods such as rebirthing, primal integration, and past life regression as well as meditations that help to neutralize the traumatic memories.

Imagine yourself as a newborn baby, an unfolding seed, a bundle of willful intent and bubbling with potential. You were born into a culture that could not accept the irrational and impulsive directives that rose up from some mysterious place within you. Have you noticed how babies are referred to as "it"? (Freud called our inner baby the Id.) You were a primal object that needed to be trained and manipulated into submission, often even humiliated. Repression, suppression, digression, diversion, castration, sublimation, and projection are some of the strategies learnt through the cultural ego, which is transmitted through the cultural acceptability that are the man-made rules born of the numbers 3 and 7.

It is this primal self that I believe Robert Bly, in his little book about the shadow, is referring to as man's "interior witch" or woman's "tyrant." He offers a helpful expression for the process of losing and regaining that part of self, which is associated with the first and last dimensions. He gives details of five stages, which correspond to the five pairs of numbers and the description that follows combines these two aspects.

The first stage is the event of casting out and exiling this inner being and hooking it onto another person, which in psychological terms is the act of projection. However, casting out can also be a casting into internal fantasy. The point is that you take parts of yourself and put them on hold, leaving them in different locations of space (which is your consciousness) and at different moments of time. You can think of it as driving stakes or pegs into the ground of your life history and there are many of them, all of which can subsequently be retrieved. The act of casting out or driving in is, however, preceded by attaching and tying a rope. This ensures the means to get back in touch with these parts of ourselves at a later date when we are ready. But be aware that some strings that are attached to you may not be your own and must be cast off rather than pulled in.

The second stage is when these pegs start to loosen up; Bly calls it "rattling." We try to make everything fixed and rigid but in the unstable journey through life we realize they are not; rather there is a "troublesome inconsistency." This is the problem stage when the tension of division and duality is experienced and felt as hunger, need, and desire.

In the third stage we seek solutions through the use of our "moral intelligence." We plan and scheme how to maintain the masks of our projections on others and get caught up in vicious circles that inevitably turn into habits. These drain all our energy even though we are unaware of the intense effort that goes into the upkeep of this projection machine. In the language of this stage and the games we play there will be a constant struggle to reshape, remodel, reinforce, and patch up not only the masks of others but also our own.

The fourth stage is the moment when we take the risk or when we feel there is no choice but to choose to give up the battle of sustaining our façade. At this moment, according to Bly, there is a "sensation of diminishment" when knowing is stripped away and we become aware of our pain. What holds us back from moving into this consciousness will depend on the extent of our enchantment with the third stage – the world where we are charmed through our fear of what friends will think when we drop the masks. But it is not until we take them off that we realize our greatest resources have been cast away on desert islands in other people's worlds. Only when we recognize from what we have separated are we in a position to choose retrieval.

This leads to the fifth stage, which is the state of retrieval itself. This stage is like a marriage, a reuniting of those exiled parts and a feeling of wholeness. Bly calls this whole process "eating the shadow" and says "we are in all five stages simultaneously" and that "it doesn't happen once but hundreds of times." This casting out is not only projected onto others but also into our own unconsciousness. It may show itself (in the rattling phrase) by our inconsistent behavior, addictions, in our dreams and fantasies, and in split personalities. The pegs are thrown in many directions and need to be reclaimed from all of them.

It is important to note that a tendency to pick up part of yourself and throw it somewhere is not necessarily a bad thing, nor is it likely to stop just because you begin the process of retrieval. It is worthwhile to practice throwing this hidden or buried part of yourself forward into the future and without a mask or projected image. This means bringing the first and fourth Spiritual Bodies together so that the soul and neutral consciousness are connected. Try relaxing your hold on projected futures, which are really just historical repetitions, and cast your hook into your unknown destiny, which is before you. The preparation for this casting happens in the short moment that you hold your breath in when you get a fright. Therefore, if you inhale consciously (briefly) and hold your points of contraction with awareness, then you can uproot your pegs from old places. You can modify their quality and place them into the next moments of your life instead of historical fantasies.

At times in your life, usually as a young child, and in moments where the survival of your integrity was at stake, you may have withdrawn or contracted from the world. Your feet may have been placed in a certain point in your consciousness and held there no matter what. This contraction is like a contract with yourself against a world that you perceived as unfriendly and you may go on to make a whole series of them thereafter. A useful outcome of any regressive work would be to identify some of your basic contracts and begin to renegotiate them.

Contracts are also contractions and some will manifest like stakes driven into the ground, creating various physical and mental points of tension. These will have some corresponding projections as discussed above and could be dealt with as I have suggested. However, it is important to recognize the value of some of these contractions for as they intensify they also transform. Some develop in response to what has been met and become seeds of a new approach to life. They may become great gifts or deeply rooted idiosyncrasies, expressions of your genius or madness. Under pressure others become diamonds, jewels, or crystals that hold great mysteries, where energy and information are stored and transformed. Realize that hidden in the muddy areas of your consciousness, which you work hard to ignore, there may be some rich jewels that could transform your survival level of existence into a thriving sense of being.

What is needling you? The Saboteur

Find your itch, your frustration, your restlessness, or irritation, which is also your madness, your craziness, or your insanity and then validate it. This is another way to retrieve the power you have tied up in contracts that may be buried deep within your unconsciousness and, therefore, ignored. They usually make themselves known through uncomfortable feelings and niggling itches that can surface on the physical, emotional, or mental levels. Sometimes the itch manifests from the outside, like when everything goes wrong the whole time and frustrates all your good efforts. This presentation gets called the Saboteur but it is your own life impulse that is prodding and poking you to communicate something about the direction you are or are not moving in.

Home and rehabilitation

There is only one thing wrong; we want to go home! The word "rehabilitate" means, amongst other things, to return home, to reconnect with your original habitat or to choose to reinhabit your own life again. It is when you do not daily choose to be at home that your existence is like an empty shell, sustaining itself merely by habit. This is related to the matter of the reference point. We rest in one point within ourselves, usually unconscious of what it is, but nonetheless it does become our home point and everything we do is anchored there. We return there again and again without realizing the dynamics that bring it about. This point is also the springboard for all our movements out into the physical, socio-emotional, and mental environment.

The process of retrieval serves to take us back through a series of secondary reference points until we realize that actually our difficulties arise because there is no substantial reference point. At this moment we might understand that the point in life is to become a point. It is to become single pointed, to focus ourselves so as to be one unit on the planet, to individualize and to give birth to the soul here on earth. The soul is normally only present as some vague misty feeling and it only becomes a solid incarnation as we learn to act on what life has to teach us.

Exercises

If you curl yourself up like a baby in the womb it will help you to be in tune with the seed quality of the soul. Practice withdrawing yourself deeper and deeper into the seed and then, still in the same position, notice the cocoon within which the seed is protected. This outer husk has the entire record of where you have been and where you are going. Rebirthing and meditations that take you back to the warmth and darkness of the womb will also help.

With your feet flat on the ground, sit in a squatting position and feel the relation to the base of your spine and feet. The feet are our connection to the earth so bathing and massaging them and walking barefoot on grass or earth will keep you grounded with a conscious sense of the soul, both personal and collective.

The numbers 1 and 9 are related to the vertical axis and so all kinds of exercises that work on the spine will have an influence on the will. When the will is weak we become spineless; flexibility and strength of the spine is flexibility and strength of the mind. Any movement that involves the spine must originate from the base otherwise there is a weak foundation. Yoga, Tai Chi, and systems such as the Alexander Technique are very useful in exercising this spinal awareness.

Qualities

Feet can be linked to the impulse to move (itchy feet) as well as to the quality of humility, seen in the act of touching or bathing the feet of a highly evolved being. Words of wisdom and revelation that pass through the threshold (5) from the spirit-mind are considered as the feet of God or the feet of the master. A back that will not bend will break so compromise and co-operation are everyday expressions of humility. However, there are times when we need the qualities of self-certainty and strength of determination. To use the power of will that springs from the body-mind, we must keep the spine straight as we engage in action. The spirit-mind, on the other hand, finds its strength in the concept of integrity. Through the ninth dimension we can be aware of the self that remains intact throughout all the changes of life and this certainty allows us to perform the most altruistic acts with complete peace and calmness.

The element earth

In the physical body the earth element is related to the spleen, pancreas, and stomach and keeping them in good health is important for the first and ninth dimensions. Sugar is one of the most damaging substances for these organs so the intake needs to be regulated. What you eat is what you are and it is in direct relation to the quality of the blood through which the soul courses through your body.

The earth is essentially a gift, as is the potential to be an individual soul. It is that part of us that we share unconsciously with all beings, which is in danger of being taken for granted and, therefore, treated with disrespect. The earth, however, needs to be cultivated wisely if it is to yield abundant fruit and new seeds. The first and ninth dimensions represent the beginning and end of our existence in the sense that prior to the seed there is no self and so there is no time or space. The seed is the beginning of time for us and our instinct for survival stems from the originating self. Self-survival as an individual body stems from the first dimension whereas self-survival as a species emanates from the ninth dimension in the spirit-mind, the Subtle Body.

It is worth meditating on the humble condition of the seed, which although helpless, contains within itself the potential of new life. When a plant dies its hopes are in its seeds. The seed guarantees the continuation of the essence of the plant yet that essence may remain locked up within the seed for an untold time before the conditions are right for its opening. This is another example in which the qualities of endurance and patience are related to the ninth dimension. It is also the durability of the husk of the seed that ensures the delicate essence is held intact.

Creatures of the first and ninth dimensions are animals that burrow into the earth and those, which are snakelike, especially worms. Rabbits also like to burrow in the earth and they are certainly famous for their multiplying capacity. Dragons that live in caves are symbolic of the ancient qualities of the number 9.

Healing and the mineral kingdom

Essential oils extract the mineral from the plant and are used in aromatherapy, which works with the sense of smell as well. There are also tissue salts, stones, and crystals. They can be used to balance and heal the effects of our karma but we must still fulfill our written destiny and purify our own crystal self. Crystals are a very pure form of the original self so they are a good medium for understanding the seed self of the spirit-mind. They contain the holographic record of events of all beings that have existed and the consequences that are yet to be fulfilled. They store karmic memories and reflect the state of the Akashic records, but take note, the Subtle Body, your number 9, is your real crystal self and it is that crystal that you need to work with.

Sounds

The seed self is silent and yet has an enormous amount of sound energy enclosed within it. The only sounds that can be made with the mouth closed are MM, NN, and NG. The chanting of OM or AUM should be understood as a withdrawal of the life force out of the seed and back into the void. Monks, Brahmins, and other male-dominated cultures that consider the feminine principle, as in Mother Earth, as nothing more than a temptation to evil or illusion, predominantly practice renunciation and retreat from the world. Perform this sound if you do not believe in the possibility of making life in the world divine, preferring instead to deny it and cutting off your relationship to Mother Earth and her natural forces. MAA or OMMA, however, open up that relationship and pave the way to pay respect to the divine qualities of the feminine energy. If you practice the contrast between AUM and ONG you will notice how AUM is a withdrawal or escape from the body-mind into the realms of the spirit-mind, whilst ONG moves in reverse, from the spirit-mind into the body-mind. We exist in a physical body and the sound of ONG is more integrated with the above and below and inner and outer realms; AUM is more of a separation of the polarities.

As I write these lines the word "enigma" keeps repeating in my mind – it sounds like an interesting combination of the seed sounds ONG and MA. Enigma means a riddle, a paradox, or something obscure. The riddles is "how does the seed, which evolved by a concentration of forces inwardly, suddenly turn inside out, back to front and sacrifice itself to become not one, but many seeds in the future?" This same enigma is found in the symbol of the oriental yin and yang polarities where the light suddenly becomes the dark and the feminine becomes the masculine. Hidden deep within one is the mystery of the other but for us it is all a paradox for the transformation is obscured from sight.

With the explosion of the seed and the expansion into the world of duality and then multiplicity, a number of different sounds can be detected. It should be noted that these sounds belong to the movement between the first and second dimensions as well as between the ninth and eighth and, therefore, not solely to the first and ninth. Many words that contain the letters B and L reside in the action of the seed self opening into the process of life and separation, which heralds the second and eighth dimensions.

With a *b*ang the *l*ife force explodes out of the seed and through the pains of *l*abor the *b*aby *b*ursts forth. The *l*ost and *l*onely seed awakens to its *l*onging to *l*ive and *l*ove, the *l*atent energy of the *l*ight of another being. Yet no sooner has this process begun than this longing becomes a lament, a song of languish and laceration, an expression of the desire to be whole again and the lunar longing for the light of the sun. With the use of certain words we can unlock the energy of the mineral forces and of our own longing for life.

Here are some magical expressions based around the principle of LA.

ULLAH, HALLELUYIA, LA IL IL LA LILA, LOVE, LIFE, LIVE

The contraction into unity is indicated in the following sacred sounds:

EK, AK, HAK, HUQ, HUQ UL HUU

Affirmations

Sometimes difficulties can be resolved by taking the right kind of action, but at other times it is necessary to clarify our understanding so that we have a more reasoned experience. For the soul it is necessary to understand the unity of the individual who exists within a finite body. However, for the Subtle Body it is important to meditate on the unity of the whole human race and ultimately of the entire cosmos.

Within the seed is the blueprint of perfection. So it is through the perfect self, which is the potential contained within the first and ninth dimensions, that we can get frustrated and angry when others do not meet our high standards of perfection. In these circumstances it is just as well to remember that everything, including ourselves, is in the process of growth. It may be very helpful to imagine our final goal but it can also be very restricting. The risk of affirming our mistakes as perfect can be very constructive for the frustrated state, which is created by the pressure of the Subtle Body and its perfectionizm. This is not a passive state for the effort that it takes to be frustrated can be freed up to discover that there is virtue in every vice and a jewel in every pool of mud.

Affirmations do not work just because someone wrote them in a book in a particular way. Of course, affirming our capacity to be calm, enduring, and peaceful will help the Subtle Body in some way but a practice of regular meditation will have much more effect in the long run. Learning to complete each task, whether big or small, before you move on to another is a very practical way of cultivating and affirming the ninth dimension and its qualities of endurance and calmness. You need patience to do one thing or to speak about one thing or to be entirely in one place at a time and to stay with it until you have achieved what was intended, but it is also the means to become patient. Skills are best developed in the same field of life where they are to be used and mastery comes only through the practice of unyielding steadfastness, which stays firm to the end.

If you want to master life take up one project, one idea, one sound, or one meditation. It does not matter which one you choose but hold firm until you penetrate into the essence of it. This essence will be the essence of everything by knowing the essence of it all. If you cannot go into the innermost being of one thing then the whole of life will remain a mystery to you. Another way to say this is to learn to see the principle behind every particular event and see the particular event within every general principle. This is the way to develop the state of Samadhi, perfect peace, which opens the door to the transcendent experience.

Finally the law of 10% and 90% must be taken into consideration. It is a law that says 10% is my will while 90% is Thy will. This 90% can be understood as the will of the collective consciousness or the will of the Divine. The personal point, however, is that individually our input is a mere 10%. This may not seem significant but it is actually essential. When we say "let me put in my ten penny bit" we are asking that our 10% might be accepted. The self-volunteering makes all the difference to the outcome of life. When we meet whatever comes our way with the inclusion of our little bit then it turns everything from fate to destiny. It is our 10% that brings things to their completion. Nothing can be complete until we stop holding back.

Chapter 23

2/8 – Negative Mind and Pranic Body: finite and infinite

The second magic is division. This mathematical function is expressed in the numbers 2 and 8, duality being the elementary division while the 8 speaks of the infinite extent of the division. To know this magic we need to reverse the divisions that we live in the ordinary world. This means we stop relating through difference; we stop splitting the world up into divided bits. Everything is one and has one taste. Nothing is there as "the other"; there is nothing with which to make a comparison and nothing to refer anything to. When there is no difference then there is no duality and we are bonded to infinity. Through this magic we cross the infinity of our separation; it is the magic of reuniting by stopping all division. The paradox of this magic is that we do this by the division of discernment, by the negative wisdom that says "I am not this, I am not that"; it is the know-how of the "no."

With the numbers 2 and 8 we have two complementary aspects of the experience of separation or division. The number 2 gives us the duality of being in a separate physical body and we seek unison with another physical body. Number 8 brings the experience of our separateness as a spirit and we seek to merge with another body of spirit-consciousness. Sometimes we call this spirit-body by the name of God but we often settle for a lesser entity.

Union between two beings requires dissolution of the individuality. We may seek this dissolution in thoughts of suicide (number 2), in daydreams (number 8), or through offering our undying loyalty to another. This death wish is the longing to belong. (In spiritual terms the death of the ego is the way to connect to the infinite. However, it is not uncommon for it just to mean a nervous breakdown, which is what can happen without appropriate spiritual guidance as well as discipline and practice.) Our physical individuality is made manifest when we are born as a finite being with a limited self of the body-consciousness. Yet with our first breath we experience the relationship to the infinite, the common link between every being that has ever and will ever breathe.

Healing, dreaming, and negation

There are spiritual healers who emphasize the love quality of the heart and those who speak more of the compassion of pure cleansing prana. It is the breath that acts as the channel for healing and when we become our breath there is no individual identity but a continuous flow between our finite vital body and the infinite life force. The more we become our breath the less we stand in the way of the flow of infinite compassion, which is not merely my love but the loving sadness of the universe for all its created creatures. In the highest level of healing work it is not appropriate to say "I am a channel." Only when I am not, then healing takes place; when I am not, then the universe is, God is, love is. This is the untwisting of the 8.

Most healing, however, does work with the channeling and dreaming, which are different expressions of engaging in the life process and its energy flow. In channeling you feel as if the energy is passing through you. Sometimes it is a relatively pure energy flow that has its own healing power and sometimes it is used as a medium for channeling information, which may be healing or manipulative. It is this information that becomes the content of dreams. Healing through channeling corresponds to the Pranic Body and requires that you put yourself in the dream state whilst simultaneously staying awake to the quality of the content as it comes through. For this question of quality you need to learn how to say "no" to the content but still allow the energy to move; it is a kind of filtering. Saying "no" is negative and negative is death.

Death is the clearing away of the superfluous, a cleansing, healing, and purifying execution.

Saying no

To say NO is to execute and to execute is to be executive.

- Practice saying NO in a way that respects yourself and others as well as inviting others to respect themselves and you.
- Practice saying NO to negate inappropriate methods, actions, and beliefs (your own and others) but not the essence of who we really are.
- Practice saying NO in a way that reveals integrity rather than hides it; this is called eliminate to illuminate.
- Practice saying NO to people's expectations of you but not in a way that prevents you from sharing.

Naivety is the absence of an educated negativity whereas wisdom is the presence of a pure but powerful and educated innocence (such is the language of the numbers 2 and 8). Wisdom is not like knowledge; it does not accumulate but empties and destroys the unreal. Being negative is not just about upsetting your friends or being inappropriately critical. Rather it can mean that you cease to co-operate with physical, emotional, or mental abuse whether it comes in the shape and content of religion, politics, cultural norms, or otherwise.

Life is an on-going detoxification process

Following on from the above, the work of learning to say "no" is really a way of engaging in a daily self-detoxification. "No" clears out and destroys. You may be worried about self-destruction but I would suggest that self-destruction is the internalization of other people's negation of yourself. To say "no" to others is to affirm yourself and, furthermore, it would be impossible to say it if there was not first of all a more basic and essential aspect of yourself lending its support. Therefore, saying "no" when it is not someone else's programed "no" is to maintain and strengthen your own integrity. It is a way to break the attachment of dependency. The know-how of the "no" is self-empowerment.

Needs

One danger in saying "no" is that you deny your own needs in order to become an austere spiritual practitioner. Death is only meaningful once you have lived, so be careful not to go for that naïve asceticism that denies water to the existing plant and never lets it come to the stages of flower and fruit. As long as you are an existing being there will be needs and instincts. The use of the negative is to have the power to say "no" to what you do not need whilst at the same time letting the vacuum in the negation draw to you, or draw you to, that which you do need. Even if you do not know what you need, you do know what you do not need. Therefore, you can always find a way forward by working from the negative principle.

Your body is a battery of energy that can be spent wisely or wasted. Wealth and vitality is often linked to the idea of a long life. Slowing down the breath, not having sex too often, regulating the tendency of the mind to burn up energy (through such things as angry thoughts), eating food which is not too heavy on the digestion, all contribute to economical living. As you may recognize from the earlier points a lot of this is about knowing when to say NO! The purpose, however, is not only the possibility of a long life but also the quality of life in the present.

Diet, exercise, sex, and breathing are all activities and needs that engage you in the process of life. Any avoidance or over-indulgence of these needs results in a depletion of the life force or accumulation of toxic and stagnant energy in some area of your life. In order to get these energies moving in a healthy manner you must attend to your body and its fluidity. The numbers 2 and 8 already tell us what is the healthy balance in our diet, exercise, breathing, and sexual activity. The material world is designed to satisfy 20% of our daily needs while the other 80% of our daily needs are spiritual and will only be fulfilled through spiritual methods.

I am quite deliberately not encouraging a path of complete non-attachment, which all too often becomes the denial of needs. It is important to come to terms with your instinct that expresses itself in various kinds of hungers and needs and to begin to realize the real nature of your needs. In particular, consider how an infinite need indicates a need for the infinite for such a need cannot be made to go away by pretending to be non-attached.

Qualities: write your own holy book

The second dimension of consciousness brings with it a childlike innocence and naivety. Within these qualities is the sadness of the soul's deep yearning and when we misunderstand that calling it can turn into depression. Yet there are also the excellent qualities of loyalty, unquestioning obedience, and discernment – the faculty of discriminating wisdom. These can be developed through a relationship with inspired writing. Such writings are like a stream of clear water running through the pool of subconsciousness, cleansing, purifying, healing, and making it possible to see our true nature reflected back. Learn to identify the purest reflections of yourself in the material you read and for each person this may be different. When you pick up a holy book, whether it is new or ancient, religious or mystical, a poem of a friend or an international bestseller, simply be sincere in your own intention and you will easily find the words that are meant for you. Going one step further record those words which you find to be a pure reflection of yourself and in this way you will start to compile your own sacred book. You may add special thoughts of your own or a comment you overheard in a conversation. The essential thing is to establish a clean and clear mirror to yourself and to look into it daily and you will find it naturally protects your innocence.

Controversial or blasphemous as it may sound I have found that putting together your own little sacred book is a profound way to meet and work with the longing that is inherent in sorrow. Buy yourself a notebook, preferably hard-backed, and try and keep it with you at all times along with a decent pen. This book will gradually become filled from a wide variety of sources. What you have to listen out for, in your conversation and in all your reading, are expressions that touch you deeply and which mirror the truest sense of who you are and what your life is about. As suggested above these expressions may be long or short; they may be found in ancient text, modern poetry, or even in a clip from the local newspaper. It may be something you hear yourself saying in the middle of a conversation or even in what your friend or enemy might say. Others do not need to realize the importance of these words for you; what matters is that you are able to recognize those phrases that really mirror you. It could be helpful to do a trial run by using a cheap notebook and then draw out the most special bits into your finer book. Now this process will already be of inestimable help in developing a discerning intellect about who you are and who you are not. This is because writing out your most important insights and discoveries is a way of distilling the essence out of your story and the world; a pure essence from which you can sip daily.

This brings you to the second phase of writing your sacred text, which is to read it. Here you are invited to notice the correspondence between the element of water and the emotions of sadness, sorrow, and depression as well as the material you have written in your sacred book. Water has some distinct properties that are relevant to the process being described. It reflects you, you can drink it, it is cleansing, you can dive into it, and finally you can float upon it. Let us take each of these properties in turn.

Reflection – every day you may look in the physical mirror but it is only to view your persona, the mask you hold up to look good for the world and at the same time to protect yourself from it. How shall you look in the mirror of your soul? When you record those words that have a feeling of depth and a ring of truth for you then you are finding one way to create such a mirror that gives an honest and clear reflection of yourself. Of course, it can be said that the whole world mirrors you in some way and that the world is the book to be read and this is the impersonal dimension. However, a private, specific, and personal level of self-reflection has its place for some people at some moments of their life.

Drinking – your daily thirst is not satisfied merely by drinking all the cups of tea that you could take in. Sometimes it is those words of wisdom that come from a pure state of consciousness that offer you a drink unlike any other. They pour easily into your ribcage like a mysterious fountain.

Cleansing – as water passes through you and flushes out the deposits (tears, sweat, and urine) you will find there are some thoughts that have the same fluid quality. As you soak them up and let them flood through you they slowly but steadily clear away the dust that gathers and sticks to you like iron filings to a magnet. Other thoughts are those specks of dust that gather into heavy burdens.

Diving in – not only can water pass through you but you can pass through water. The flow of water is like the flow of time, rivers of consciousness in an endless flow to the same ocean from whence it sprang. It is reasonable to be selective about the flow of consciousness that you dive into and in which you swim around. Wisdom works on the negative principle where it negates the unreal and fantastic, thereby discovering the real; this is also its cleansing property.

Floating – there may be times in life when you just need to be carried across for a while. The right words can do this.

Breathing – there are some interesting correspondences with the breath and the properties of water described above. The breath reflects your emotional state. Conscious breathing leads to more intake and movement of prana or chi, the vital energy available in the atmosphere, and this equates with drinking the breath and breathing the fluid of prana. Diving into the breath is to realize that we are always in a sea of energy, while finally floating is a matter of trust and allowing the breath to support you.

The Orient

Different religious and cultural communities tend to emphasize different pairs of numbers. The 2 and 8 are numbers that have been central too much in the oriental way of thinking. The association of the Tao with the element water, the study of the polarities of yin and yang, the eight trigrams of the I Ching, the eight spokes on the wheel of dharma in the Buddhist tradition, and the deep meditation on the great void are all powerful examples of this relation. Nirvana is the number 8 in its purest state. The Bodhisattva principle and practice of non-attachment serves to transform your personal suffering into an awareness of the suffering of others. This awareness further evolves into compassionate being. If you wish to deepen your philosophical understanding of the numbers 2 and 8 then I would suggest you read about Buddhism as it uses the negative principle and the not-self to considerable lengths.

Death

Death is the last problem that you have to deal with while you are still in some relationship with life. Yet death affords a solution to our problems. If you were to meet your death now then a certain freedom would be experienced. Death of dis-ease is healing, as the old patterns that trap us fall away and the energy that was absorbed in these patterns is set free.

You may have heard about people who have clinically died and come back to life and how everything is changed from that time on. There are also those who have been told that they have a terminal illness and only then do they really start to live. Well, why not imagine yourself to be in this kind of position and realize a new lease of life right now? Death meditation means making friends with death as a dynamic flow out of which life is rediscovered. It does not mean making the death instinct wrong but learning how to keep it in an intimate dance with the life instinct.

One way to meditate on the death process is to imagine the elements dissolving into each other starting from the earth element. As the earth dissolves into water the stability of the body breaks down and the life impulse disperses. The water then dissolves into fire and the fluids dry up. Next the fire dissolves into wind and the habits of existence can no longer sustain themselves; at this point the rhythm of breathing is difficult. The wind or air dissolves into the ethers and the last breath is exhaled. Finally, the consciousness has the opportunity to dissolve into "brilliant luminosity" and attain enlightenment. In most cases, however, the karmic identity has been gradually taking over from the biological dynamic and this will set you up for another incarnation.

Sometimes the description of death may be unclear because it mixes the descriptions of different cycles of exchange between the elements. For example it could go like this:

3 – The body goes cold as there is a loss of the fire element and perhaps a manifestation of anger as the third karmic identity tries

to resist. Or it may be that you have understood that this is the right moment to forgive and forget the past.

1 – Then comes the dispersion of the life impulse and a lack of capacity to concentrate with a degree of resistance expressed in an ineffective frustration; this stage may also be accompanied by sleep and calmness.

4 – Now there is a kind of awakening as you realize you really are dying and you do not know anything; this might be accompanied by panic or faith.

2 – After this the life force, known as prana or chi, leaves from every bodily exit and does not return.

5 – The threshold is crossed and there will either be a merging of consciousness into the totality or a karmic return.

Exercises

The organs related to numbers 2 and 8 are the bladder and kidneys so any exercises for these will be beneficial. Notice all the places where there might be a figure 8 in the flow of energy around the body like your hips and shoulders. Are there areas where you are too stiff or loose or not aware of? How might you change that? The 2 and 8 are the numbers of the left and right axis and, therefore, exercises and movements that connect the two sides of the body are useful, as well as various types of breathing which involve alternative nostrils, for example hip rotations. There is an energy flow around the hips that follows the pattern of the figure eight. It is the second dimension of body-consciousness that experiences and holds the frustrations of the life impulse, which moves from the base of the spine, and in our modern lifestyle we do not move this area enough. We sit around in offices, cars, trains, and at home and the energy that resides in this second dimension has to seek some way of resolution. The result is an over emphasis on sexual desire and instinct, sexual restlessness. The solution is not to deny sexual activity but to balance it with things that bring us into contact with nature (the second and eighth dimensions relate to the natural world of plants).

Certain forms of martial art exercises, which work on the thighs, hips, and lower stomach area, are designed to strengthen the chi or prana, the etheric energy of the second and eighth dimensions. Try sitting on an imaginary chair with your spine straight and your feet flat on the ground, about shoulder width apart, and do not hold your breath. Imagine your two legs as roots in the ground drawing up the moisture of the earth and transforming it into the life force.

Therapies and exercise systems, which work on the understanding of a vital energy that is constantly in process, all speak the language of the second documentary. Acupuncture, Shiatsu, Shen Tao, Jin Shin Do are examples that work on the energy flow through the meridians. There are an increasing number of classes available in exercise systems such as Tai Chi, Aikido, Che Kung, all of which stem from the Orient. From Asia come the systems of yoga, which also work on this energy flow, here under the name of prana and kundalini, moving through pathways called nadis. From the western therapies there are the systems of bioenergetics, which work on the vegetative aspect of the body and refer to the energy as orgone energy or just as energy. Whatever it is called and however you engage it, your health and well-being depends on the harmonious flow of this energy and by learning the exercises you are less dependent on a therapist to do it for you.

Breathing is the reflection of physical intercourse; in our breath we are continuously having intercourse with the universe. There are a wide variety of breathing patterns each having their own effect and the science of breath, also known as pranayama, can be learnt at yoga or meditation classes. Some conscious breathing practices work with the oxygen in the blood and the opening of the heart (see 4 and 6) while others work on the energetic or pranic quality in the vital fluids.

If you experience the number 8 in the sense of having high ideals and wonderful dreams but cannot ground them, then breathing out is important. On the inhale hear a sound like ssooo and as you exhale, hear one like HUNGGG, and use it to help you completely expel the breath. Try and do this breathing in and out of the nose for about three minutes. You may know of other sounds that have a special connection to the breath and you could use these instead. For example, inhale with the sound SAT and exhale with NAM.

When you need energy repeat the pattern of breathing in and

holding the breath for the count of one second and then let the breath go in a relaxed manner. This exercise, however, will bring a fair amount of tension into the body if you do not know how to relax. Throughout the day we tend to unconsciously hold the breath in and absorb a lot of tension, which our environment produces. Breathing in and holding the breath in is a way to integrate spirit-consciousness with body-consciousness (above and below). But the fact is the way we habitually hold our breath in tends to separate us from the body experience. It is as if to breathe out is to allow ourselves to fully experience the death which complements the life force. Our excessive attachment to life is actually killing us. Therefore, it is best to first learn to break this unconscious habit by focusing on letting go of the breath as freely as possible and ultimately to establish a breath pattern which is long, deep, continuous, and steadily flowing. It is a good idea to let yourself yawn more often and to daily practice letting the breath out with a sigh.

Breath exercises that involve holding the breath out are aimed at triggering a more subtle breath of the organic/plant nature, which is the second dimension of body consciousness. Whatever you do with the breath, remember at least that the rhythm is of the utmost importance. Whether we are engaged in a physical or mental/spiritual activity doing it in rhythm will be more energizing, whereas a lack of rhythm will be de-energizing. Breathing in rhythm is helpful because the rhythmic breath will gradually bring our body-consciousness and spirit-consciousness into rhythm and effective relationship. Furthermore, rhythm will help to bring about a balanced flow of the energy between the Negative Mind and the Pranic Body.

Breath meditation. Using the image of an egg timer, where there is a two-way movement through a small passage, imagine yourself with these two dimensions between your head and body or your two eyes or ears or nostrils. Then feel the exchange of two qualities as they pass through each other, synchronizing this with the flow of the inhale and the exhale. Now expand the sense of two dimensions to exist between yourself and the room you are in, another person, a group, the earth, or even the whole universe and feel how the consciousness flows out as the breath comes in and how the consciousness returns as the breath flows out.

A meditation with a special mudra for the 8 is to place the thumb tips on the tip of the ring fingers on the opposite hands and then to move and twist the hands to the maximum capacity, like a dance, without separating the thumbs and fingers.

More on water

The flow of waters from the body is the expression of cleansing and healing taking place. Through tears, sweat, and urination we put our past behind us and distil the essence of our history; we use the negative principle to eliminate the unnecessary accumulations of the luggage of life. The experience of time flow, the rivers of life, is related to the water element and the second and eighth dimensions. The breath also counts time. When the waters of the body and the breath is not in perpetual flow then the pool of consciousness start to stagnate; mud settles to the bottom, full of bubbles of air that frighten us when they come to the surface and pop! Little creatures (our thoughts) start to be born out of nowhere and having nowhere to go begin to multiply. Why the water element should be connected to the breath as well as the element of air can be easily explained. The air element is the breath of our future; it is the breath we have yet to take. But as we distil our experience into the future, or breathing the future into ourselves, we condense it, drawing out the lessons to be learnt from it and our exhale becomes moist. Thus the water element is the breathing out of the present, allowing it to become the past, part of our historical essence. In meditation it can be helpful to think of consciousness as an infinite ocean, which is both broad and deep without end.

Swapping places

There is another aspect of the hydraulics of life that it would be useful to understand. That is the law of supply and demand in relation to the principle that "nature abhors a vacuum." The application of this law is useful when it comes to making changes in your life. Think of a figure 8, and again the egg timer, and imagine that you want to change something in one of the circles. The result is a displacement of some kind into the other circle, but what we often forget is that this displacement will be reciprocated by a reverse displacement from the other circle to the one in which we have been operating. So for example, if you want to introduce some order into a part of your life that is chaotic you will be more effective if you also move some chaos into an area of your life that is too ordered. Another example is commitment. You can only manifest a new commitment if, at the same time, you release a commitment elsewhere in your behavior or thoughts.

Energy is not all there is

Water, prana, chi, life force, and other terms used in this section are all expressions of energy. Energy is not only a medium for communication but it is also a power in itself that most people desire more of. In itself it seems to be formless, like water, lending itself to any form. Yet beyond the fantasies projected by our ego-mind that we try to realize with whatever energy we can muster, there sleeps a primary intelligence that we are often reluctant to hear. If we could listen beyond the chaotic void that swirls beneath the surface of our man-made order we would hear an innate order. It is not an order that we like to listen to, however. To hear it would oblige us to obey it. Instead it seems that we prefer to manipulate the energy to nourish structures of secondary intelligence while anticipating the terrible possibility of being overwhelmed by the underlying magic that we cannot master. To fall into the shapeless energetic ocean is to risk drowning, and certainly this is the final end of the ego-mind anyway.

Energy problems

In general we can say that problems are problems of energy. Its properties have been compared to water. Flowing in spirals it can be directed, interrupted, slowed down, accelerated, or otherwise regulated. To make it move in an alternative direction than its inclination at any moment requires a special effort. Energy can also be stored but may also stagnate, dry up in certain areas, or flood. It can be flavored and colored with different qualities and in this way it may act as a carrier of more or less desirable ingredients.

In the diagnosis of a problem attention is given to the nature of flow between different areas or zones (rooms in a house or organs in a body) such as difficult, easy, fast, slow, narrow, wide, as well as the frequency of flow between each area. We may also be concerned, not only about the energy but also the things that might block, control, direct, hold, attract, or use up the energy.

Manifesting in the tension between polar opposites energy moves back and forth in an alternating rhythm of charge and discharge. The first polarities we meet in life are female (mother)/male (father), night/day, hunger/satisfaction, awake/asleep. Each is known only in relation to the other. In each of these polarities there is a different quality of energy; some other examples include hot or cold, still or moving, emptiness or fullness, and spiralling up or down.

Gathering profit and regulating the flow – you should give attention to the charge and discharge of energy and the possibilities of stagnation or loss. Your measure of health and wealth is not given by what sits in the bank but by how it flows through your lives. It is not what we store in the body, which generally becomes tension, but how we do so and how much we allow the energy to flow through our system. So pay attention to any tendency to build reservoirs, which then become stagnant, crystal deposits that can lead to arthritis. Try to move some of the unmoving energy. Then ask yourself how you are with debt. Do you pay your own debts or avoid responsibility? And do you know when a debt is fully paid? Do you think in terms of indebtedness? Be careful – there are some things that can never be repaid. No amount of trying to compensate for certain favors, or God-given gifts of life, could ever be enough; no compensation is adequate so let it go. Work instead on infinite pardon of your own and other's debts. Even if you are in debt, try assuming that you are in credit. Credit is an attitude – can you risk having such an attitude? What stops you? Ask a lot and offer a lot. Do not forget nor be afraid to speak what you want. Do not forget or be afraid to listen to what others want (or give them reason to be afraid to speak).

Healing and the plant kingdom

Plants are the second realm of the four planes of existence and as creatures we enjoy a special relation with them. The carbon dioxide that we breathe out is taken in by plants, which in turn breathe out the oxygen that we need to survive.

Food is medicine, especially the organic food we eat. Herbal remedies have a special value for healing energy problems. The second stage of the plant is the shoot or sprout, which holds the most water. Sprouted seeds and beans, all kinds of leafy vegetation, and seaweed are, therefore, the closest to the numbers 2 and 8 and probably offer a great healing to people who want to work on these aspects of themselves. Such foods are known to benefit the kidneys and bladder, which are governed by the water element. They are both the weak link and the power organs of the body and often the first to suffer from too much stress. For example, the fear related to the numbers 4 and 6 can lead to an excess of water flow, whilst impatience and other related problems of the 1 and 9 can result in an excess of water retention.

The quality of our organic life is enhanced by the presence of plants in or around the house and we can help to tune into the qualities of the numbers 2 and 8 by working in the garden and preparing raw food meals, especially salads. If you live in the city then think of the buildings and streets as trees and bushes or the hills and valleys of the land – a kind of concrete garden growing out of the earth level. The roads are like rivers. Ancient roads followed the pathways of the flow of energy in the earth and these lines of energy have been called ley lines.

Plants provide a natural form of ionization but can be usefully supplemented in the city with electric ionizers; chanting SUCH is the human being's own way of ionizing the atmosphere. Other water activities to keep in mind are swimming, hydrotherapy, flotarium, bathing daily, being near the river or sea, and drinking plenty of water.

As the second kingdom, the world of plants clearly illustrates the first level of separation. That is to say it is at the level of plant forces within us that the duality of sexual interaction and reproduction takes place. Hence there is an important relationship between the quality of food eaten and your sexual appetite and potency. Plants are more influenced by the seasons than any other plane of existence. This suggests that if our internal plant forces, our sexual instincts, were less influenced by the excess of psychological stimulation of the modern media and the like, then perhaps they would be expressed in a more rhythmic and balanced manner. Another point is that intense sexual desire can be transformed by going into nature and taking delight in the flow of life forces that abound there and by being attuned to the seasonal changes.

As has been suggested many of the oriental practices of traditional medicine work on the organic and etheric levels of our being. Kinesiology and all its various branches is a science of muscle testing and belongs mostly to the realms of numbers 3 and 7 but provides information about the state of the energy channels known as meridians. And then there is a breath therapy called Vivation, which is a recent addition to the modern world of therapies and highly recommended. It is a supervised way to complete the tendency to inhale and block in the face of difficult experiences.

Water-based animals are strongly associated with the numbers 2 and 8 and reptiles are of particular interest in the way they use their tongue to taste the air. Dolphins are excellent examples of compassion and masters of the breath and the only creature other than a human that can breathe consciously and voluntarily. They can choose to die by stopping their breath, something they often do when taken into captivity.

Sounds

I have mentioned that the sounds L and B are related to the move from the seed (1/9) to the shoot (2/8). I also gave some examples, mostly of the sound L. The duality of the organic realm and of life in general is commonly expressed through the sounds VI and BI. Think of words such as biological, bicycle, and binary. In ancient times ABA meant setting out, beginning a journey which later transformed to ava, via or the "way." Once you set out on a journey and you take your first step out of the door the distance between you and where you have come from is like a **v**ast chasm or **v**oid. To begin a journey is to step into a potential chaos and a**b**yss. "**B**ye **b**ye" expresses the sadness that is experienced as you step into the void and immediately long to return to unity. However, there is only one way to go and that is forward. To go forward with the intent to arrive back where you started is a difficult and paradoxical task that requires continuous attunement to the voice of yearning that lies deep within. Many **b**oundaries are crossed and **b**orders **b**roken through. Through **b**isection and **b**ifurcation the world of duality is the world of **b**ecoming.

To deal with the sadness of the negative aspects of consciousness it is important to recognize that we must go through it to get clear of it. The separation is a necessary stage on the route to flowering and becoming, not one, but many seeds and discovering the unity of these with the whole. Rather than suppress desire and have it surface in a distorted fashion, we might do better to acknowledge the true nature of our seemingly insatiable hunger. Our emptiness, which we experience through the second and eighth dimensions of consciousness, is truly a longing to link back to the universal source out of which we arose. Just as our infinite need is a need for the infinite. Our sadness is not just our sadness but the sadness of the universe, which is also suffering from the pain of duality. One drop, one taste, of a tear of sadness tastes the same as the ocean of universal sadness; it is of the same essence. Our tendency is to personalize it and interpret our individual loss as wrong, calling it things like depression. When we realize its true and universal nature then we realize that it is the condition of all separate sentient beings and this awakens our compassion. The yearning is not to be avoided but understood as the power of attraction, which will ultimately guide us on to a successful reunion.

There is a simple exercise, which can help you to get in touch with the deeper levels of this longing and to use it as a force that will propel you on. Close your mouth and breathe in and prepare yourself to say the word BANG or BABA. Before letting out the sound take about eight to eleven seconds to allow the throat to relax and open up and as you do this you should feel the cheeks expand, the great void making itself known. Feel the sadness of it and let out the word and be prepared for a surprise.

Rocking from side to side and rhythmically repeating the sound HNG, HNG, HNG as in HUNGER will also provide a means to give expression to your deepest need, which only the universe can fulfill.

During relaxed breathing learn to listen to the sound of your breath, sometimes hearing a particular mantra in time with your breath but at other times hear it rise and fall like the waves on the beach. This natural movement of the water is another reflection of the second and eighth dimensions of being.

Affirmations

There has been an over-emphasis on the concept of positivity in recent years and no fashionable or socially agreeable term has been coined for the healthy use of the necessary opposite principle of negativity. The importance of resolving this situation cannot be sufficiently stated. The attainment of women to their full power will not be possible until this is understood. Sexism in society will not be eradicated by masculine-style demands for equality or by women taking on the ways of men or their activities. This does not mean that women should not be more active in the world or in politics or whatever. What I am saying is that women's involvement in what has until recently been a male-dominated society will not bring about the real changes that are needed. Rather the real impact will come about when women learn to use their negative power to say "no." A woman's real power lies in her privilege to withdraw consent from the male. This does not just mean on the sexual level but in all aspects of life. If a woman withholds her co-operation in the man's game then he will change to win her. A woman who knows how and when to say NO and be heard has the world at her hands and feet.

It is true to say that everything we negate must sooner or later be acknowledged as a part of the whole and so a part of us. Remember that the practice of saying NO is to be directed, not at objects or people so much as the thought forms or energies that they might call into being. It is also true, however, that while we are still in a body, which is distinctly separate from other bodies, we are identified as much by what we are not as by what we are. If we do not take a conscious part in this process then other people will decide for us what we are not. To try to be whole and beyond duality is a noble project but only attainable when we fully enter into the experience and learning that the condition of duality brings with it. It is a question of not trying to be an adult before you have been a child or not trying to be a master without first of all being a student.

The Buddhist practice of non-attachment is an application of the negative principle in a very pure form. It is designed to get you in touch with the infinite energy of the great void and to cross the gates of death. The practice of negation is very useful in meditation, sleep, or death itself, when images come before you that wish to draw your attention away from the pure essence of reality, the still sea of consciousness from which all things arise and return. It is not to deny that these things exist but to realize that all these images are just temporary. They are not illusions but they are not permanent or lasting and this gives their reality only a relative value. To negate wisely is to be able to free yourself from attachments to things, which are just passing and not of the pure nature of your timeless and infinite essence.

Death can only occur as an event in time and to things that occupy a limited space. The use of death as a meditation is very powerful and the Zen question might be phrased "what is the form of time?" or "how fast does time move?" Resistance to the falling away of aspects of the self, which are not of a timeless form, merely establishes further suffering. If on our last breath we try to hold on then we create a mandala of the self, which will be carried over into the next life. Immortality of the self can be achieved by such attachment and recycling of the self through endless lifetimes. Be sure, however, that the suffering of separation is an inherent part of this experience. Dying to the past and dying to the future is real dying. Such a death embraced with every breath brings you into the eternal here and now. Death is mastered by being here and now as if you have been living forever and will live forever by living fully.

Chapter 24

3/7 – Positive Mind and Aura: action and belief

The third magic is addition. The numbers 3 and 7 govern this mathematical function; 3 adds the three-dimensional world of space and form while the 7 adds the seven colors that make it possible for the forms to be visible. Generally we live in a world where everything is complicated by the eyes through which we perceive. We always add something more – a little story, a lie, an explanation, justification, exaggerations, fantasies, inventions, judgments, or reasons. In other words we add more to the world than it actually is. The magic of addition is known when we can see what is and add merely the smile. This requires that we stop all the other forms of adding and in this way return again to the world as it is and then to see the one light shining through all. It is related to the magnetic field, the Aura, and the mind with its projections. All this becomes transparent in the third magic. By undoing all the temporary additions we realize the nature of the divine addition just as the creative myth describes how God on the seventh day added the first judgment – that all was well. When we come to this realization we are ready to make the final judgment, which is an agreement with the first one; that all is well.

The numbers 3 and 7 correspond to the fire element. Money, like water, can be destroyed by fire, but it can also destroy fire. There is a lot of fire in our lives so the alchemic mysteries included the contemplation on how to bring about a marriage of fire and water. Certainly anger, judgment, and resentment, as well as revenge, are fires that burn up our vitality and leave us depleted without any profit for our investment. Pleasures can be another kind of fire that burn up our vital supply, especially the pleasure of the proud ego when it seeks praise and status.

There is a use of the positive or affirmative consciousness, which unlike affirming praise or blame, can bring about a mystical meeting with water. This meeting permits us to go through the ring of fire and beyond it. It is to let all the fires reduce everything to ashes and then let the ashes be moistened by the waters of compassion and in the clay that results you can refashion your life. This is an activity of consciousness that does have radical implications for the practical life – including that you stop worrying about many things. This works because in the process of burning all is reduced to the same ground, the same common substance. From that basis the positive realization comes that all is equal and that "more" or "less" are temporary beliefs, which, having become transparent, no longer act as the guiding principles of your life.

Numbers 3 and 7 are the positive dimensions of consciousness and experienced through dynamic enjoyment of the physical body as the karmic car and the confidence to take your own counsel. Through the positive experience of the body we enjoy being physically active, inhabiting the body, and valuing experiences that stimulate the bodily sensations. In the ego-mind we enjoy creating a positive self-image, an identity that creates its own philosophy of life and indulges in the pleasures of different realities known as fantasy.

The adventures of the body lead us to live dangerously on the physical planes whilst in the ego-mind we like to live dangerously on the planes of intellect. Playgrounds, fairgrounds, adventure parks, and sports are examples of environments that stimulate our three-dimensional existence, whereas drugs, movies, and scientific speculation are among the things that stimulate the mind. The activities are all space fillers, each with their own consequences. There are other space fillers, which can have less detrimental results and can even produce pleasant effects along with healthy side effects. That is what this whole book is about, giving some clues to ways of living and understanding that will shape our lives towards our greatest destiny.

The rational consciousness

The numbers 3 and 7 are busy wanting to understand and to be understood. Always seeking a sense of proportion and perspective their oft-repeated question is "why?" Everything is to be explained and can only be done in relative relationship to everything else. The questioning consciousness is most at home in the numbers 3 and 7 but this can be a state of kidnap unless it goes beyond the limits of "why? – because." In trying to piece together the jigsaw puzzle of your life there will be many complex combinations of questions and times when you ask one thing but mean another. It is useful to realize the mental activities you engage in as you try to sort out and simplify the crossed wires that you might get into when you build question upon question, for you are in danger of becoming trapped in vicious circles. You may use questions to defend your structure and build layer upon layer or you may use them to challenge someone else's structure. Questions can also be tools to destructure and restructure the shape of your belief system and personal life philosophy. One way or another you use questions to give some kind of order and apparent understanding in your life.

Your life drama

The language of 3 and 7 is very much like a drama script that we act out after having first written and read the text. Role playing, acting out as well as watching or reading archetypal expressions of different characters, helps us to formulate and retell our own drama in a way that redefines its meaning. A drama can either imprison you into the limitations set upon each role or it can help to make these roles more transparent. Only in the transparency of the roles you play can it become possible to introduce changes.

Image

Drawing, painting, and getting a sense of color in your life brings your attention to space and your place within it. When you are able to see your place in space you can then work on clearing out old images that may not function very well anymore. It is a practice of revisualizing and learning to use vision as an affirmative restructuring. There are plenty of books and tapes around addressing this approach to changing the way you see your life and consequently how we behave in the world. There are books on affirmations and technique after technique on how to be more positive and change your belief structure. However, your image of change that these books may have introduced is not your own but a borrowed one and this limits the effect. Furthermore, image or belief is only a vehicle to get around in or a coat to protect you from the weather; it is not you. How you drive the car or wear the coat can make a lot of difference, as can the direction in which you travel. The image is not you and though you may create your own reality, you cannot create reality through the image. You may, however, be able to be real in the process.

Realizing a vision

Realizing a vision is a creative journey, which progresses through the bodies (and numbers) in a particular route. This route is 3/7 – 1/9 – 4/6 – 2/8 – 5/10 (or fire, earth, air, water, and ether). Starting with 3/7, there is the inner vision (7), which will be somewhat idealistic and gets projected into the Aura and there will be what you are prepared to accept in practical reality (3). The fire of vision acts as the catalyst for action and the Positive Mind gives hope and encouragement. This is followed by the stage of 1/9, which challenges you in regard to intention, personal and impersonal, and requires that you make contact with the resources available. Your personal resource is your own soul (1), while the impersonal resource is the collective soul, related to the Subtle Body (9). Without this connection there will be confusion between the structure of the vision and the objective it is intended to serve. It is the loss of contact with soulful intention that leads to dogmatic idealism where you worship the vehicle and forget the destination.

After this stage you are invited to be clear about your priorities, make a commitment, and take responsibility for the consequences.

This requires the qualities of the Neutral Mind and the Arcline and it includes the attitude of service and prayer as well as the consciousness to be met by grace. This stage will also confront you with your fears – when you feel that nothing is happening ask yourself what is stopping you and this will show you your insecurities. To follow on from this you can ask yourself what you need to commit and invest yourself fully. Your response to this question of needs will move you on to the next stage of 2/8, which will include the consideration of *how* to proceed. This step adds the process of longing (2) and energizing (8). It is a time of not doing but allowing the vision to be purified and empowered. Sometimes this means completely losing the vision in order for it to gain a deeper quality. The whole process is brought to fruition through the numbers 5/10 where either it is fully realized or nothing is realized (10) but whatever way there is a lesson learnt and integrated (5).

(Note: This is just a rough summary, which can be expanded on considerably by reflecting on the qualities of the different numbers and bodies as described throughout the whole of this book.)

Psychic cafés

The third and seventh Bodies and all that goes with them become heavy if you cannot accept a transparency about your games. This also means to be able to laugh at yourself. Each quality of your consciousness that you find yourself in (each affirmation, its image, and the state it produces) is just a psychic café that you have breezed into. Changing the shape of your worldview permits you to pick up the vibe and perhaps develop a certain skill while you are there or maybe just to check out what the world is like in this space. It is a chance to try out a different act, though strategically each act is really just a variation of the same theme. You explore the tourist outlook to the world and enjoy being an astral traveler, which does not in most cases involve leaving the body, lying in bed, and shooting off to the stars.

Many people use up most of their seemingly busy days checking out different psychic, astral, or mental places and spaces. The language in each space may change a bit as you try on the variety of costumes. Even the qualities associated with the other Spiritual

Bodies are played with through the dramatizing nature of the third and seventh Bodies. Some examples are as follows. In the fear café you can build up your courage a little. The hopeless café is where you test out the world to see if it can still give you a little encouragement. In the depression café you might be testing to see if the world will feel sorry for you, compensate you, or help you boost a false sense of value. Think about the many cafés you have passed through and continue to do so – like the apologetic café, the victim café, the rescuing café, the why me café or the café of searching for the answer.

The impersonal dimension includes the possibility that you may become a customer in a café for others. Whole hosts of entities may come and play out their scenes within your consciousness (usually in the inner mental realm of unconsciousness). This psychic intrusion may be a kind of possession facilitated by drug use or other kinds of trauma. On the other hand it may well be some great godlike archetype playing out its ancient myth. Sometimes, however, it is just people that you meet in the day and let into your mind without the capacity to put them out again, though people who can have this effect on you are usually themselves mediating some kind of demigod. Think about whose story you want to be in and whom you want in your story.

Exercises

The associated organs are the heart and small intestines so exercises for these are recommended. The healthiest and most natural expression of the 3 and 7 is laughing. Through the number 3 we have a strong sense of fairness and unfairness. This very easily leads us to be quick in passing judgment, both on ourselves and on others. Judgment without action, however, is slander. When we can laugh at the situation we open up the potential to lift others and ourselves out of the oppressive environment, breaking the victim habit. Laughing is also the best way to free ourselves from the past; 7 is that aspect of consciousness that tends to accumulate the past and wants to take revenge for unresolved issues.

Whether we are blaming others or ourselves it is of no advantage to continue with resentments. Laugh and create a situation where you are free to live more fully in the present. If you take action about the things that stimulate your caring qualities in the present environment, it will ensure that your caring does not become locked into passive aggression and subsequent feelings of helplessness and impotence.

Writing is a good exercise for the number 7, which has a tendency to record everything. It will be easier for your consciousness if you record things in a notebook rather than try to keep it all in your brain. The externalization process can help to put things in a different perspective.

Practice exercises that work on the belly and make you aware of the power point out of which the laughing energy is generated. Leg lifting, rolling on your stomach, pumping the navel point in and out, breathing out as you pull the navel in and relaxing the navel to let the breath come in by itself are all exercises to help you with this. Also try lying on the back and then push the navel point into the air as you breathe in and as you relax down, breathe out. Practice the reverse of that; lying on the back, raise the head and legs ten centimeters off the floor and breathe long and deep.

For the Aura practice exercises, which use the outstretched arm, swing the arms left and right and backwards and forwards and swing them whilst walking. Bend your body, exhaling as you bend down with the arms going down to the floor and stretch up and back with the arms over your head as you inhale. Clasp your hands in front of the body, stretch out the arms, and inhale while you raise them above the head and exhale while you lower the arms down, level with the navel point. If laughing is not easy and there is deep anger, then punching an invisible beanbag with alternative fists will help; powerfully exhale out of the nose each time you punch forward.

Sight is the sense related to the third and seventh dimensions and so eye exercises are beneficial. The deeper advantage of the exercises, however, is not so much to stimulate these dimensions, but rather to regulate a tendency to indulge in semi-conscious fantasy; in other words to use sight in a disciplined way. The eyes will be stilled and thereby bring about an awakening of the fourth and sixth Bodies, which are related to the sense of touch and intuition and awakened when we are in the dark. The importance of this process for spiritual development cannot be underestimated. I have, therefore, included eye exercises also in the section on the fourth and sixth dimensions.

Qualities

The very term "quality" belongs to the numbers 3 and 7. It is through these that we judge the quality of our experiences, our environments, and our relationships, along with our own and others' personalities. When we encounter or personally experience inequalities in life then the 3 and 7 are called into play, usually in defense. From the 3 comes the caring quality and the enthusiasm to give encouragement to those on the suffering end of oppression. When supportive action cannot be exercised then the feeling of victimization takes hold.

From the 7 our attention is focused on those who are seen to be the causes of the suffering of others. We learn to recognize their suffering and to be merciful and forgiving. We also learn to see and know the law of karma. It is the law that states "as you sow, so shall you reap." We can, therefore, relax in the confidence that it is in the nature of the universe to resolve all imbalances. Furthermore, we may even be able to understand that those who are suffering today might well have been the ones who were causing suffering yesterday. Such reversals may take place within one lifetime or over a succession of incarnations. Through the number 7 we can grasp conceptually, though not experientially, the idea of going through repeated cycles of lives and deaths. The experience is more fully grasped in the movement between the eighth and ninth dimensions.

Bringing hope and understanding into the lives of other people rather than looking for it from others is an important transformation for the Positive Mind. Bring quality into life and inspire those who feel hopeless to have a sense of self-esteem and to recognize their self-worth. Learn how to treat the precious jewel of the physical body with more respect by supporting others. Through the seventh dimension discover how to become free of guilt and shame and sin. Do not wait for God to forgive you – forgive yourself and forgive others. God is the image and structure of our total condition and just as we are said to be modeled on God's self-image so we make many gods according to our own images. By elevating myself to be equal with all others, I elevate the whole because I am a participant. By forgiving all others I forgive myself because I am all. Forgive and you will be forgiven, understand and you will be understood, care and you will be cared for, be hopeful and there will be hope, support and you will be supported, be strong and there will be strength. These statements illustrate the nature of the fire element, which is the element of the numbers 3 and 7.

Fire element

Thinking of the fire element and the language of the third and seventh Bodies you might realize that qualities such as judgment, anger, humor, and forgiveness are all expressions to be found here. Fire as anger is very controlling; as forgiveness it is thought to be freeing but forgiveness can also be a form of control. The most effective forgiveness is the one in which you release the initial judgment that something or someone was wrong. You are only likely to do this when you no longer believe that you need the control mechanisms that you have set up. I am not going to try and convince you that now is the moment, even though it could be. Fire, whether it is active as anger or warmth and caring, is a display of your current beliefs and image about yourself and the world. Humor also releases heat and may be expressed in the form of slanderous humor that brings an angry and defensive reaction, or as light-heartedness that can melt down people's resistance to human contact.

Fire may be stored up as in judgments about the past that you do not wish to release until revenge has been taken. Another way you might store the past is in souvenirs, which you believe hold a good image of yourself. The rules that govern the way you do this are learnt and internalized when you are quite young and you learn some of these well enough to become your own policeman. In other words you end up with both the good and the bad within you, forever arguing about why you should or should not do any particular thing. It can help to arrange a friendly meeting between the different parties to this struggle, which may be the child and parent, the rebel and the politician, the judge and the victim, or the rescuer and the rescued. The point is to reconcile with your enemy and realize that in struggling with you, they have served to make you stronger – they may turn out to be your best friend. The enemy may take other shapes such as the government, a drug, your past, or whatever. In educational terms this meeting means bringing the playground culture to the classroom and the classroom culture into the playground.

Fire is the catalyst to action; it is the motivating power, which makes the fulfillment of any plan possible. A burning flame represents the continuation of life, the undying spark, the will to go on, the hope for the future. Our own hope kindles this flame and keeps it burning. When our flame goes out, we go out. This is not to be taken as a good or bad thing but simply a statement of the dynamics of existence. Fire can also get out of control and fail to see that it is burning up the air of other people's freedom. So long as there is fire there is a chain of cause and effect. Fire is the medium through which karma is processed and the heat of the moment is a challenge to really be ourselves and acknowledge our motivations, their causes, and consequences.

Anger is generally considered to be an undesirable state. However, we must recognize that its source is also the flame, which motivates us to do something positive about what caused the anger, what fanned the fire. To deny, suppress, or otherwise dampen the flame is to limit our power to create change. There are, of course, moments in life when it is not for us to be the creators of change but to acknowledge the true creator and absolute doer. In these moments, however, the fire still does not necessarily go out but instead becomes a comforting glow of warmth around which others may safely take shelter. Fire may be smouldering embers, hardly visible, or a raging furnace that can be seen for miles and is too hot to approach. Unless the fire is dying out then sooner or later and one way or another the fire will display itself to the public view. When our fire is not a source of warmth for others and is not dying out, then it will inevitably become the catalyst for social conflict.

When the fire is too hot it can be cooled by breathing in through the mouth and breathing out through the nose. For the inhale the mouth should be pushed forward and rounded as if you were trying to whistle, only you will be inhaling in this position instead of exhaling. To enhance the cooling effect you can link your thought processes to the water sounds such as breathing in with the sound soo and breathing out with the sound HUNG (see above sections on the second and eighth dimensions). If you feel that you need more fire then see the section below on sounds and the exercises described above for the navel energy.

The kingdom of animals

Animals are the third plane of existence. Uprooted from the earth they enjoy the illusion of freedom. As an enchanting and strategic intelligence this finds expression in competitive activities. The predominantly masculine activity of sport is a human expression of our animal nature. Fight or flight is the natural animal instinct corresponding to the third dimension. We humans, with our reflective capacities, complicate this instinct with such things as anger, guilt, and revenge.

Animals are great sources of warmth and in many cultures people still sleep near animals or above their shelters in order to benefit from their body heat. It is not only bodily warmth that we gain from animals though. The presence of animals in our life asks us to find our sense of caring and mercy. The fact that people can so easily kill and eat animals in such excess and without any sensitivity to the creatures suffering indicates a distinct lack of compassion. This is not necessarily to advocate vegetarianism but just to point out the nature of our relationship to animals in general. There are people, rare though they may be, who can take an animal's life with the utmost compassion. Such an act leads to a very great karmic development for the spark of consciousness of that specific creature. The karma of the human race is very tied up with our relationship to animals. The animal liberation movements are trying in their own way to awaken us to our right relation to animals and a time may come when no animal will be afraid of human beings and no human being will be afraid of animals. At present, however, our relationship with the animals of this earth is perpetuating our fears, inhibiting our collective destiny, and creating the seeds of further karma.

The symbolic use of animals in the spiritual practices of certain cultures offers an inspiring alternative to the mainstream western attitude toward most creatures, Native Americans being a very good example. Systems that work with animal symbolizm such as the zodiac circles, both western and Chinese, are also stimulating to the energies of the third and seventh dimensions of consciousness.

Healing

Naturally being with and relating to animals in a reasonable manner is very therapeutic for the Positive Mind and Aura. Any healing practice that works on the Aura will have a direct influence on the Positive Mind. Radionics, for example, works on the electromagnetic field. Color therapy influences all the dimensions but does so through the numbers 3 and 7, and the Aura can be strengthened by wearing clothes of the same color at any one time. The above-mentioned therapies work on principles of frequency, vibration, and resonance as does geometry and the use of geometric forms and diagrams. All these have a significant effect on the electromagnetic qualities of the 7, providing some kind of cleansing and strengthening of the Aura. Aura massage is also a practice that can be done with the hands.

The numbers 3 and 7 are additionally the realms through which we experience the diversity of visual stimulus, our sight. It is interesting to note that our ancestors seem to have perceived three primary colors and that the development of our visual ability did not rise steadily from three to four, then five, and so on. Rather it took a leap to the seven colors of the rainbow. Medical, religious, and spiritual practices that are based on the models of trinities and septeneries clearly rotate around an axis of 3/7. Meditations, which use visualizations or special focus on objects or images, help to bring the wandering mind back to its home. The seven chakras or energy centers of the human being are the ones that are visually accessible, so working with the visual qualities of these seven chakras will prove worthwhile.

Dream work and astral traveling also belong to the same realms. If you recall, the 3 and 7 are related to the laws of cause and effect (karma) so dreams and astral travels, which are not very different from each other, provide ways to gain insight into the underlying karmic causes for our present and even future experiences. It must be pointed out, however, that much of our so-called seeing into the future is just a reading of the past coupled with a creative ability to construct the most likely outcome, given the historical details. A fortune-teller is one who sees into your seventh dimension and if this is clear from complications from the past then it will be difficult for them to see anything. Instead, what is experienced of the future is a sensation, which then requires a picture for the ordinary ego state to understand.

Furthermore, when we have astral experiences, which are in fact visions, and assume them to be totally new, we are forgetting that we will interpret the future with the visual data from the past, from our library of historical images stored in the seventh and third dimensions. Remember, even animals dream and travel in the astral worlds, the worlds of visual experience. It is a rare, difficult, and extremely evolved state to move into the future without the familiarity of the past and to see the reality before us, unconditioned by historical patterns. Our present vision is largely influenced by past experience of patterns as well as denials of all that could have been seen; that is to say negations of parts of reality. This is a necessary process involving the use of the energy of the 2 and 8 for the establishment and maintenance of our positive personal identity. Our future vision is also inhibited by unexplainable fears of encountering the unknown as it really might be. Such fears, therefore, also prevent us from encountering the truth as it actually is.

Note: Past life therapy used wisely can heal the trauma dramas stored in the Aura very effectively but not before healing the present life and awakening the soul from its paralysis.

Sounds

If you can roll around on the floor and laugh from your belly then go right ahead; you clearly do not have a lack of energy in the positive aspects of consciousness. If you laugh a lot and it is not from your navel then the laughing is a cover-up for a lack of self-confidence. To learn to laugh just take a relaxed breath in and start repeating the sound HAR HAR HAR HAR as fast as you can while you let out most of your breath; breathe in and continue to do the same again. The sound HA is a positive expression of the self coming into being. RA can also be an expression of *r*uthless *r*age and *r*ampage, or it may be a *r*ay of hope or the branching out into *ram*ifications; a bringing of some *r*ationality into the *r*andom *r*anting of a flame lost in the void.

Related to the seventh dimension we can be *r*uthless (lack of pity) or *r*epentant (to feel guilty). There may be a *r*elease (letting go of), *r*evenge, *r*eprimand, *r*emorse, *r*esentment, and *r*etaliation (all to do with holding onto the past).

The hiss of fire is different from the whish of the wind although both seem to be connected to the sound SSSS or SHSHSH. The difference is distinguishable in various ways. For example, the SSS sound of the fire manifests out of or after the sound H or from certain other consonants – *h*iss, *h*uss, *h*ustle, *h*assle, *c*uss, *c*urse, *k*iss. While in the SSS sound of the air the H sounds follow the SSS – SHSH, SUCH. Making the SSS sound on the exhale expresses a lot more fire, whilst drawing in the breath with a sound SSS is more cooling. This effect is increased when the breath out begins with the sound H and the breath in begins with S and moves towards SO or SU. In some teachings the vowel sounds have also been linked with the different elements. Here it is sufficient to state that sounds like EH, I, and EE are vowel sounds that generate or control warmth.

Affirmations

Affirming the self is a practice that is developed hand in hand with discriminating wisdom. In the progressive sense it is natural for a baby to first find itself through negation, "I am not my mother," and then learn to affirm itself through positive expression of its name and its needs. Equality, which is an important issue for the third dimension, will surely include your own equality. To care for others requires that we care about ourselves and to want to bring quality into other people's lives requires that we know what quality is in our own life. The first affirmation, therefore, is really one that affirms your own existence and right to be who you are. Also it will be more effective if it is kept simple. Try any one of the following phrases:

I AM OK, I AM ADEQUATE, I AM ENOUGH, I AM SUFFICIENT, I AM FINE, MY EXISTENCE IS A SUCCESS, I AM HAPPY, I AM.

The ultimate affirmation is positive action. If our actions confirm our understanding of forgiveness then our self-affirmation and ability to take our own counsel become a source of confidence in times of trial. When our self-value and worth is established in positive action then we are able to take pleasure in our own company. Making it OK to let go, to say goodbye, and part company is a quality of number 7 but is effective by the action of moving on. Having the insight of infinity allows you to realize that in a certain sense there is no real goodbye until the final dissolution of the self. Until then an expression like "see you around" is more appropriate.

An affirmation can be expressed in words or actions and clearly indicate a resolve to break past habits and establish new ones. In a very tribal and instinctive sense we are creatures of habit. It is a part of our nature to form habits and it is around the routine and ceremony of these that much of our life revolves. In the right balance and realms of existence routine and structure is a useful tool, a relatively stable point of reference from which we can operate. Out of balance our habits become neurotic patterns of behavior, which imprison us in our own suffering. Habits that we serve are prisons while habits that serve us are the best affirmations.

We will end this section with the understanding and affirmation that 70% of our happiness depends on our state of mind, right thinking, and right understanding. It follows then that 30% of our happiness is a result of right action.

Chapter 25

4/6 – Neutral Mind and Arcline: stillness and movement

The fourth magic is subtraction. The mathematical function that strips away the form is born by the winds of 4 and 6. 1 + 2 + 3 + 4 = 10 demonstrates that the addition of 4 returns to the original zero and 6 is the grace through which we remain in the openness of the formless. We try so hard to get to the essence of things by removing what we suppose to be obstacles but in the end we often end up also removing the essence itself. The magic is to stop trying to remove anything, to stop trying to take away from life what simply is. It links to the realization that there is no such thing as injustice; what is just is. To make it wrong is to take away what is and to try to add something else in its place. So it is another way of the magic to return again to the realization that the world is just as it is and to subtract nothing. The consequence is that the false is effortlessly subtracted, the layers of the veil are naturally stripped away, and a direct perception of reality is experienced.

The complementary nature of the 4 and 6 lies in the fact that one is the consciousness of the heart while the other is the heart of the consciousness. (Note: This does not refer to the heart organ but the fourth chakra of energy, which is sometimes experienced approximately in the center of the ribs.) Number 4 is the realm in which we seem able to go beyond the basic likes and dislikes of the body. Intuitions and feelings that stem from the body instincts have their own wisdom and it is the neutral mind that acts as the highest aspect of body-mind. It exercises its capacity to spontaneously select the most balanced action in response to the body's (the heart's) experiences. In other words it brings the insight of the spirit-mind to bear on the body-mind's choice of action.

The number 6, on the other hand, acts as the heart of the intellectual faculties of the spirit-mind. That is to say it brings a balance into the positive and negative aspects of spirit-mind by relating spirit-mind spontaneously to the practical issues of bodily existence. With this interaction a balance is brought about between the qualities of commitment and trust, otherwise understood as responsibility and faith.

Flower and the sword

A common experience that inhibits the awakening of the Neutral Mind is that you may feel oversensitive, overexposed, vulnerable, and in danger without a sufficient sense of guardianship offered by the third and seventh Bodies. It is a kind of raw and painful feeling, which makes you shy, reserved, and afraid. You are like a flower opening up revealing your beauty, though you most likely feel you are only showing your weakness. Encounters with human beings, especially insensitive ones, hurt, like when a petal is touched and it turns brown and drops off. From the position of the number 4 you may talk of each encounter as a searing pain, a stripping away of your preciousness. The process, however, can be likened to the tempering of steel. Each burning encounter prepares the steel until it becomes sharp as a sword. At this point you discover the strength of opening rather than the vulnerability; you discover that the human heart can flower perpetually. For every petal stripped away there are ten more opening up and in the very center of the heart is the sharp precision of the sword. Love, you realize, has these two qualities – embracing and gentle like the petals of the flower and piercingly sharp like a well-tempered sword.

Child of the future

We have a strange tendency to walk into the future backwards. This sensation is partly a true correspondence with the fact that the future is not visible to us. Our fear, however, leads us to reinforce this sensation by looking to where we have come from rather than looking into the darkness in front. By looking backwards we can at least see something. We then attempt to project the past into the future and make, what we believe will be, controllable limits upon it through our plans.

When psychotherapy speaks through the second and third dimensions then it will spend a lot of time dwelling on the inner child of the past, concerning itself with its unmet needs, and trying to understand what went wrong. Much of this time is useful and well spent and life is manageable. It will not take you on toward your destiny but it might create a sense of safety from which new risks can be taken. It is not enough, however, just to take the child of the past and set up its safety and well-being in the future based on past images. In this way you are left constantly in the past, never catching up with the moment, never mind facing the moment that is your future. The projection of the historic child into the future totally stifles the person you are becoming.

Psychologically we often walk into rooms and other spaces backwards holding onto the past as a crutch, which we can still retreat to if the new space is too threatening. The child of the past belongs to the numbers 3 and 7 and instead of being a victim there, can become our sturdy friend and support. It is the one who knows what we have been through and, therefore, can offer its understanding and encouragement. The child of the past is, in fact, not just a child stuck through trauma or other bad experiences. After all it has been through it is worthy of being recognized as someone who has matured through experience.

From the perspective of numbers 4 and 6 the child is the child of the future, just as children are our future. The true child is what you will make of your destiny, your aspirations, and your flowering. The attitude of the number 4 is brought into the therapeutic discussion by those who attend to whom they are becoming as opposed to whom they have been. When you walk into a room of your house you generally look in front of you, not behind. You look into the room you are entering, not the one you have left. This future orientation is an important invitational expression of the number 4 and a receptivity to the consciousness available through the number 6.

Crisis management as a way of awakening

Crisis management is a useful method for people who see everything in life as a crisis but also for those who try to ignore the crisis of life. A crisis is a moment of decision and every moment of decision is a moment of crisis. Life is full of decisions and so full of crisis. Even death sometimes seems to hinge on decision. When you are faced with decision you may find yourself thrown back within and down through your well of emptiness to find out who you really are and what you really need to be doing or not doing. You tend to call this dilemma a problem and often choose to get depressed about it. I say "choose" but I must point out that this is the passive choice that happens by default because by not engaging in the world in some way you are choosing inevitably to go inward. This is not wrong; it is just one way to go. Inward can also take you upward, instead of down, into daydreams and inner fantasy.

Sometimes the choice to go in and up or down is an active and conscious choice but it is usually a choice by default, resulting from your insecurity about engaging the world. Difficulties arise when you also fight against this inwardness, not allowing it to take you in to find your buried resources with which to meet the world again. It is this multi-directional resistance that contributes to the central realm of unconsciousness where you remain numb to the experience of relationship. This kind of approach is not the management of crisis except by attempting to ignore it, though perhaps that is all a person can do at certain moments in life. In a crisis you may feel locked in the room of your fear, which you hope someone will open and set you free, but the key is on the inside.

Number 4 and the Neutral Mind are about choosing to face the crisis of life, making decisions and choosing to make those decisions. This is where management comes into the picture. To manage means to use or to handle, to have in your hands. So to use crisis is to allow yourself to come into contact with the uncertainty of decision, to take the decision in your hands and hold it in front of you; this is crisis management. It is not the same as coping or organizing or regulating. It is handling and making use of the tension that is there in the critical moments of decision and finally it is being decisive.

Decisiveness arises when you recognize the tension of your doubts and fears as the energy that charges your intuition. The ultimate decision is to trust, or in other words, trust is an active decision, not just a cosy feeling. A decision is always a risk; you develop your involvement and participation in the fourth Body to the extent that you learn to take appropriate risks. You might say you first need to feel safe enough to take risks but consider what it would be like to have the courage enough to choose to feel safe.

Intuition

Intuition is another way of saying "feeling your way into the future." It is not clairvoyance, seeing into the future. Intuition works with the sense of touch more than with sight. This means that your intuition will give you a feeling of what not to do, which way not to go, rather than what to do or which way to go. Following your intuition is not as easy as it is often made out to be. It means working within the realm of your fears and doubts, it means taking risks and consciously applying your trust and faith. Intuition is to relate the heart of the mind to the mind of the heart.

Choices are either dictated by your programing or inspired by your intuition. The question of free choice is not just an abstract philosophical debate, but is biologically grounded in the activities of the brain. It is the primal back brain that operates on learnt patterns, while the forebrain activates you toward future alternatives. Between the two there seems to be a struggle. The back brain is concerned with basic survival priorities while the passively frustrated front brain allows programed stress to interrupt its freedom to choose differently. The real risk is to choose to choose which would bring the front brain into active life and open the way to an intuitive approach to life. This is one of the physiological effects of meditations that focus on the brow, the area associated with the sixth chakra, which is also known as the third eye.

Poetry, music, art, and beauty

The experience of life through the numbers 4 and 6 is best told in the language of art, which expresses the transformation of the struggle to express beauty, whether through music, dance, painting, song, or whatever. The expression of beauty and the appreciation of beauty help us to awaken to what has been called the "fourth way" and links to a sense of discovery, surprise, and wonder. Such an approach is not about curing our problems but finding creative expressions out of the tension.

The impersonal, silence, and prayer

One of the impersonal expressions of the 4 and 6 is luck or Lady Fortune. Spiritually this is experienced as the hand of grace. Moments of silence are moments when the Neutral Mind awakens within and touches out lives. As the number that sits closest to the number 5 (the threshold) it can be considered as a gateway to the impersonal dimensions of 6, 7, 8, 9, and 10. For some people, passing through this gate is like a spiritual conversion, an unalterable and irreversible transformation where the language takes on the quality of prayer.

The unknown

The task of the language of 4 and 6 is to facilitate a meeting of the situations where your rational knowledge does not work. It is a stepping into the field of discovery, acknowledging that we never actually know. Every moment we maintain an attitude of receptivity and responsiveness to all that we might meet. All is possible and every meeting is an opportunity as we are constantly allowing our normal view of the world to be stripped away. It is a dynamic state of permanent revolution and radical transmutation within which the stillness of trust and faith gives stability.

Community

It takes the humanity in you to heal the humanity in others and it requires the humanity in others to heal the humanity in you. Human relationships are experienced in community and there is a great need for new approaches to community in this modern world. To work with the numbers 4 and 6 is to be committed to become an innovator in discovering the way forward through community.

Exercises

As part of the alchemic practice it is with our own hands that we must labor for our liberty. All work is worship and carries a prayerful attitude. As an extension of the fourth chakra our hands are made to perform a labor of love, which is the true quality of presence in the atmosphere that can bring about the condensation of compassion. Exercises for the Neutral Mind and Arcline focus on rotating the upper body. They will include movements for the shoulder blades, ribcage, and upper spine, meditations with the arms raised above the head, placing the palms and hands flat together to balance the circuitry of the left and right hemispheres, and graceful dancing with the arms and more especially with the hands. The lungs and large intestines are associated with these dimensions and exercises that strengthen and tone these organs will be of benefit.

Eye exercises

1   Look down the tip of the nose and from there into the ribcage where the eye of the spirit-mind penetrates the body-mind.
2   Having closed the eyelids and whilst keeping them gently closed, go through the internal motion of closing them again and stepping further back into yourself and repeat this as often as you feel comfortable. Imagine that behind every set of eyelids there is another set of eyelids to be closed and another door into the heart of your spirit-mind to be entered. Entering backwards is an expression of faith, which is an important quality of the sixth dimension of human consciousness.
3   Close your eyes gently but definitely whilst in a public place, like waiting for a bus, and now become aware of your fears. Learn to trust yourself, to be at ease and yet alert. Let the feelings of the body become as eyes to perceive the world. This is simply a reversal of the normal process where our eyes operate like arms

reaching out and touching the world so that the spirit-mind can experience the outer world.

4 Place the fingers gently over the closed eyes to invite them to become still and relaxed while not losing consciousness into the dream and sleep states.

In what way does sight relate to the sixth dimension? It is not just a matter of seeing but more a question of what is seen and how it is seen; in other words feeling seeing. Eyes display our fears, our trustworthiness, and our ability to trust others or God. It is with our eyes that we see injustice and through its negation begin to build up a vision of a more harmonious future. With our eyes we see ahead but we also face the unknown before us. Beauty is seen in the eyes and with the eyes. Through the sixth dimension we can come to see that part in everyone that is beautiful. This need not inhibit us from negating injustice but rather it should stir us on to cultivate truth and beauty. In the practice of negating we do not negate what is beautiful in a person but the ungraceful way in which they attempt to bring disharmony into the flow of life and death.

There is an interesting relationship between the numbers 3, 6, and 9. The number 3 permits us to see our individual self in a positive light; we discover our own beauty. Through the sixth sense, or third eye, we find the beauty of ourselves in the community to which we belong. And with the subtle nature of the 9 we find the beauty of ourselves in every individual, regardless of their status or cultural background.

Meditation and prayer are both important for the dimensions of 4/6. Prayer is the quality of calling out from the ribcage and preparing an intuitive state of receptivity and silence. Meditation involves more awareness at the forehead where the mind is held steady and awakening of the state of wonder takes place. To align yourself with the number 4 inhale in four steps and exhale in four steps. Meditate on the mantra "silence," half on the inhale (si) and half on the exhale (lence) or chant SA TA NA MA, which corresponds to the numbers 6, 7, 8, 9.

We find it hard to stop in our lives since stopping is to arrive in the storm of our fears and to let the future catch up with us. When we stop we cross a line from the past into the future and then the unconscious habitual activity of maintaining our projections stops. It is these projections that do not permit us to have a future but when we do stop the future is set free to arrive and we can tune into the flow of time and use its power instead of being unconsciously swept along in its many undercurrents. Moving with time we find ourselves staying still and in this stillness we can direct the time and invest the time.

A meditation in how to stop: Take the time, wherever you are to do some not-doing.

For example, become aware of your breath without trying to breathe and without trying not to breathe. Become aware of your eyes and the activities of seeing and seeing who is seeing you and with this awareness do not try to focus on anything and do not try not to focus on anything. Become aware of your feelings and whatever they may be in relation to and do not try to feel anything specific but also do not try not to feel anything specific. Become aware of your thinking process and its contents and do not try to think of anything whilst also not trying not to think of anything.

Remain in this mysterious state for three to five minutes and then breathe very deeply in and out a few times and forget what you have just been through. If you do this on a regular basis you will find that you open up greater access to your energetic resources and an innate sense of peacefulness without trying.

Qualities

Like the numbers 2 and 8 there are also feminine qualities associated with 4 and 6. The daughter and mother energy belong to the 2 and 8, while the princess and warrior woman correspond to the numbers 4 and 6.

The ability to be a confidant, to win someone's trust, requires that you are not motivated by principles of self-interest. To take up struggles of social justice involves a negation of the individual and an affirmation of the community. Justice is, furthermore, built upon choosing what is ethically good or right by deciding what is wrong or undesirable and that is by a process of negation. Where there is harmony, injustice is not an issue; where there is disharmony, justice is established by negating the disagreeable factors. It is with issues of justice that you may become dogmatic. Rules of ethical behavior can take over from a felt essence of truth as a dynamic principle not confined to one form.

Structure was the issue in the dimensions of the third and seventh Bodies but can become a means of sabotage in the fourth and sixth where feelings and experience of truth outweigh the enforced code of moral norms. Freedom, though, must not only imply the freedom to do what you feel without regard for others; there is a danger of false spontaneity here. Freedom to be free of fear of others must include the acknowledgment that others are to be free of fear. This presents a natural check on your behavior so freedom is not really absolute for a self that is limited. Freedom also includes the ability to step beyond the prison of your social training and habit. You confirm your freedom when, at any random moment, you can stop and consider an alternative course of action or attitude other than that which is being adopted or about to be undertaken. Then, if appropriate, it is to express this alternative in word and deed.

Spontaneity comes from feeling the truth rather than discovering it through dissecting the ins and outs of an issue. Learn to distinguish between feelings, which have simply been culturally interjected, they manifest as emotional reactions, and feelings that are more lasting, more deep, and, therefore, more real. Learn to feel in your bones the extent of any truth within a thought. Let the will of the blood and body rise up to your ribcage and see what truth rests hidden there. What is the true direction to steer in order to serve the true needs of the true self?

No amount of debate will answer this kind of question. Set aside doubt, which arises from and perpetuates a dualistic and dilemma-orientated life pattern. Do not trust me or another human being who is caught up in the world of pros and cons, good and bad. No, trust yourself in relation to totality, yourself in relation to all and everything. Above all trust the sincerity of your own intention. If that is difficult because you have not yet clarified your own intention, then trust for the sake of trust, for the sake of your soul, which cannot rest until you trust it. Without clarity of intention spontaneous choice followed by spontaneous action is not possible.

To clarify your intention begin by negating so that you cast aside and vanquish into thin air those intentions that you do not feel comfortable with and which do not strike you as being beautiful.

True faith is not blind faith. Rather true faith is the expression, which arises naturally when we realize that we have reached the edge of the knowable. Just as in a game where we learn the rules before we start to play, a point is reached when we may not have the whole picture but know that we can only learn more by jumping in and going through the experience. There is no clear marker for this stage where we decide "OK, let's throw a six and begin." It is purely a felt moment and one we have probably passed many times but held back from because of fears. Fears are indeed justified for who knows what lies beyond the cliff edge. But like an actor on stage, the power of our fear can send us into shock or empower us and carry us through the game of life.

Air element

Air is the nature of the breath yet to be breathed, the feeling yet to be felt, the thought yet to be thought, the experience yet to be experienced, the decisions, choices, and commitments yet to be taken, the responsibilities yet to be acknowledged, the projects and projections of life yet to be given birth to, the hopes and aspirations of our intuitively felt destiny, the empty bubbles of our future, which have yet to surface and explode into wonderful moments of existence, and the children of tomorrow, gone no sooner than they appeared. Air, like the future, is hard to grasp. Air slips through our fingers and is gone before we realize it.

Air has often been linked with the mental plane of existence. This does not, however, refer to the ego-mind. Rather the fourth plane of being is the state of awareness known as consciousness. As I have indicated, all dimensions are actually dimensions of consciousness. The important thing is to understand the different nature of consciousness in the different realms. The air element is associated with the sense of touch, which means that in the fourth dimension consciousness is experienced through touch; intuition is our sense of touch. Through the Arcline the wisdom of spirit-consciousness touches us and the result is inspirational thinking; such a thought becomes an experience.

With the number 6 thought is awareness and manifests as a feeling, thought is felt. The inspirational quality given by the 4 and 6 is a wind that fans the flames of the mind machine that produces static thoughts with which we create ideologies. The true realization of the air element is to be in a state of spontaneous flow. It is to trust the next breath we breathe in to bring with it the inspiration and guidance needed for the action, which will flow out of us as we let that breath go. The numbers 4 and 6 bring the inspiration to forever go beyond all boundaries and limitations, to forever reach out (and in) further and further to grasp a little bit more of what is infinitely ungraspable. It is through these dimensions that we come to realize the truth "the more we know the less we know."

Air condenses and produces water. From the 4 and 6 comes the 2 and 8. The immediacy of the moment is a 4 /6 quality and from this comes the sense of flow and continuity that we call time, i.e. 2/8. Time is energy; it waters the seed of 1/9 and it fuels the shapes we make through the time, our projects and projections that inhabit the spatial realms of 3/7. These are the branches and trunks, the forms and structures, through which the sap of life, the vitality of the pranic breath, surges in and out of creation. The air element returns in the presence of the flowers of life, flowers that begin to fade and wither no sooner than they have come into full bloom. This is quite a different situation than that of the first and ninth dimensions where the seed may rest stationary for any length of time. The branches of the plant, on the other hand, are a positive expression of the established existence of the plant; that is to say the third and seventh dimensions dry up and become firewood upon withdrawal of the pranic life force (chi).

Speaking of flowers, it is in the flower of the fourth chakra, often known as the heart center, that the emotions of love, awe, fear, pain, and hurt are experienced. When we are hurt, usually by someone's excess of fire (resentment, slander, or aggression, for example), we tend to identify with the crushing of the flower and the associated pain, and fear develops in anticipation of further pain. What we forget is that it is in the nature of flowers to dry up and make room for the fruit. The burning heat of the autumn sun need not present such a threat and less so for human beings. Why is this so? Well, just as we are able to mate and produce children all year round, independent of the seasons, so are we able to perpetually flower. The attachment to old flowers only slows down the endless flourishing, which is our nature. Slander is a blessing in disguise, which reminds us to be free of old opinions of who or what we are and to make way for the continuous moving out of wonder and beauty from the dimensions that express our distinctively human nature. We have some choice as to whether we identify with the apparent pain and hurt of the old and drying up flowers or the spring of love, which flows all the more favorably by letting go.

Healing and the kingdom of human beings

The air element finds representation in the flower stage of plant life. Flowers open up the heart, not the organ of the heart but the heart of body-mind and spirit-mind, the heart from which stems creativity in its most beautiful forms. In flowering, human beings have the potential to distinguish themselves and to make the distinct mark that fulfills the human project. Flowering is the nature of being human. To be human is to be a beautiful, soft, and delicate flower, to invite the busy bees of love to alight on our petals, taste the nectar, and carry the message of love onto another flower. The opening of the heart of consciousness is indeed as magnificent as a flower.

A man brings flowers to a woman to express his love but it is often just a token gesture, a social habit, or an attempt to gain less than love. A woman tends to keep flowers in the house more than a man because she intuitively knows that they will sooner or later open the man's true heart. A man flowers according to the advice of a woman, which may be to his advantage or disadvantage. Men who campaign for the protection of plants and trees in the environment are men who have begun to explore, rather than avoid, the feminine qualities of their own nature. This is a healthy expression of that exploration and not one to be blocked or criticized. I would, however, point out that the success of this project is primarily dependent on the giving over of the ownership of the planet to woman. Woman will sooner or later learn the power of negation and withdraw their passive co-operation with man's political and business projects, which pay no respect to the feminine qualities of nature and existence as a whole. This withdrawal will ultimately oblige man to hand over the power to woman. Woman in turn will use or abuse their status according to the general state of their evolution.

Massage practices usually work on the fourth and sixth dimensions through the sense of touch and human contact. Counseling of most varieties is a kind of holding that depends on the qualities of the fourth and sixth bodies. In other words most practices, which help to break down inhibitions in human communication, have a significant effect in encouraging us to feel our thoughts; processes that open up trust between people are important. Art expresses thought in a way that touches the one who is receiving. It follows that the performance of the arts is particularly valuable in opening us up to what makes us human. The kingdom of birds, which is most beautiful and various and whose wings are like flowers, are a reminder of the soul awakening and developing when we open up the fourth and sixth dimensions.

Sciences of all types could also be said to be uniquely human, but it is how we engage in these practices that make the difference. When we are tuned into the feelings of the discoveries that our apparent intellect falls upon, then we will also know the full implications and outcomes of unrestrained application of the scientific mind. What makes us truly human is not just the ability to uncover and seemingly master the laws of the universe but our ability to feel the thoughts behind science. When we experience a thought we are more likely to maintain a healthy sense of wonder as well as acknowledge our responsibility to carefully use the wisdom given to us. It is then, in the fourth and sixth dimensions, that religion meets science and science becomes poetry.

Technology becomes more than dangerous when the majority of people prefer to remain in tribal and robotic life habits according merely to social conditioning. This allows the responsibility of the whole to be in the hands of the few. Opening up to our feelings means awakening from our paralysis and discovering a new way to respond to life's experiences. Fear is simply a manifestation of presence and can become the weapon of faith. New ways to respond are discovered by jumping into life, by taking responsibility for our own existence and for the fruits of all that we do or do not do. Again it is by fully engaging in the game of life that we cultivate a feeling for the game. There would be no fear if we played life to the fullest and this is because our intuitive sense would find the grounds in which it can expand and become the master. Getting a sense of movement is only achieved by moving, yet we need to feel the still point within that provides the springboard and point of reference for our orientation.

Sounds

Throughout this book the material has been presented using language that is very specific to the numbers that are being described. For example, to speak of truth and trust is to invite the reader to attune to qualities within that are part of the experience of the numbers 4 and 6. Notice how the addition of the letter T changes and softens the meaning of the word "rust." Then rifle becomes trifle, a rack becomes a track just like rail becomes a trail and ram becomes tram. With the T there is a kind of overcoming of things, just as faith allows us to hold in our heart what the mind cannot deal with. Put the T at the end of the word and labor becomes liberty. Yet without a clear, conscious, and educated faith, that gives the readiness to find the grace in any crisis, the T can strip away and shock. So we find that rebel becomes terrible, rouble becomes trouble, and rage leads to tragedy. Whatever happens, the T will bring a dimensional shift.

A common expression of trust is the giving over of the small i into the hands of the big I (the God, spirit, or soul within). "Thy will be done" places the emphasis on Thou, Thee, and Thine and the Latin and Sanskrit origin of this is tu, tuhi, and tera. Even the more modern word "you" is effective in awakening the more essential aspects of the fourth and sixth dimensions. Ya is a more ancient form of the sound Ja and YA HO WAH is a more ancient form of JEHOVAH. Yahowah uses the vowel sounds more and consequently brings us closer to the essence and life of the word. The capacity of a creature to say "I" is unique to human beings and so indicates a relationship between the sound I and the numbers 4 and 6. Saying "I" is a form of self-remembering, it is the remembering of the truth and who we truly are.

As language migrates across borders there are subtle shifts in the use of sounds. In the more northern parts of Europe the T often is transformed into a D. So "du" is the same as "tu." There is a relation of these sounds to the numbers 2 and 8, as in the nature of **du**ality. However, the longing that is felt in the Negative Mind (number 2) is a movement that takes us towards the opening of the fourth chakra and the Neutral Mind.

- Dumfounded is the inner paralysis of the number 4.
- Dwelling within is the temple bud of the heart.
- Donations are truly given and received through the Neutral Mind.
- Danger is sensed through the presence of intuition.
- Dance is the art of a loving relation.
- Daring is the risk to be open to all.

On the other hand, if fear is used to manipulate others then there is **d**rama, **d**ogma, **d**omination, and **d**amnation. The natural spontaneity of the breath is **d**amned up and the inner **d**omain loses the opportunity of **d**elight.

Silence is a quality of the number 6. Being in silence can develop the sensitivity and awaken the Arcline. Stopping the chatter of the mind is not an easy task. Each dimension of consciousness, whether of the body or the spirit, is engaged in its own forms of dialogue. Intuition is the ability to listen whilst in motion.

As there is often a confusion between need and love so also the sound S might originate from or influence the numbers 2 and 8 as well as 4 and 6. SO is more representative of the 2 and 8 while SA has more relationship to the fourth and sixth. Salt, salute, sane, sacred, Sabbath, salaam, saint, saving, salvation, and sacrifice are examples of words that express the qualities of the 4 and 6, both in the everyday meanings of these terms and in the esoteric. Words that begin with ST are also significant – state, status, stir, stimulus, strategy, stratum, street, still, stay, stable, stamina, satisfy, satiate, saturate. And certain words where the H follows the S – shanti, share, shame, ship, shrine, shudder, shy.

Affirmations

The greatest affirmation for the number 4 and 6 is to realize the law of 40% and 60%. This law states that in every situation you are 40% responsible and God is 60% responsible. In this way you do not blame anyone else for things but neither do you take the whole thing on your own shoulders. There is nothing to fear, there is no reason to be afraid. In the state of faith in the absolute, infinite, eternal presence of a cosmic force and intelligence, what is there to fear? In the fear of God all other fears are diminished to nothing. These are examples of the use of negation in order to strengthen the fourth and sixth dimensions. Likewise other qualities of the 4 and the 6 that we wish to affirm will be best done so through the use of the negative. For example, trust and faith are, in fact, arrived at through the negation of unnecessary and groundless fears. Furthermore, given that 4 is 2 + 2, then the double negative is even more appropriate. So you could try "no, I have no fear" or "I do not not trust."

Doubt is another polarity of trust and faith, which may or may not be based on fear. In certain schools of thought faith is seen as an escapist route and something for the masses that do not have the capacity for an awakened mind. Such teachings may go on to recommend doubting everything, even doubting your own doubts. Doubt, however, is only understandable in contrast to faith or some other term indicating the absence of doubt, so to let go of faith would be to let go of doubt also.

Doubt is clearly the use of a negative principle and used in the appropriate manner can only facilitate our development. Doubting what we commonly take for reality may open up the possibility to recognize its temporary nature and come closer to a more lasting reality. Or in other words, doubting the known leads us into contact with the unknown. Once we come into contact with the lesser-known aspects of existence and non-existence we might also note its potentially infinite and eternal nature. Now something that is infinitely large, infinitely small and subtle, endless in time, without a knowable beginning or end, something that might be considered as the essence of all other things as well as the essence of the absence of things, something that is nothing knowable in the ordinary sense, or perhaps in any sense, something that is free of the conditions that our limited senses might impose on it, that potentially chaotic, unstructured, and formless something that is unidentifiable, that sum of all the unexplainable forces – what relation do we or could we have with it?

If we, who appear so definitely to be something, doubt the reality of the known self, the I, which we so easily and semi-consciously declare to be the operator of all operations in life, what then? Shall we deny the existence of a nominal reality? Shall we live in fear of a something, which seems only to be identifiable by stating what it is not? Or shall we throw caution to the wind and accept that what is unknowable in the absolute sense will remain so? Shall we accept that the undiscoverable factor, which penetrates the whole of life and death, will always leave our final questions unanswered? Shall we accept and have faith that whatever it is or is not, it alone knows its nature?

OK, I have been pointing to the idea that if there is faith then there is also doubt and vice versa, the question being how to apply these qualities of consciousness. What we doubt and what we have faith in is going to play a major part in how we experience and understand life and death. In the study of any teachings that may use the terms "doubt" and "faith," often making one of these qualities a sin or error, it is important to understand what activity or process is being spoken of. The use of the words in accordance with particular contexts will suggest a certain definition. Interpreters and translators of ancient teachings will often transform the meaning of a text into something quite different from that originally intended. It is possible, however, through clear thinking to identify the inconsistencies, unexplained contradictions, and one-sided nature of teachings that have become dogmas.

Using the concept of non-attachment and negating what is temporary in life, we can begin to explore our relationship to that which is more permanent. Affirmations about truth are limited in their success because we do not have a clear definition of truth. Any absolute truth can only be that which survives all changes and goes on through all time and fills all space. We may construct all kinds of virtual realities, but we do so within the context of a greater reality. And even though little or nothing can ever be known about it, we can nevertheless enjoy an interesting dance with this unknown lover.

The affirmation of truth depends on the negation of untruth. Consider the confusion present in the multiple meanings of the expression that "nothing is not true." To choose truth is to choose the spontaneous and unplanned expression of each moment of time meeting each particle of space. To discover the unknown is to turn away from the known. It is a meditation on divine darkness.

Note how the prefixes DE, DIS, and DI before a word emphasize negative qualities. Most of the words beginning with these prefixes will be found to have a significant relation to the numbers 2 and 8 through division or the numbers 4 and 6 through subtraction. Some examples are debar, decamp, decease, decline, defend, deflate, deflower, delete, deliver, depart, desist, destroy, detach, detract, deviate, dichotomy, differ, difference, dilemma, disagree, and disallow.

The even numbers are divisible by two and, therefore, in those dimensions we are more likely to experience a duality, which engages us in endless debate. The dimensions identified by odd numbers will tend to show a stronger sense of action because of the uneven distribution of energy. In other words, it is more likely that a certain quality will gain the upper hand and this will enable activity to arise. The following words are suggestive of the second, fourth, sixth, and eighth dimensions in their discursive aspects: define, deliberate, divide, distinguish, discern, discriminate, detect, determine, discover, diagnose, dialogue, discourse, discuss, dispute.

The purpose of listing these words is to give you an idea of the range of terms, which can be utilized in structuring or restructuring your own dialogue with yourself and others. Some people are quick to declare negativity as a bad or undesirable attitude of consciousness, yet our language is full of negating as well as affirming terms. Also, most terms that are not neutral, can only be meaningful by a contrast to terms that are the opposite in meaning. If you take the time to reflect over the various possible applications of the words listed and others like them it will become clear that in certain contexts, in certain situations and settings, their use will be entirely appropriate.

Chapter 26

5/10 – Physical Body and Radiant Body: center and circumference

We live our life stretched out in time and space and it all gets very complicated. Yet within this complexity, as a kind of backcloth, there remains the very simple concept of multiplying, dividing, adding, and subtracting, nothing more and nothing less. Of course, as we continue multiplying, dividing, and then adding what we have divided and subtracting what we have multiplied it can develop into a huge mathematical complication. But the basis is always simple and if we can develop an intimacy with this simplicity our management of the complex is also easy. The fifth dimension is the quality of our integration of the four mathematical functions.

Life becomes really interesting when we have exhausted all activities of subtracting, adding, dividing, and multiplying. There is no greater meditation than this. You take away nothing, you add nothing, you split nothing, and you multiply nothing; all just is. This is the zero state and allows us to really listen; when we do that our word is our single reality. We are what we speak, nothing more and nothing less, this is the sum total of the equation on completion of the four phases of natural magic. Completing the equation is the fulfillment of the adventure of the possible human. Then we are a 10-in-1 being. Transcending the human state we return to the unity through community with the word that is divinity itself.

As students of our experience, 5 is of central importance. 5 is the harmonization of the five elements, five senses, five planes of existence, and the five states of consciousness that correspond with the five pairs of numbers. The totality that is 10 is spontaneously realized when all the other numbers are brought into balance. As the link between all the other dimensions 5 is the gateway to achieve this. Through the number 5 we can influence every facet of our being, keeping them apart, or keeping each part in relation. Therefore, the emphasis in the number 5 and for the highest level of self-help is through the word.

The synthesis in sacred chanting

The sacred, the holy, the consecrated are terms that indicate that there is a part of yourself that cannot be violated. Many things or places deemed sacred are only so by human law, but that which is most sacred and genuinely worthy of our reverence is not governed by the same man-made laws. The truly sacred is that which cannot be violated by virtue of its own innately sacred nature. Simply speaking it needs no one's law to protect it. The unconditionally sacred maintains its own integrity and purity by being inaccessible to all of us until we equal it in purity. This is not said with intent to judge the impurity within us, nor to slander those who mark out times and places as holy and sacred. There are perhaps degrees of sacredness yet the most sacred will, by virtue of its infinite depth, always be infinitely beyond the limitation of any shrine or holy day or specific prayer, no matter how special. Yet by infinite yearning, dedicated devotion, and grace (amongst other things) any of these sacred tools may be transformed into a gateway to the beyond.

Chanting is an act of faith. When all rational means fail we turn to the non-rational and attempt the impossible. Chanting is a naming of that which cannot be named, an acknowledgment and a praising of the sacred. In naming some of the endless qualities of the ultimately intangible we solicit or invite the manifestation of these qualities. Their sublime nature results in what may be perceived as a spiritual rather than material manifestation. The naming of less subtle qualities, which impose a more concrete limitation upon our perception of the ungraspable reality of the most sacred, results in our attending to more physical forms such as saints, symbols, idols, and mandalas. The trap of the more physical form is that we may forget that it is a mere finite representation of something beyond the form. The difficulty of the most sublime qualities is that they are so abstract and refined as to be out of our reach; hence the need of some form of guru to act as God in focus, the narrow gate to the Divine. The ultimate quality of Guru is a word. The mystery of the sacred names is that though they are a form they are not fixed into a rigid material form. Each word is a most short-lived expression of that which never ends. Sounds are the middle field, the means of meditation and relationship between the two poles of the endlessness of the sacred and the narrow confines of each crossroads in the matrix of time and space, between the impersonal and the personal, the infinite and the finite.

Chanting and singing is the flower and the fruit of speech, which gives a melody to the soul as it struggles to find its way in free flight. Chanting is the expression of Soul rather than bodily needs and fulfills the needs of Soul by their very expression. There are things that need to be said and yet words are not quite enough. It is the mood that demands expression and this is done through song. Song may carry beauty, pain, joy, sadness, anger, love, and fear.

Words are only of value when heard by another person and yet somehow we never quite feel as if we have been heard. In chanting and singing, Soul is called more into presence where it both sings and hears; then there is no question of whether we are heard by another. The birds sing each morning simply because it is true to their nature and they have little concern for who is listening. The absorption in their song is the experience they seek. At the closing of our many long, dark, and lonely nights we, too, may burst out in a flourish of song or drone on in repetitive complaint, never being heard and never hearing ourselves until this complaint becomes our song.

Chanting brings us into relationship. It relates the aspects of our personal duality to each other. There is also the duality and polarity of our individuality and the endless universe – a fiery ocean crossed by the tracking of a sound current that relates the two. And chanting will bring us into relationship with anyone else who is willing to communicate from the real source of their experience, from the nakedness of Soul, knowing it cannot be violated.

Being extreme

An extreme situation requires an extreme approach. If you have a tendency toward extremes there is no point in trying to moderate your extreme nature. Why not find the asset within this tendency and cultivate it? Any extreme behavior or thinking pattern will be resolved by another extreme act or thought. The extremes of religious life are simply the means for extreme people to become extremely balanced. If you also feel that life has been radical to you then consider being radical in return. This is the role of a teacher, to offer the insight of radical transformation and self-realization.

Maps of self

Another useful way to begin the synthesizing process is to work with creating maps of the self. This is done simply by taking any issue and placing it in a circle with your name or some indicator of your identity and then to draw lines reaching out to all the aspects of this issue in your life. This will remind you of who you really are amidst all the opposing forces. It is like drawing a mandala of yourself and can be quite dynamic in that you can modify it as and when you wish. Contemplating these maps of self can help you to see things in different perspectives and opens up the possibility to change the shape of things. When you introduce these changes on your map it also has an effect on the territory. By regular practice you find a greater sense of alignment of all the parts.

Exercises

All kinds of exercise that work on the nervous system will have some effect on the fifth dimension. The nervous system is the communicating link between the worlds of inner and outer, body and mind. Many yogic exercises strengthen the nervous system while at the same time increasing its sensitivity and capacity for energy flow.

Exercises for the neck help the fifth dimension of consciousness. This is because the thyroid and parathyroid glands, which are situated at the throat level, have an important function in regulating the nervous system and effecting communication. Furthermore, at the back of the upper neck the nerves from the two frontal brain hemispheres cross over to the opposite sides of the body. Here is a sequence of exercises you could try:

1 Inhale and turn your chin to the left shoulder, exhale and turn your chin to the right shoulder. Repeat at least twenty-six times.

2 Now breathe in and drop your head backwards while lifting the chin up and then breathe out while you take the chin down to the chest. Repeat at least twenty-six times.

3 Roll the head slowly round in circles, inhaling as you rotate one ear to the shoulder on the same side. Continue inhaling until your head is all the way back, and as you rotate the other ear down to the other shoulder, start to breathe out. Continue breathing out until your chin has come down and round to the chest. Repeat three to five of these circles and change direction, rotating the head for the same amount of time.

4 Hold the head straight in the center, without dropping it from side to side or backwards or forwards, and start to move the neck in a figure 8 (a bit like Egyptian dancing). Continue for up to three minutes in both directions.

5 To finish, focus on the sound of the breath as it passes in and out of the throat. Bring a small degree of friction into the sound of your breath; this will help you focus and balance the thyroid and parathyroid glands.

Tension in the throat indicates problems in the fifth dimension. Since this dimension holds such a central role it is clearly important to work towards keeping it free of tension build-ups. In addition to the exercises given and others like them, singing and yawning are good ways to release tension in the throat. As the fifth dimension is a center of communication in all respects it is no surprise that when one person starts to yawn other people in the same room soon join in. Likewise with singing, it is hard to resist joining in with someone who is genuinely enjoying a good song.

Communication games, which often tend to be a part of group therapy, are aimed at opening up and balancing the fifth dimension. However, if such games are not utilized responsibly it is possible that our communication may open up too much or even close down in reaction to inappropriate stimulus. Learn to listen, both to the mood as well as to the content of what people say. Practice saying what you really mean and really listening to yourself as you speak. Communication with yourself is the most important relationship and if you were to be honest you would realize that all relationships are really just mediums for intimacy with self. It is often the case that when we feel like we really want to say something it means that we really want to hear it. Listening is an important activity in itself. An informal and intuitive study of body language is very interesting but it will be more valuable and challenging to translate your own and others' body language into words. This brings to consciousness what tends to fall into the subconscious.

Qualities

The most essential quality of both the fifth and tenth dimension is balance. It is a perpetual sacrifice of imbalance. To find the middle ground we often need to go toward the opposite extreme from where we are. So if you find that you tend to overdo it in things like eating, speaking, and sleeping then you might gain from occasionally underdoing it a bit. Some people, however, find it easy to go to both extremes, feasting one day and fasting the next, being lazy today and overworking tomorrow. This can be addressed by applying the intensity that manifests with the tenth dimension to the concept of balance. That means taking the quality of the tenth dimension, which influences us to go all the way into something or not to go at all, and go all the way into balance.

The Japanese art of Feng Shui implies everything in balance; the right things in the right place, the right actions at the right time, practical, decorative, with quality, fluid yet stable, and based on a holistic encounter between the limited and the unlimited in all things and in all ways. A very important point to consider in seeking balance is to remember that it is a process rather than a static point. If we take balance to be a set condition to be achieved once and then held onto, we are in danger of falling into petty forms of obsession and fanaticism. This is especially so as the set conditions that we might apply tend to include aspects of the impermanent world, those parts of the world that are forever in flux. In some cases it might help to think of balance as being a place, like the center hub of a wheel around which the world revolves. This center, however, is not tied to one location, and is, anyway, only one small center revolving round a more important center, which itself rotates around an even more significant center. Questions of location of identity are only relative and although helpful, need to be recognized as limiting.

The perfection of balance can be referred to as the Golden Mean, the achievement of excellence. Through educational systems, whether spiritual or otherwise, the educator is trying to facilitate the student's realization of the Golden Mean. There are general guidelines as to what this might be but it is equally the case that each individual finds their own personal expression of what the balance is in their life, given all their particular circumstances. Not only do we need to consider the physical and social environment, the details of timing, and other external particulars, but we must take into full account the circumstances of the individual person. Both the historical and the present inner state of the individual play a role in establishing the balance for any occasion. The whole sense is required in order to determine what would make the doing or not doing of any action a balanced procedure. This whole is grasped from within by virtue of the Neutral Mind. Getting the whole picture constitutes and establishes the extent of the Radiant Body, which is a dynamically organic ecosystem that is stable through perpetual change.

You are the relation of all things to all things. This is so because you are consciously present in a Physical Body. It is who you are at the center of your existence. Here in this center of relationship is also the center of experience. It is the realm in which all experience is processed and integrated as a part of the whole self. The fifth dimension is the center in which all learning and teaching really takes place, where old models of reality are destroyed or, at least, turned upside down and where the self is continually sacrificing itself in order to be made new. The art of the fifth dimension is to surrender to the whole rather than just a part. In this way you will realize the self that is the total self, more than all the parts put together. It is you that holds it all together. You are the circumference and you are the hub of the paradox.

Through the number 5 you cannot stand outside of yourself but you can give voice to every part of who you are. The number 10 applies the boundaries of consciousness, and even though this is also who you are it is not an easy identity to rest in. There is more of a tendency to feel like the nothing of the zero than the greater unity. For this reason the appropriate move is to actively surrender the central self to the tenth dimension by addressing it as "you." It is to create a personalized relationship between you as your experienced self and its partner, the transcendent unity.

Other key qualities of the fifth dimension are synthesis, integration, harmony, health, wholeness, communion, and relationship.

Ether element

The ether element is of such a nature that it cannot be found separate from the other elements. It is by virtue of ether that the other elements can be distinguished yet related to each other. It is out of the ether that the various parts emerge as apparently separate realms and merge again into each other. The self that both separates and synthesizes does so in order to meet itself through the parts. The periphery is the limit of the extended parts; the circle's boundary is created by the extensions being called back to the dynamic center.

There is no beginning or end, no final boundary in space or time, the presence of every color and form as well as the absence of any of these things. These discoveries tell the central self something about its own nature. There is no realm of mind or consciousness that is not filled with the presence of ether.

Continuing the analogy of the plant, the fifth dimension finds expression in the fruit, which follows the blossom. The fruit is the final outcome of the plant's existence and at the same time it is the necessary condition for the beginning of many new plants. The fruit contains the end and the beginning within it. The gift of the harvest is not for the fruits alone but for the seeds, which guarantee the continuance of life and future nourishment. This is an important point, which is lost in many forms of celebration. Celebration is intimately tied to sacrifice and because we do not recognize the nature of the sacrifice required to move from flower to fruit to new seed, we stage-manage unrealistic and superficial sacrifices or impose the ritual of sacrifice on others rather than go through it ourselves. It is interesting to consider that Christ was born in August, the harvest season. He was harvested from the moment of birth; his birth was already the sacrifice. Death is within life and life is within death. Mastery of the fifth realm is when we can equally celebrate life and death while experiencing the paradox of both. Who we become when we embrace the paradox is the greatest secret and is implied in the symbol of the golden fruit. It is a fruit that is no longer to be eaten but instead remains forever in the glory of the final state. Just as the ether element is associated with the plane of the gods, so fruit is also considered as the food of the gods and naturally they become what they eat.

Some other things to do

Being in the center, the 5 is a place where mixing and separating of all the elements take place; it is the alchemic laboratory. A practical expression of this is the preparation of food. By getting involved in the whole process of food preparation we mix the elements of earth, water, fire, and air. The activity of cooking can, therefore, naturally tune you in to the numbers 5 and 10. Life itself can also be approached from the same perspective as the preparation and enjoyment of a meal. That is by being experimental, searching out and preparing the ingredients of life, mixing them up in various combinations, and throwing in something new from time to time. It is bringing the whole to be greater than the sum of the parts.

Cultivating and maintaining an explorative and experimental attitude of healthy curiosity is good for the fifth and tenth Bodies as long as it does not become obsessive. The opposite extreme of this is where we assume to know everything, to have been everywhere, and to have tried all things. Life becomes boringly familiar and we do not find newness in each moment; the flow stops. "Familiarity breeds contempt" but familiarity is also an illusion. All things that manifest for our knowing are caught up in a process of coming and going. They are, therefore, never stable and consequently never absolutely knowable except for the recognition of the constant change that is going on. The object itself can never become familiar to us because of its ever-changing nature. What of the process of change and the source from which all things come and to which they return? The process has only a degree of predictability and, therefore, it also maintains a contingent factor, which prevents us from establishing any familiarity. The source of all things is itself not knowable in any ordinary sense of the word and its unlimited nature makes it impossible for any conclusive familiarity to be declared. It is only our ignorance, our tendency to ignore the unknown factors, due to fears, attachments, or whatever, which lead us to set up a relationship of assumed familiarity. This relationship first of all provides us with a false sense of security but sooner or later develops into ingratitude, insensitivity, unawareness, laziness, boredom, and contempt.

Becoming aware of the links between the body and thought processes is a part of consciousness of the fifth realm, combining physical movement with breath exercises whilst at the same time being aware of thought patterns. Another way of saying the same thing is to mix the body movement with emotive expression (feelings) and directed intellect (mantras and affirmations).

In order to exercise the synthesizing skills of the fifth dimension we go out and about seeking knowledge, which may be through physical experience or other various forms of gathering knowledge. It is possible, however, that we just collect experience after experience, knowledge upon knowledge and do not pass on what we have gained or share the discoveries of our experiment of life. It is as though we are afraid of being empty and proudly hold on to our knowledge and await recognition for something, which we keep hidden. What we have yet to learn by diving deeper into the nature of the fifth realm is that we are constantly being refilled. It is the nature of things that when we give out something, a space is created for more to come in. Even if we believe we have so little to give, the giving of it opens up the possibility for more experience to flow in and more learning to take place.

Teaching is the principle means for the flowing of all kinds of knowledge and is, therefore, the principle means of learning too. There are many formal and informal methods of teaching and learning. We all teach by our example and learn from the examples of others, only we are not conscious of this process. Becoming conscious of all that takes place in the flow of knowledge in the combined processes of teaching and learning is what brings us to the more than human plane of being. The fifth dimension is what makes it possible to turn an experience into a thought and a thought into an experience. Anyone who has understood this will have a natural capacity to teach and anyone who wants to understand and master this process should get involved in teaching.

Sounds

The number 5 is basically about communication and, therefore, all sounds will have some impact on the development of this dimension. As we become more centered, we also become more connected. Then, being more connected, we are able to hear more clearly. We increase our awareness of what we say and how we say it, as well as of what others say and how they say it. A most effective way of improving communication skills is to listen more, and this includes listening to yourself, especially listening to your listening. In order to become aware of the many aspects of sound it can help to take one word or phrase and repeat it over and over again. You can also learn to notice the words you repeat most often and ask yourself what kind of identification of self-identity is implied. There are words for different moods but there is also a vast range of moods that may lie hidden behind any one word. Sensitivity to the feelings behind words can be cultivated by keeping the spoken word the same whilst varying the emotional expression of the word. This is one of the values of mantra, to be able to express every emotion through a simple sound.

The sound HA has a very throaty quality to it and can be stimulating to the thyroid glands, which are associated to the fifth chakra in the neck area. Other variation of the HA sounds that are often present in mantras include:

HO, HAM, HUM, HUNG

These sounds are linked to the sense of celebration – Halleluiah – as well as the moment of meeting, merging, and identifying with the other (friend, partner, or God).

All expressions of polarization and all forms of linguistic opposites are held distant yet also held in relation through the properties of the numbers 5 and 10. The totality is a self-regulating unity whose ways and means we hardly guess. It is often said that cannot be spoken about and yet is constantly pointed to by the paradoxical use of language. Well, it is what we experience and so it is no surprise that our language born of experience tells something even without trying to tell it.

The number 5 is the experience of being at the meeting place between the two sides of an hourglass – while the sand moves through into one side the air is moving through to the other. It is in the place where they meet and mingle that creative sound is generated. The two sides of the hourglass represent the two sides of each of the polarized dimensions.

Affirmations

I am my word. This is the final affirmation. What is the use of affirmative words if we are not ready to identify with them? State your case then affirm that you are the very words you have just spoken.

Every word we speak is either the expression of an established habit, whether desirable or not, or it is the expression of something new, which is trying to be born, and something old, which is dying. Speech that is habitual is often a semi-conscious process of repeatedly giving birth to the same self over and over again. Repeating a prayer every day can become a habit or it can be the daily birth of a renewed self; the difference is decided by the mood and awareness with which we speak out.

Habit tends to become empty of mood and empty of our full presence. In habitual action and speech we work in a form of automated existence while the major proportion of our awareness is buried in the subconscious occupied with other things. The body generally benefits from the routine of habitual and organized living, presuming the habits adopted are healthy. Some habits, however, are extremely detrimental to the body and accelerate the degenerative process into chaos and untimely destruction. The spirit on the other hand appears to get stuck when it tries to organize its understanding into a cohesive system. The spirit-mind is expansive and potentially infinite. It knows no restraint and, in fact, does not realize the suffering that it imposes upon itself by attempting to bring order into realms that have an order beyond our reasonable understanding.

Here again is the paradox that while in the realms of the spirit there is no order that we can declare with any certainty, it is nonetheless filled with multiple holograms of any order we may look to find there; this is the astral fascination. The whole situation is made complex and paradoxical by the fact that these two polarities of body and spirit are intimately linked to each other via the interface of the fifth realm with its 5 senses. With words we bring together all the qualities of the pairs of numbers:

- The primary information that directs the intention is 1 and 9.
- The secondary information that gives form and structure, like grammar, is the 3 and 7.
- The flow of energy that empowers the word is 2 and 8.
- The presence of breath and awareness is 4 and 6.
- In every word we speak there is a mixture of all these ingredients. The sum total of this in its synthesis is the 5, while the listening is the 10.

Though I may repeat the same word with every breath, the self that is born out of that will depends on the quality of consciousness of the eight dimensions (1, 2, 3, 4 and 6, 7, 8, 9) and their cohesive interaction in the center. Were I alternatively to move into diversity and expansiveness, never to repeat the same combination of words more than once and to keep inventing new words, the self that is created will still be as profound and full or empty as the reflective boundary that becomes my world, the boundaries of my language. This boundary is, of course, the boundary of my listening, especially how completely I hear my own words.

Finally let's be clear that the word that created us must one day be returned. It may be taken or we may voluntarily give it. This difference is all the difference there is. After this has been decided then there is no difference.

Section four

Chapter 27

Applied numerology: the application of number awareness

Warning: Since any number is always the same no matter what situation we find it in, then to speak of number is somehow also to say the same thing in so many different ways. This section deliberately states and restates the basic virtue of numbers.

Earlier in the book it was suggested that the importance of numbers in our life, like the ground on which we walk, is taken so much for granted that their significance is concealed by their familiarity. But why should we make any effort to become aware of numbers?

When we leave this life we pass through a stage when our life movie flashes before us. The next stage is when we then pass judgment on our life. Here it is quite likely that we become fascinated by our successes and failures and become trapped in what are known as the astral planes. If, however, we are blessed with the clarity of awareness then we can break through the clouds of the astral planes to arrive on the lonely mountain peak. There, at the gateway to the transcendent, we will not be asked to explain or justify ourselves or to display all our great and terrible deeds or to convince the heavens why they should or should not let us in. No, we will be asked only one thing ... "what is your number?" Don't wait until then to find out. It is only whilst alive in the human form that we can make this discovery and end the climbing and falling game once and for all. Here on earth we can collect the true treasure of our spiritual essence, remember who we really are, and go home with grace and dignity.

The heavens above us, like the ground upon which we walk, are constituted from a basic or primal substance. The dust of the heavens is numbers. What we build up from the ground, whatever its culturally modified form, is basically made up of the one dust of the earth and whatever vision we bring down from the heavens is also constituted out of one common substance; it is number. In the heavens this base is an abacus, from Abba meaning father grid, whereas on earth the base is termed a matrix, from Mata meaning mother grid. Whatever we call them they are, in fact, identical in essence, "as above, so below."

Numbers are a personal and global language through which we can discover our relationship to all things including the Divine. Numbers give the gridlines on the multi-dimensional map of consciousness; they show the way we need to go and the work we must do. At the same time, however, numbers might appear decorated as guards on the paths we are not yet ready to follow. Each number is only valid and bears meaning by its relation to all the other numbers and so everything in the universe is meaningful only by its relationship to the whole. The communication between the parts honors the interdependent relationship. The study of life through numbers and numbers through life (in other words demystifying the mystery of numbers) brings us into the conscious experience of the underlying beauty of the dynamic connections within ourselves and to the world and wider universe.

Numbers have their own qualities but are so abstract that they are only made visible when attached in a particular context, like one object, one person, one day, and so on.

The art of applied numerology is to be able to extract the basic quality of the number from its concrete and specific environment so that it can be recognized in all its other manifestations. This changing environmental context does not only refer to different times and spaces but also different dimensions of reality. So, for example, in simple terms we can start with the physical manifestation such as three people and examine the type of interactive life game that a group of three people are naturally inclined to engage in. Then moving on to the emotional content of these three people's experience that arises from the triangulation we could explore the energetic processes that take place between father, mother, and child, or persecutor, persecuted, and rescuer. After that there might be the mental construct of 3 within a person's logical processes including the equation of A + B = C. Then going into a deeper psychological level we might hear a person talk about a theme that clearly links to the number 3, such as feeling like a victim (two against one) and equality or self-respect as in an equilateral triangle.

So clearly the art and application of number awareness to life requires developing the capacity to move between different levels such as physical, energetic, behavioral, mental, psychic, thematic, symbolic, and conceptual. Then to move the awareness of number through different moments of time as well as different locations in the spatial environments and still be able to identify the expression of the number in that new context. The possible variations are immense yet the number remains clearly and distinctly the same number. This integrity of the numbers can actually facilitate the shift through different dimensions. If we have taken the numbers as our essential reference, if we have learnt to be at home with the numbers, then the numbers become a point of stability in every case; they are a homing signal. Once you learn to recognize the number wherever it appears you can then develop an intuitive sense of selecting the contextual level and its appropriate language at which you wish to respond to any situation. The skill of number awareness is to link particular occasions of the ordinary world with the world of complete abstraction where the common or global language of number exists. The result of this meeting could be described as an alignment between heaven and earth, the universal and the individual. It reinforces the capacity to transfer significant insights drawn out from one environment and to offer them into another completely different one where you think it might be useful. The first section of this book has done that by taking the example of the lives of the ten Sikh Gurus and relating them to the ten Spiritual Bodies. The common ingredient that made this possible was the number. In the next chapter we will look at another example by applying number awareness to the comparison of the body organs and the rooms in a house with numbers as the uniting link.

Applied numerology is a sophisticated method of taking consciousness of the given laws that are innate within all things and realizing these as primal laws that cannot be changed but which can be aligned with or struggled against. Take, for example, the law of cause and effect. It does not so much give us a choice about the primary cause but leaves it open for us to choose how we respond or react to the effects. Our responses are themselves further effects. All we ever do is play around with effect yet we rarely manage to take full advantage of this law of cause and effect because we do not respect the ultimate cause. By this I refer to the unknown cause that all philosophies and religions speculate about but struggle to live by.

The application of number awareness to any system or model, including the apparently complex human being, provides an intelligent and adaptable insight into the essential components. It allows first the deconstruction and then the reconstruction of a wide variety of models, each a diagnostic window into a different facet of the system being studied. This activity gives an intuitive depth to any situation and maximizes the possibility of a generous and prescriptive response.

Numbers are the spiritual ground of all souls, the footprints of the Divine, the backbone of our life, the bricks with which we build our structural identity, and the essential and common ingredient in every spiritual philosophy. Therefore, they are also the abstract basis for all spiritual practice and the difference between vertical and horizontal living. Numbers are the spiritual reference in a material world. Alone they are very abstract and difficult to relate to. But, when recognized and respected in the world, numbers provide a solid and enduring reference for all our understanding.

Every situation, group, or person is like a puzzle, each one a different picture. If you could look on the blank side of each piece of the puzzle you would find numbers. And if you looked at both sides of puzzle after puzzle you would begin to recognize a consistency of association of certain aspects of imagery with certain numbers, as well as certain patterns of how the numbers fitted together. Eventually you would become so familiar with these patterns that if you were given a puzzle and only had access to the blank side with its number and no idea of the picture, you would nonetheless be able to put together the picture perfectly. The objective, however, is not to put together puzzles without access to the imagery. In real life situations you have this access but it is often a picture with pieces missing or in the wrong place or still loose by the side and not fitted into the whole picture. With training you can turn over a few pieces and recognize by the numbers underneath where these pieces fit or what pieces might be missing.

When reading someone's date of birth we are in a position to help him or her reshuffle the pieces of their puzzle. Our study of numbers does not give the right to impose but merely to propose alternative perspectives. We might ask "did you try thinking of it like this?" Or we could point out areas that don't make sense and ask the individual in question to take another look to see if they can recognize the incoherence. If so, are they then prepared to dismantle this area of the puzzle to get a better fit? For the missing pieces, remembering that the numbers give us a general clue as to what they might be, we will have an idea of what kind of questions to ask in order to bring out an awareness of these missing pieces. Furthermore, we are equipped to help the individual to get a sense of where these newly discovered pieces fit, although it is usually appropriate to let them first try to work that out themselves, giving intuitive clues where it feels appropriate.

The rest of this section applies number awareness to the rooms of a house, the organs of the body, the five senses, language, money, life cycles, and relationships.

Chapter 28

The numbers behind the puzzle: the grid of nine

3 is the number that makes construction possible and, therefore, the trinity is the base of several religious creation myths. Repetition is the activity that builds up the construct from the base of 3 and the most potent repetition is multiplication. 3×3 is the first constructive multiplication that produces more than repetition by addition.

$1 + 1 = 1$ and $1 \times 1 = 1$

$2 + 2 = 4$ and $2 \times 2 = 4$

$3 + 3 = 6$ but $3 \times 3 = 9$

Hence with 3×3 there is a greater magnification. It may be applied microscopically or telescopically but it does allow a more penetrative insight. Furthermore, it gives x-ray awareness. The subtle and invisible becomes present for us and we perceive the nine integers that are normally beyond our grasp. What was a vaguely intuited abstraction becomes something that has actuality. In mathematics the numbers are considered to be the only things that have real integrity and substance.

This deeper vision is outlined below in the descriptions of the eight different sets of 3 that are contained within the grid of nine squares. It will be noticed that there are horizontal, vertical and diagonal sets of three numbers each.

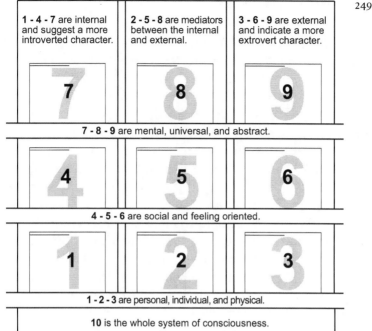

1 - 4 - 7 are internal and suggest a more introverted character.	2 - 5 - 8 are mediators between the internal and external.	3 - 6 - 9 are external and indicate a more extrovert character.
7	8	9

7 - 8 - 9 are mental, universal, and abstract.

4	5	6

4 - 5 - 6 are social and feeling oriented.

1	2	3

1 - 2 - 3 are personal, individual, and physical.

10 is the whole system of consciousness.

Horizontal lines

The horizontal relationship is one of progressive movement from beginning to end. There are three steps to this linear development. They represent three phases of a seed's journey towards multiplication of self, from one to many (1 to 9).

1, 2, 3 is the journey from seed to branching out.

4, 5, 6 is the stage of the bud becoming the flower.

7, 8, 9 is the final stage of departure from the bush as the many new seeds are thrown to the mercy of a random law of survival.

1, 2, 3: these first three numbers are indicative of the will to individual existence being realized. In the date of birth they are very personal and practical numbers. They relate to the will to act, the desire that empowers, and the action itself. These three numbers could be said to link to the three gunas, which are qualities or modes of energetic states that make up the fundamental forces in nature. They are tama, satva, and raja. Tama is the state of inertia, satva is the state of purity or innocence, and raja is the state of dynamic activity. In the mental plane this would be in the order 9, 8, 7.

4, 5, 6: these second three numbers represent the development of our social and emotional being. Beyond the individual or personal life there is the sense of others and community, though this is not a global or universal quality; it tends to be more localized. The detached clarity and search for the truth is the expression of number 4 and provides the capacity for neutral thinking. Fearlessness and the search for beauty that is part of the Arcline or halo relates to the number 6. The relationship between this inner and outer sensitivity is mediated in social intercourse by the nervous system, which corresponds to the number 5.

7, 8, 9: the third three numbers indicate the development of our awareness towards a higher self (or another self – God). It is with these numbers in the date of birth that there will be an inclination to global or universal thinking and feeling. This can show itself as being spaced out and very dispersed on the personal level unless some of the lower numbers are present for a person.

7 is the son, the ego-hero on his quest for the treasure, the questioning mind.

8 is the mother, infinity, and the ocean of empty time that the hero must traverse.

9 is the father, home, the higher self, and the completion of an intention.

9, 8, 7 is sometimes interchanged with 1, 2, 3 as father, mother, and son.

Note: The Holy Ghost is actually number 6, the aerodynamic presence of grace – a wind that blows where it will. Therefore, the trinity of Father, Son, and Holy Ghost is the numbers 9, 7, and 6. This is an unusual set of three numbers that are not evident in the grid of nine as being in any obvious triune relation. It can also be noted that the mother is ignored in this trinity.

Vertical lines

The numbers which lie on the same vertical lines will be found to vibrate at sympathetic or harmonic frequencies. Any activity in one of the numbers will then have a resonance in the other numbers in that vertical line.

1, 4, 7 are three levels of impulse, inspiration, and insight that are behind us.

2, 5, 8 are the process, interchange, and flow through which energy comes and goes.

3, 6, 9 are the physical action, the emotional presence, and the intelligence principles that pervade the environment around us, either as products of our existence or external influences upon our existence.

1, 4, 7: these three numbers are the sources of the generation of new levels of self-identity. Through each of these numbers a new level of being takes a hold of the individual. These numbers express the introduction of a new level of manifesting the life impulse. They are indicators of major motivational factors, reasons for being alive.

1 is a physical impulse indicating the will to survive.

4 is the feeling impulse known as inspiration, like the inner feeling of being in love.

7 is the development of inner vision, the ways that we put things together into an understanding from where we can again engage in the world. Here we produce assumptions and working hypotheses to motivate ourselves in going out and seeking proof.

When we return back to 1, 4, or 7, rather than being motivated from them, sometimes we withdraw from the world either through 1, sleep, 4, meditation (inner prayer), or 7, inner visualization (fantasy and astral travel).

2, 5, 8: these numbers are the mediating channels through which the impulse can find its way into some form of manifested action. They express our bonding, internally to the physical impulse, inspiration, or inner vision, or externally to the results of our actions, the romance of presence, or the mountains of our philosophical aspirations. Through these numbers we will experience the tensions of the push and pull between inner drives and outer influences.

It is the mediating aspect of these numbers that makes experience possible. 2 is related to the physical experience of need, 5 is the movement into or away from social intercourse (the words with which we carry our inspiration to others), and 8 is our spiritual and mental vitality which makes dreams possible. It is the wisdom or the power (money) that fuels our vision. 2, 5, 8 can be experienced as the emptiness of unstructured chaos or the fullness of pure bliss. Number 2 is the Negative Mind as the instinctive chaos or our craving and hunger as well as the breath, which offers the rhythmic link into infinity. 5 is a most significant number since it is the only location where polarities meet together within one human being. This is represented by the mouth (feminine) and the tongue (masculine) and explains why it all started with a word. 8 is the infinite ocean of chi from which we all drink and in which we all swim; the pasture of common passion and the fountain of compassion.

3, 6, 9: these three numbers are the final outcome or expressions of each level initiated at 1, 4, 7. They are also external forces that introduce us to each level from without as opposed to within (as happens at 1, 4, 7). 3 is a physical activity that may be an extension of a physical impulse from 1 through 2, or it may be an action (such as an imitation) which then travels back through 2 to effect the formulation of further inner impulses. 6 is the expressions of beauty, art, justice, and social freedom that may follow (through 5) from inner inspiration or that may enter into us (through 5) to touch us in an inspiring way. 9 is the general or universal principles that are perceived in coded forms in our inner visions and symbols.

The diagonal lines

The central significance of the number 5 and the complementary aspects of the number 10 are further understood by reflection on the diagonal lines, all of which pass through 5. The horizontal line of 4, 5, 6 and the vertical line of 2, 5, 8 also pass through the 5 giving a total of four axes of consciousness, four pairs of numbers that revolve around the central hub of 5.

1, 5, 9: these three numbers are the central axis of the soul and spirit. They indicate the journey of the soul from being seeded in the physical body to the maximum expansion of consciousness and self-completion. Number 1 is the will to exist as an individual self, complemented by the number 9, which is the carrier of the finite individual until it achieves self-mastery, right understanding, and realizes its identity as a part of the absolute whole. 5 is the transformational gateway or threshold between the personal and the impersonal.

3, 5, 7: the physical body and its five senses is the means for right action and right understanding. Right action is the creation of habits that serve us rather than habits that we serve. Right understanding is to be able to see the natural order and let it inform our contextual expression in daily behavior.

These numbers represent full recognition of our individuality, complemented by full recognition of all individual sentient beings. 3 is the sense of equality implying not only shared success but also shared pain. This relates to 7 as the expression of mercy and forgiveness for all and a sense of fairness, self-respect, and dynamic optimism of the Positive Mind of number 3. 7 is the inner thought pattern while 3 is the outer behavior pattern and 5 is the two-way communication between these. 7, 5, 3 connects to the trinity of perceiver, perceiving, and perceived or the looker, the looking, and the looked at. It is also the trinity of Generate, Organize, and Destroy and Brahma, Vishnu, and Shiva.

You are encouraged to begin to build up your own dictionary of numbers. A very helpful practice would be to draw out the grid of nine squares again and again, inserting a range of information about each number in the relevant boxes. Here is an example to close this chapter.

7 · Judgment · Mercy · Vision · Understanding · Knowledge · Status · Positive thinking · Revenge or forgiveness	8 · Power · Wisdom · Purity · Money · Force · Healing · Death · Authority · Compassion · Negative thinking · Discernment or solemness/ seriousness	9 · Calmness · Impatience · Subtle · Vague · Persevering · Enduring · Mastery · Integrity · Completion
4 · Trust · Doubt · Choice · Indecision · Neutrality · Inspiration · Service	5 · Teaching · Learning · Transformation · Communication	6 · Fear · Faith · Freedom · Justice · Beauty · Silence · Suspense · Responsibility
1 · Individuality · Self-will · Survival · Humility · Originating · Seed · Intent · Intensity	2 · Duality · Sorrow · Attachment · Loyalty · Need · Negation · Passion	3 · Equality · Fairness · Respect · Deserving · Affirmation · Positive action

Chapter 29

The mansion of consciousness

The way to learn about the numbers is to meet them again and again in many different settings. This section and the chapters within it do exactly this. Working with the general idea that consciousness is all pervading and that it can be mapped most deeply yet most simply with the numbers, we will take a look at a few more life examples through the window of the grid of nine squares.

We simultaneously inhabit several spaces at the same time. One is the physical body; through this we live in the external space of our environment and this outer expanse reflects the nature of the inner psychic realms. The body is a temple and our house is a body. Both contain an organization of areas that together make the whole system function more or less effectively. In one, the areas are called organs and in the other, they are called rooms. Numbers provide the lowest common denominator that enables us to identify the links between these two different systems and by this link, to understand each one more deeply.

Your environment, especially your home, reflects your physical, emotional, and mental state of affairs. When things are well placed at home it is easy to find your way around, to find the exits and entrances, and to feel comfortable enough to relax.

Your work is to identify the parts of each room (especially in your inner life) that have been ignored or over-emphasized and find ways to introduce some meaningful change. In the external world you may not have a basement in your house but there will be a cupboard, garage, box, or even a neighbor that provides that location in your life. Likewise, with each of the other rooms, identify the issues related to each number and find in your world where the corresponding space is located and then decide if you would like to introduce some changes.

Each room contains a treasure but it is often buried under a pile of junk or it may be something so obvious that you take it for granted. It can also happen that you try to accomplish something in one room that would be better accomplished in another. In a small house one room has to take the place of several but it can still be helpful to have some clarity about each aspect of your consciousness and the different spaces within one room.

The following chart (see next page) is just an example of the correlation that can be found between the rooms of the house and the organs of the body. The principles that have been applied here can be developed in several directions, both in terms of diagnosing and helping the person or the building. It is most valuable to maintain an awareness of the relationship between the building and the people who manifest their presence within it. The number arrangement used is the magic square in which each line adds up to 15.

Note: The gall bladder is not in the grid but stands outside. It has the qualities of the number 10, that is the sum of the whole.

The garden can be included in this grid in several ways. One method is to extend the grid to cover the whole plot of land, which may contain the house and garage as well as the front and back gardens. Another method is to consider the nature or use of the garden and determine if it is an extension of one of the areas indicated. For example, a vegetable garden is like an extension of the kitchen (number 8) while a flower garden might be an extension of a meditation space or reception area (numbers 4 and 6).

Large Intestines 4	**Spleen and Bones** 9	**Bladder** 2
· shock absorbers that assimilate and eliminate, the dumping ground, receiving garbage, storing and eliminating.	· produces blood, the transporter of energy, the distributor, influencing the center.	· stores overflow and fluid secretions, eliminates fluid wastes, regulates vaporization.
Reception Room	**Bedroom**	**Bathroom**
· living room, inner garden (flora), the area where energy is received and assimilated once it enters the house.	· place of rest and recuperation where we rest and regenerate our inner resources; the fountain of wealth - it is the father.	· cleansing with water and eliminating. The area where there is necessary drainage but where there can be other losses also; too much / too little.
Small Intestines 3	**Liver and Nervous System** 5	**Heart and Muscles** 7
· heat and digestion, trusted with the riches. The safe keeper, assimilating, separating, and redistributing.	· regulates the metabolism. The strategic leader, dwelling place of soul.	· keeping order, officiating over circulation. Controller, conductor of the other players - team leader, organizing influence.
Games Room	**Hallway**	**Study / Office / Balcony**
· can include cooking area of kitchen. The play area where excessive entertainment may be burning up the money or objects may hold it stagnant.	· the overall regulation of energy depends on the state of the hallways, corridors, stairways, and thresholds between spaces.	· administrative area (where you keep your check books, bills, and accounts), for overseeing the cash flow.
Kidneys and Body Fluids 8	**Stomach** 1	**Lungs, Skin and Glands** 6
· store of chi, the energetic workers, regulating the fluid, storing the vital energy.	· first entry of food to inner body, accumulating and supplying, rotting and ripening.	· airing and refreshing, the receiver of pure chi, interpretation and conduct of official jurisdiction - natural sense of justice.
Kitchen / Food Store	**Entrance**	**Art / Music Room**
· store of energy, water flow, where energy is transformed to nourish the household; the waterfall of wealth - it is the mother.	· and foundations, basements where money/energy comes in and out, watering the latent potentialities that reside there.	· meditation space, an added presence, breathing of the walls. A sacred area where grace is acknowledged and thanks offered (lady luck, Guru's Grace - all is just).

10 is the Gall Bladder which governs the overall metabolism. 10 is also the whole house.

Problems at home

The grid of nine squares can then be used to represent some of the problematic manifestations of energy in a house.

Note: The grid layout here represents an organic spiral of the numbers. Different arrangements can be utilized for different purposes of diagnosis.

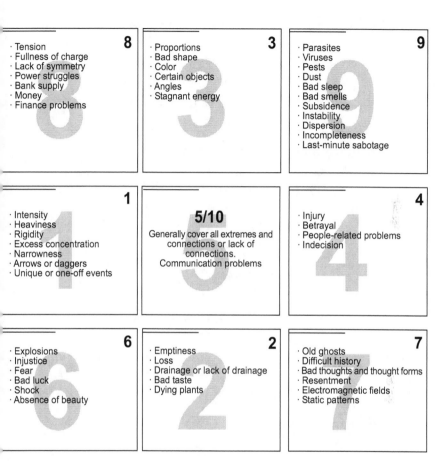

· Tension
· Fullness of charge
· Lack of symmetry
· Power struggles
· Bank supply
· Money
· Finance problems

8

· Proportions
· Bad shape
· Color
· Certain objects
· Angles
· Stagnant energy

3

· Parasites
· Viruses
· Pests
· Dust
· Bad sleep
· Bad smells
· Subsidence
· Instability
· Dispersion
· Incompleteness
· Last-minute sabotage

9

· Intensity
· Heaviness
· Rigidity
· Excess concentration
· Narrowness
· Arrows or daggers
· Unique or one-off events

1

5/10

Generally cover all extremes and connections or lack of connections.
Communication problems

· Injury
· Betrayal
· People-related problems
· Indecision

4

· Explosions
· Injustice
· Fear
· Bad luck
· Shock
· Absence of beauty

6

· Emptiness
· Loss
· Drainage or lack of drainage
· Bad taste
· Dying plants

2

· Old ghosts
· Difficult history
· Bad thoughts and thought forms
· Resentment
· Electromagnetic fields
· Static patterns

7

Problem solving is not just about clearing away stagnant or undesirable energy but how to do so more economically and where reasonable, to transform it, recycle it for other uses or to exchange it for another manifestation of energy (trading). The recycling approach will also have the effect of confronting the primary cause of the problem. We would profit from remembering that problems are not always to be solved. One of the biggest problems is that we are too busy trying to solve problems. Death is inevitable and struggle helps us grow. The struggle caused by problems and the endless, insurmountable struggle to solve them is more interesting than all the solutions we can come up with. Some struggle, however, is more useful than others and, therefore, it requires an intuitive approach to identify creative tensions and maintain a moving equilibrium; an appropriately balanced flow of energy.

Example of tools for sorting out your own house

Note: A different grid arrangement is given below according to the theme of tools for sorting out your own home.

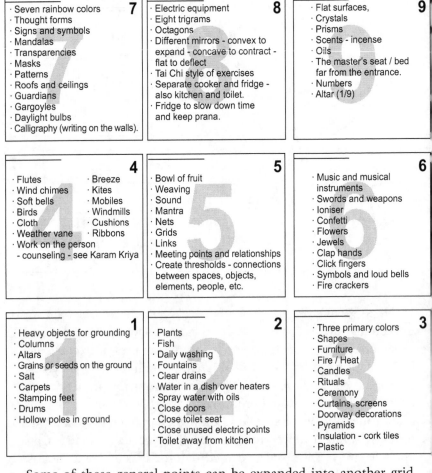

7
· Seven rainbow colors
· Thought forms
· Signs and symbols
· Mandalas
· Transparencies
· Masks
· Patterns
· Roofs and ceilings
· Guardians
· Gargoyles
· Daylight bulbs
· Calligraphy (writing on the walls).

8
· Electric equipment
· Eight trigrams
· Octagons
· Different mirrors - convex to expand - concave to contract - flat to deflect
· Tai Chi style of exercises
· Separate cooker and fridge - also kitchen and toilet.
· Fridge to slow down time and keep prana.

9
· Flat surfaces,
· Crystals
· Prisms
· Scents - incense
· Oils
· The master's seat / bed far from the entrance.
· Numbers
· Altar (1/9)

4
· Flutes   · Breeze
· Wind chimes   · Kites
· Soft bells   · Mobiles
· Birds   · Windmills
· Cloth   · Cushions
· Weather vane   · Ribbons
· Work on the person
  - counseling - see Karam Kriya

5
· Bowl of fruit
· Weaving
· Sound
· Mantra
· Nets
· Grids
· Links
· Meeting points and relationships
· Create thresholds - connections between spaces, objects, elements, people, etc.

6
· Music and musical instruments
· Swords and weapons
· Ioniser
· Confetti
· Flowers
· Jewels
· Clap hands
· Click fingers
· Symbols and loud bells
· Fire crackers

1
· Heavy objects for grounding
· Columns
· Altars
· Grains or seeds on the ground
· Salt
· Carpets
· Stamping feet
· Drums
· Hollow poles in ground

2
· Plants
· Fish
· Daily washing
· Fountains
· Clear drains
· Water in a dish over heaters
· Spray water with oils
· Close doors
· Close toilet seat
· Close unused electric points
· Toilet away from kitchen

3
· Three primary colors
· Shapes
· Furniture
· Fire / Heat
· Candles
· Rituals
· Ceremony
· Curtains, screens
· Doorway decorations
· Pyramids
· Insulation - cork tiles
· Plastic

Some of these general points can be expanded into another grid. Obvious examples would be color, electrical equipment, flat surfaces, shapes, rituals, music and sounds, plants, animals, weapons, signs and symbols, and working on the person. By a combination of your own research, intuition, and the utilization of the numbers as a cross-referring tool, it will be possible to build up a large number of various grids for different fields of specialized application of some of these general tools. This is what creates the expertise of color therapists, aromatherapists, herbalists, etc. It is legitimate to choose your own areas of specialized interest and knowledge according to your own constitution. If you go into it in a complete way you will still touch the whole.

- Whichever numbers appear in the person's date of birth, special attention is to be paid to the themes corresponding to these areas of the home or organs of the body. Sometimes a certain number seems to be dominant in the date of birth, either through repetition or because it just seems to be the number that talks the loudest.
- Each aspect of the date of birth can also be related to specific rooms. The day relates to the kitchen and bathroom, the month relates to the playroom and the study/office, the last two digits of the year relate to the entrance and the bedroom, and the full year of birth relates to the reception room, guest room, and sanctuary. The total number of your date of birth corresponds to the corridors and connecting spaces.
- Following the above approach you can try to investigate whether the energy of the numbers of the date of birth is influencing the organs. The day governs the kidneys and bladder, the month affects the small intestine and heart, the last two digits of the year influence the spleen and stomach, the full year relates to the large intestine and lungs while the total date of birth is in relation to the liver and gall bladder. So, for example, a person born in the eighth month is likely to have a strong heart while a person born in the second may have to be careful of energy depletion in relation to the heart or small intestine.
- The absence of certain numbers in the date of birth might suggest rooms or organs that are ignored or not given enough attention in the overall flow of energy.

Some general points in relation to applying cures

The grid of tools is not a comprehensive list and should not be interpreted too rigidly. It does, however, point the way toward the range of curative actions that can be taken on different levels. Let each situation, each place, and each person teach you more about the variety of problems and possible cures. When you meet a problem ask what has already been attempted as a solution and what the outcome was. In certain situations the presence of some tools can also be problems just as some problems may also be tools.

Solutions to problems are never permanent. The context in which they are applied includes the moment, the season, the people, and many other changing factors. Life is always in a transition from past to future. The artist is a negotiator and arbitrator between the changing and the unchanging as well as the changeable and unchangeable. The nature of the balance between these factors is that we human beings have a 40% influence while the other 60% is given by the heavens. It can help, therefore, to know something about the heavenly influences though this mostly requires as much an intuitive knowing as a scientific one. This also means that no cure is final and there will always be something we do not know or miss. There is never an adequate excuse for blaming the environment or others for things that we, ourselves, have to take responsibility for.

Many tools and the cures on offer are also bound up with cultural perspectives and values but the deeper cures are not culturally bound. As is suggested in the section on numbers, it is possible to identify the common principle behind different forms of cures and then find a culturally relevant form of the same cure. This takes time and practice. Use a long-term preventive approach, as well as treating emergency symptoms in the short term. This also means that you do not just aim to solve the existing problems but that you consider the future. In addition to a preventive approach the importance of a future orientation is related to the fact that we are in a cybernetic relation to our environment. That is to say it is our own life impulse that provokes and creates the environments in which we can be reciprocally provoked to release and realize our innate potentialities.

Note: The diagrams above may give the impression that the relationship of each part to the other is static but this is not the case. There are creative and inhibiting interactions between various parts of the whole as well as a variety of relationships between different numbers, influenced by different arrangements of the grid. So a problem that is identified as a number 8 type of problem does not automatically call for a number 8 type of solution. Our attention, at least, needs to go to the numbers before and after the 8, which is the 7 and 9, as well as to the opposite number, which in this case would be the 2. By studying the parts and their relationships in detail you can return to a greater sense of the whole. Each area can itself be further detailed by the use of the same grid; this is the holographic principle. For example, take the aspect in area number 8, which relates to wealth and money. In addition to identifying the specific area of the house where the wealth corner may be, it is useful to consider each area of the house in relation to money.

Chapter 30

The five voices

The five pairs of numbers live in the body through the five elements and their associated five senses and organs. This section brings you into a new level of intimacy between your house and your body through the number pairs and the experience of the five senses and the five voices that speak through us.

In making yourself available to help someone through reference to numbers, including the numbers in their date of birth, you must use your voice to speak the numbers. In addition the person's own voice can give you a lot of information about how the numbers are manifesting in their life. By listening to the quality of their speech, both in terms of its mood and the content of their conversation, you can get a picture of what is happening within the inner and outer house and, therefore, give helpful feedback on each pair of numbers. When you can read the world and hear the numbers in all communication you will bow to the ingenuity of God's design. When you recognize these voices within yourself, then in just a few words you can offer a great gift to others.

The voice of numbers 1 and 9: foundation, basic substance

This voice is the essential matrix that is the skeletal framework, the basic backbone of all, the earth, dust, and rocks that provides the bricks. These numbers are the basement of the whole, the bones and feet that give the worldly and heavenly foundation, the pillars or columns, attic and chimney. Subsidence and sabotage might happen on or under the ground and will be related to geopathic stress, fault lines, and the quality of building materials. As the foundations of the body house, the bones also work with the spleen to produce the basic blood quality.

Related to the base numbers 1 and 9 are the stomach and the spleen. The stomach has the function of absorbing energy through the food and drink that you consume after birth and during life. Your stomach is a point of focus in which energy is gathered before being dispersed and distributed in various directions. It is also the first organ in your body to receive the food.

The first voice is primal and impulsive. Its objective is survival through the alchemic refinement of baseness into sophistication, lead into gold. It is an evolution from grunt to the sweetness of Guru. When you speak the language of the stomach and the spleen your conversation will be about giving and receiving nourishment. The internal process of gathering the substances and letting them rot in order to begin transformation starts in the stomach. Problems with the stomach can lead to impulsive eating and impulsive speech. When the stomach is too empty it may become even more primal and result in survival concerns, which could be an intimidating and forceful demand for some kind of nourishment. On the other hand, your will to survive can be weakened to a point where all motivation is lost.

The essential ingredients of your food intake contribute to make the essence and the lifeblood that has its source in the spleen. In this aspect your conversation might be about drawing out the essence in what other people are saying or only speaking the essentials. Again, however, to live only by the essence can lead to an inappropriate withering away of your more substantial qualities. The spleen is the foundation and your blood is the primal fluid, which carries messages of all kinds to all parts of the organism. In this sense the first voice is the foundational aspect of your conversation, though often ignored or taken for granted, it is the medium through which you carry subtle ideas and messages to others. It is the basic intent and lifeblood within all your other aspects of conversation. The pancreas also needs to be mentioned here as contributing to the enduring nature of the essence. It helps with the sugar balance and so the sweetness of speech and humility.

1/9 is smell and it is a good idea to smell food before you take it into your stomach. If the smell is agreeable then the food is right for you. The strongest and first impact upon entering a house is the smell. And you will find that you sleep better if the smell in your bedroom is light and pleasant. Smell is a primal sense and it stimulates the will to get somewhere, which is no different from the will to live. Through this sense the baby finds its mother and the mother knows her own baby, sometimes finding it so sweet that she has the impression that she wants to eat it. The sense of smell is more subtly expressed in our sense of direction, which is a mental as well as a physical sense. When you want to find your way it's often best to just follow your nose. In our behavior associated with smell there is a very primal expression of the individual's survival instinct. Yet when we are captured by a smell we will lose all sense of our individuality and become immersed in the outer realms, which are filled with the fragrance. Hence, in one moment smell is our very individual sense and in the next, we completely lose our sense of self through the sense of smell. Therefore, our sense of smell is also tied to our sense of what is most particular and individual about the other person.

The voice of numbers 2 and 8: force of bonding and separation

The infinite duality of these numbers provides the tension as cement, the life force that is the glue that holds the bricks together. They are the water supply and drainage, the body fluids. Each room of the house is like a body organ and these numbers are the flow of energy between them. Organically the building is influenced by the compass orientation of the entrances and exits and how they direct the flow of chi or water (flowing or stagnant). Biologically it refers to the fluid systems that are involved with cleansing – the lymphatic system, mucous systems, and the bladder and kidneys. There is a link to the doors and windows through which energy and fluids pass and all the passages in and out of the body.

Related to the energy numbers 2 and 8 are the kidneys and bladder. The function of your kidneys is to cleanse and purify the blood and this involves a constant flow of fluid and energy. Another important role of the kidneys is the energy they store that accumulates before birth during foetal development. The nature of the energy stored in the kidneys is like a reservoir of vital life supply, which is gradually used up during your life. Excesses, especially sexual, use up this energy very quickly and it is not easy to replenish this supply, though things like changes in diet or exercise can compensate for the emptiness.

The second voice is the one through which we cry out. It can be the voice of emptiness and longing or the voice of fullness and power. It is the language of the bladder and the kidneys. For example, conversations about your bank balance reflect the quality of the kidneys that act as a reservoir of the vital force. Cathartic conversations, through which you cleanse yourself of built up energy that waits for release, are also a part of the second voice. You can imagine the gates of a dam that often stand after a lake and every now and then they are opened and a flood of water comes pouring through. This last activity is especially reflected in the function of the bladder, which stores up the waste fluid until the moment comes for release. Sometimes your conversation will be like this – building up and emptying out. Too much release, however, leads to loss of energy and dehydration; you get tired and your words or your throat dries up. Release is not always the answer and the energy can be retained for other uses. Practicing certain sounds or breathing exercises can be a way to build up energy and vitality. As a result your conversation will also become more energized and can even be energizing for others. This then is the voice of healing and compassion.

2/8 is taste and links to the water element. How a person keeps their bathroom is the best statement about their taste. And, of course, the kitchen is all about cooking up the best tasting energy called food. Our sense of discrimination is closely linked to our sense of taste. These senses of taste and discrimination are most awake when there is something wrong rather than when things are

OK. A young baby, as it transits through the stage most influenced by this quality, will cry a lot if things are not well. The rest of the time the baby is happy to sleep or gaze into infinity. When food is well flavored with a mixture of different spices and herbs we do not distinguish the specific ingredients but simply feel our needs are being met. If, however, the combination does not result in a smooth blend then we clearly identify a range of unpleasant tastes. This discriminating faculty is no different when it comes to the realm of thoughts and concepts or music. When the mix is not working our sense of taste comes alive and guides us back to combinations within which we can once again lose ourselves and feel satisfaction. At the moment of satisfaction the pain of discomfort abates and our consciousness of taste merges into unity with what is being tasted. The water in our mouth is essential for the ability to taste our food.

The voice of numbers 3 and 7: form and function

Once we have the bricks and the life force we then set about, in three-dimensional space and with the seven colors, constructing the forms and shapes of our lives. These numbers provide the heat that holds our cultural images, the flames of our designs and appearance, the circulation of our symbols. They are the phantoms that inhabit our semi-autonomous and mechanical creations, our fantasies, and relate also to the garage, shed, car, and pets. It is at this level that major changes can be made to things like cultural forms, historical patterns/imprints, characteristic features, objects, colors, the placing of things and the influence of electromagnetic fields. The heart is strongly influenced by electromagnetic fields while the musculature of the body takes on the patterns of our habits and gives us our characteristic shapes.

The numbers of form and space, 3 and 7, relate to the small intestines and the heart. The heart is a structure designed to carry out a mechanical function but also to accumulate a store of energy during the pre-birth period. This is like a machine that stores energy, which is then released through the operating of the machine. Another manifestation of this stored up energy is heat, which is released when you feel warm-hearted to another person or when you feel other forms of heat such as anger. Whilst being in the magnetic field of your mother you also absorb magnetic energy, which is then expressed or released in certain patterns of thought and behavior after birth.

The third voice gives the rational control over your life energy. It creates and maintains the boundaries of your temporary identity known as the ego-mind. It is the voice of the fire element and so qualities such as humor or anger will also be a part of the third voice. Here you will speak the language of the small intestines and the heart. The small intestines assess the appropriateness of the food passing through and judge its value. It is a caring and attending attitude that can become over-reactive. Political correctness and its language game is an example of an attitude of social concern which has become over-reactive and excessively scrutinizes every word a person speaks for hidden values of prejudice or inequality, separating the good from the bad. A deficiency in the small intestines expresses itself in the victim consciousness, which then uses the politics of right and rights as a means to attack and defend. This is further exaggerated by the contribution of the heart, which assumes itself to be the autonomous king with all powers of control.

The heart's function is to introduce order and this is what gets expressed in your rational conversation. The heart operates like an overseer who monitors the program of your life and it is through the heart that you establish yourself as a witness to your life and to others. This does not so much refer to the physical eyes as the inner eyes of your mind. With these eyes you monitor and evaluate all that you can or will bring into your vision. As the observer you may range from qualities of judgment and punishment to understanding and kindness and this will be expressed in the nature of your conversation.

Another quality relating to the heart is the seeking and storing of knowledge and information. The muscles around the heart can become overburdened if you rely too much on knowledge. What is called the heart protector in Chinese medicine is related to the way you use knowledge or belief as a psychological defense line. In your conversation you may notice the ways in which you use your knowledge as a kind of armor or buffer against attacks from others.

Too much knowledge, however, also becomes a heavy burden and imprisons you in your own illusion of safety behind the bars of what you believe to be knowledge.

3/7 is sight and to be kind-hearted is to look upon all with a merciful and forgiving eye. Strangely the play area and office area look most natural when they are in a mess. The link with entertainment and the eyes is strong and obvious and the office is where you keep an eye on your affairs. Sight is the sense related to the fire element. Through our eyes we perceive and create shape, form, and color. Seeing is our most valued way of knowing and understanding, though it is also often the most deceptive. Seeing is our rationality and, therefore, our sense of ratio and, therefore, our faculty of judgment. The logic and grammar in language is an expression of our way of seeing and understanding. Sometimes our sense of understanding, linked to the fire element, extends itself beyond the rational and analytical toward a sense of warmth to another person. Seeing and understanding is another way of referring to our sense of meaning and purpose. It is our capacity to put things into place and, therefore, also gives us a sense of place.

The voice of numbers 4 and 6: freedom of presence

These are the numbers that give breath and consciousness to the spirits of the man-made world. They correspond to people, presence, respiration, breathing, porosity, permeability, wind, and atmosphere. Within the body system is the sense of touch and the sensitivity of the skin and the sophisticated chemistry of the glandular system.

Problems arise with underground cavities (trapped air pockets), movement of gases, and mineral deposits (6 being related to metals). Relating to the air element are the people whose presence lives, breathes, and moves in the house, their life events, objectives, tensions, illness, relationships, family roles, and attitudes. The body also hosts the presence of other beings in its large intestines and this organ, as well as the lungs, deals with the winds and gases. The skin is comparable to the walls of the house that also must breathe.

The numbers of presence, 4 and 6, are related to the large intestines and the lungs. The lungs are the medium through which you have a moment-by-moment encounter with your existence and the future. Through the breathing process, which begins after birth, you absorb energy from the atmosphere, not just in the form of oxygen but also from other people's emotions such as love and fear. The large intestines are the final organ of receptivity and assimilation. This part of the body acts as a host to many bacteria and functions according to our ability to host others as well as neutralize unhealthy attacks.

The fourth voice is the voice of the poet, warrior, and artist. It is sensitive to possibilities and it is future-oriented. It can be fearful or faithful, clear or confused. For a counseling conversation the large intestines are of particular interest since they function as the dumping ground for the waste produce before it becomes eliminated. Many counselors too easily limit their work to this function and simply act as the receiving bowl for the other person's junk without being sure of how to eliminate it afterwards. They dump it on another who acts as their dumping ground and so it goes on as we continue to pass a lot of junk amongst each other. Effective decision-making utilizes the function of the large intestines. If you can first gather up all the unnecessary items or issues and cast them into the dumping ground for elimination then what remains will be clear and decision will be easy.

It is the lungs that then take the responsibility and provide the energy to carry out the decisions and to exercise justice. It is in your lungs that the wounds of injustice are held and any associated pain that you may have will be expressed in your communication of hurt feelings. The quality of your lungs and the corresponding conversation will also express your capacity to trust and be present or of your doubt which leads you to be less present.

4/6 is touch and the lungs bring you an innermost touch of the outer world. The artistic or meditation area of your home is where you get in touch with yourself. The reception area is where you allow others to get in touch with you. Touch can range from a sword-like penetrating touch, which goes deep into the secret places within us, to an embracing touch that wraps itself around us as a blanket. The sword may be deadly or it may be healing like the surgeon's knife. The blanket may be safe and trustworthy or it may be suffocating and imprisoning. Sometimes we feel touched as if by a warm or cold wind which either goes right through us or tries to pick us up in its arms.

Along with the sense of touch comes our sense of beauty and wonder. A moment of beauty touches us deeply in hidden places and awakens a sense of inspiration from within. It is from the mysterious place of our inspiration that our sense of truth and justice manifests and guides our responses to the world around us. Otherwise everything is just a program of reactions. As justice is the beauty of events and beauty is the justice of events, so truth is the melody of events and melody is the truth of all things. Our sense of melody is our true common sense and is no different from our sense of humanity, our human nature. It is the sense of ourselves as human beings rather than simply creatures and, therefore, also the sense of the humanity in others (We-in-me and Thou-in-all).

The voice of numbers 5 and 10: fulfillment

The 5 and 10 give the all-encompassing medium for the other four levels to relate to each other; it is the connecting and communicating systems. The circumference is held by the number 10 while the number 5 is the central connection of all parts to each other. These numbers, therefore, are the whole house, the whole of you, which is more than the sum of the parts. They bring balance, synthesis, communication and regulate the process of change. Physiologically this is the nervous system and to some extent the glandular system, although that also plays a role on the fourth level.

All of the modifications of energy that take place in each organ are balanced by the function of the liver, which regulates the metabolism and transforms the energy. The gall bladder is related to the number 10.

The fifth voice is the sum total of the other four voices as they combine together in our on-going communication between each other. It is the voice of integration or exile. It is the voice with which we speak about the voice. The ability to converse in the first place is related to the liver, which governs the overall metabolism of your organic system and the flow of chi energy in all directions. A sluggish liver gives sluggish speech; you may feel tired, lazy, and unbalanced with a kind of stagnation. These issues would be the topic of your conversation and also influence the style of your speech. If the liver is functioning well you will feel centered and well regulated. On other occasions you may feel like a lot of transformation is going on in your life and you talk about change all the time. This reflects the activity of the liver to release stagnating blood for elimination of toxins and to rejuvenate the system with fresh blood. The liver is your only organ that can reconstitute itself and the practice of certain types of vocal exercises or meditations are designed to do this. This voice is the voice of flexibility and could be said to be like a chameleon, changing according to its environment.

The gall bladder is also linked to the fifth voice and has the function of maintaining the total balance of your organic system. This organ is associated with the quality of the number 10, which is the unity of all parts. This means that to speak with the consciousness of the gall bladder is to speak with your total self. It is an extra-ordinary organ, standing beyond the whole like the unit that transforms 0 into 10. Your speech may also be extra-ordinary and stand outside of the whole and you may not feel understood by others. It requires a lot of courage, or gall, to be whole and to wholly engage in life. Sometimes conversations about bravery are compensation for a lack of real courage while other times your talk about really doing and being what you are is a way of generating the courage to follow through in your life. All of this will be related to the condition of the gall bladder.

5 and 10 are related to the sense of sound. 5 is the speaking while 10 is the listening.

In the house it is the thresholds between the areas where the sound can be closed off or allowed through. Our sense of balance and harmony is the sense through which all other senses are regulated. Just as the ears contain the secrets of physical balance so our listening holds the secret of balance for the soul. A little known fact is that our third ear is made up of every hair on our entire body. Listening with our every hair brings us to the ultimate sense of wholeness and unity.

Application for the date of birth

There are several approaches to interpreting a person's date of birth in relation to the organs of the body and corresponding styles of speech.

- See Chapter 29 for the relation between the time cycles and organs.
- You may feel that one number is manifesting itself strongly in this person's life. This will be affirmed by inquiring into the health of the corresponding organ as well as by listening to the quality of the person's speech, both in terms of its mood and the content of their conversation.
- The absence of certain numbers in the date of birth might suggest organs that are ignored in the overall flow of chi.

So remember that the numbers give you a common link between the organs, the rooms of a house, the ten Spiritual Bodies, the ten Gurus, the sacred Mul Mantra, and the many themes discussed at various stages throughout this book.

A short note on the chakras

Since we are on the subject of the body and its mysteries we can take this opportunity to clear up any questions readers may have about the correspondence of the numbers and the ten Spiritual Bodies with the chakras.

The seven chakras are frequently thought of as the steps up the ladder of attainment and there is often a special significance given to the number 7 as if it stands out from the other numbers. In fact, each number is equally sacred and can manifest in equally mundane ways. The seven chakras are only symbolic of the journey and not the whole journey itself. As symbols they are signposts that point to something beyond themselves. Their colors and forms are projections, archetypal manifestations and not the essence. It is the numbers that are the building blocks for the images and structures of the chakras. The numbers are the permanent, invisible matrix while the chakra is a temporary constructed appearance. If you wish to study this relation in more detail then you can begin by exploring the relation of the chakras to the numbers in the following manner:

First chakra is composed of a mixture of qualities from the numbers 1, 2, and 3.

Second chakra from numbers 2, 3, and 4.

Third chakra from numbers 3, 4, and 5.

Fourth chakra from numbers 4, 5, and 6.

Fifth chakra from numbers 5, 6, and 7.

Sixth chakra from 6, 7, and 8.

Seventh chakra from 7, 8, and 9.

Chapter 31

Life stages and the passage through the ten Spiritual Bodies

We have the chance to evolve progressively through the qualities of each of the Spiritual Bodies as we pass through the life stages marked by the seven-year cycle. Upon reading through these stages it should become evident how each corresponds to each of the Bodies, from the first to the tenth. By the time we reach the Golden Years we might be lucky to have become a 10-in-1 being. More occasionally, but possible enough with the right application of consciousness and discipline, we could reach that integrated state earlier in life.

The solar and lunar cycles

"Three score years and ten" is 70 years and gives ten stages of 7 years each. These seven-year cycles also provide information about the numbers as the numbers provide information about each stage of life. Numbers will help us to understand the deeper significance of the seven-year cycle and show the relation between the solar and lunar cycles.

Life begins at the moment of conception. Since the period of ovulation follows the lunar cycle, then the period of gestation is, in fact, ten lunar months, not nine solar months. On this basis, let's call a lunar year ten lunar months. It can then be noted that nine lunar years are more or less equivalent to seven solar years. On investigation this last point will be found to be of great value in understanding human development. The significance is that each seven years we pass through the nine numbers.

The seven-year cycle starts with the earth element in the first seven years, the water element in the years 7 to 14, fire during 14 to 21, air between 21 to 28 years and ether through 28 to 35 years. Then the process returns and we meet the unresolved issues of our past as we go back through the air element from 35 to 42 years, fire in 42 to 49 years, water 49 to 56 years, earth 56 to 63 years and back to our final path in ether at 63 to 70 years.

The first seven years of life are very much a given thing, like the earth element. In those first seven years we are still in a certain sense under the protection of Mother Earth whose natural instincts within us are awakened or suppressed according to the type of relationship we have with other people, especially our personal mother and other women. From the age of 7 to 14 we are learning to master the water element in our lives and our relationship to masculine forces becomes more influential in our development. 14 to 21 is the period in which we really struggle to find our position and shape (culture) and life is catalyzed by fire. 21 to 28 is the beginning of taking life choices seriously, our teenage heroes lose their value and there is a turning inward.

The turning point of 28 is doubly significant because it is close to the cycle of Saturn, which makes for a sort of natural rebirth experience. 28 to 35 is a period of transformation. Sometimes a person feels their whole life is turned inside out and upside down. Life can teach us many lessons at this stage and we may well be teachers ourselves to the children in our families. During the years 35 to 42 our children and projects of life should be manifesting in such a way as to work back on us – perhaps making the past worthwhile, perhaps inhibiting our further growth and more subtle developments. In this period we meet the consequences of the decisions taken in the period 21 to 28.

42 to 49 is a period of success and status but also of resentment at all those obstacles that have stood in our way. Sometimes we feel that we have missed out on the fun and try to be teenagers again. At other times we may enjoy the position of the accomplished professional.

In the years 49 to 56 it is interesting to note how many people do not go on to grow into their spiritual path after 49. Instead they attempt to take a physical or psychological shortcut in this eighth period. What they do not realize until too late is that they are caught up in a cycle of eternal return. It is a mistake made by all systems that hold the seventh stage to be the highest attainment. We repeatedly make the blind jump into the seventh heaven and consequently experience many rude awakenings, finding ourselves not in heaven but immortal only through reincarnation. Hence, we arrive back in the constriction of the body and declare, in accordance with the separation produced by the Negative Mind, "oh no!" If, on the other hand, we are blessed to remain awake in consciousness after the age of 49 we may find ourselves breaking through the time cycle, which bounds all beings. We may then pass through a much more subtle form of completion (number 9) and emergence into a higher being (number 10). Experience is the teacher, so it is only through the cycle of many births that we cultivate the ability to give up our expectations and assumption of what is and what should be in order to discover what actually is. The years of 49 to 56 will then find us either as half asleep and vacant bodies living out the last years in absence more than in presence, or in renewed vitality where we break traditional boundaries and become teachers by example of our own life.

56 to 63 are years of completion and peace or frustration and irritation. The impatience stems from not having completed as well as the fact that at this age we begin to lose the faculties with which to finish our life projects. It is the ninth cycle and influences us to look towards the end of life, either in a restless or resignational manner or with a contented sense of fulfillment.

63 to 70 is especially the time for emergence into a higher personality, the unity of all the parts which is more than their sum. Known also as the second childhood, this tenth cycle may either be a reversion into the childhood that never really happened or an expansion into a realm of joy known only to a few. Either way, unless the soul has already abandoned its project at 49, the last years of life offers the opportunity or the trauma of a total breakdown of most, if not all physical, social/emotional, and mental limits.

The above descriptions of the life stages are brief but hopefully indicate an area well worth studying in greater depth, especially by observation of people of all ages. There are other cycles, which can have an influence such as 9, 11, 12, 18, and 36/37 years. For a beginner, however, it is best to become familiar with the seven-year cycle first.

When exploring the meaning within someone's date of birth it can be an added point of awareness to give consideration to the age of the person and where that places them in the seven-year stages. This will help you to be conscious of the kind of issues that are of predominant concern in this person's life at this stage.

We will again use the example of the date of birth date 14. 1. 1957.

Last two digits of the year of birth: 57 = 5 + 7 = 12 = 1 + 2 = 3

The last two digits of the year of birth (earth element and base numbers 1/9) govern the first and ninth cycle, which are the ages 1 to 7 and 56 to 63 years. During these periods of life the person with a number 3 will have a lot of fun, feel like a victim, or undergo some serious skill training. They will experience issues such as fairness or unfairness, respect or lack or respect, joy or repression of joy.

Day of the month: 14 = 1 + 4 = 5

The day of the month (water element and base numbers 2/8) governs the second and eighth periods, which are 7 to 14 and 49 to 56 years. In these periods the person with a number 5 will develop strongly in communication and either have a lot to say or feel that there is not the language to communicate adequately. The strength or weakness of the person will be in the voice.

Month: 1

The month of birth (fire element and base number 3/7) governs the third and seventh cycles, which are the ages 14 to 21 and 42 to 49 years. The person born in the first month and having a number 1 in this area will find these stages of life the most solitary.

Full year of birth: 1957 = 1 + 9 + 5 + 7 = 22 = 2 + 2 = 4

The full year of birth (air element and base numbers 4/6) governs the fourth and sixth ages of 21 to 28 and 35 to 42 years. The person with a number 4 in this area will find these years to be the most poetic, revolutionary and decisive.

Total date of birth: 14. 1. 1957 = 1 + 4 + 1 + 1 + 9 + 5 + 7 = 28 = 2 + 8 = 10

The total date of birth (ether element and base numbers 5/10) governs the fifth and tenth periods, 28 to 35 and 63 to 70 years. To have a total number of 10 radically increases the intensity of these years.

Another way to interpret the date of birth could be that a predominance of any number might indicate the tendency of the person to want to live in just that stage of life, no matter what age they are.

Section five

Chapter 32

Introducing
Karam Kriya

Because the psyche of the intermagnetic related personality at the collaborative time of interaction at the frequency in which the magnetic field inter-exchanges and inter-relates at the speed so provided by the neutral atmosphere of the planetary magnetic field is got to be under the circumstances an actoreactive relationship in which the neutral point and the nucleus has to be found. This is the law. This cannot be changed. This statement is forever. This is God. You have to memorise it, you have to understand it, you have to understand it forever. And you have to deal with that understanding all the time. Don't forget it.   (Yogi Bhajan)

This is a most profound statement, which is very difficult to understand; indeed it could take lifetimes. Yet the living of the wisdom it encompasses is an elementary reality to which even children have an innate inclination. It is an inclination that we live naively as children and, therefore, lose touch with as adults until the moment comes when we begin to reclaim our inner integrity. This inner integrity is always in a resonant harmony with universal integrity. The conscious meeting of God within and God without is an art and science that can be studied and practiced. Karam Kriya and the science of applied numerology are a unique yet global expression of this. By being introduced to the principles of Karam Kriya and applied numerology you are offered a path that is based in natural law and invites you to walk in the footprints of the Divine.

Yogi Bhajan's words refer to the unchanging law of cause and effect. This law can be respectfully and consciously worked with to adjust our psychic field by action and thought patterns in such a way as to harmonize the quality of the relationship between the individual (you and me) and the universal psyche. The difference between the individual, which is finite, and the universal, which is infinite, is neutralized by entering into the time stream at its own pace. It calls on its energetic flow to empower space to adjust its shape so that the lower and upper astral gates are unlocked. Essence can then converge to a unified point of self that remains stable in the overwhelming encounter with the Almighty One. We become a conscious 10-in-1 being where the all-pervading light of God focuses to a zero point within and our radiance shines through.

This is not going to change so we might as well come to terms with it and just get on with it.

The study of Karam Kriya is a journey, which will take you to a different state where you will discover the power of the word. Our language must be redefined so that we stop and listen again for we have forgotten how to do this; rather we interpret and filter what we hear. Numbers guide the way into a new territory with words and it is said that when you know the number of something you have mastery over it. To know the number is also to know the name.

This is for people who relate with love to the mystery of life and cultivate the art of living the paradox rather than trying to resolve it. It is for those interested in the magic that made man rather than man-made magic. It asks for the humility that few know unless they have passed the threshold of humiliation to a point where they recognize a deeper level of being that nothing and no one can crush. It is for anyone who is ready to take a good look at themselves and realize they do not need anybody to give them anything more than a pure mirror to their own essence. It is for those who are shocked and who do not yet know they are here to shock the world because it is their destiny to do so. It is not for the clever intellect. To get back to the fundamentals means becoming simple and totally available; it is like a seed bursting open and enjoying the awakening of its potential. Inside all of us lies the possibility of every virtue and every virus and a true understanding and respect of numbers provides the space in which virtue can unfold. The text of this book has worked with language and important concepts in some new ways that invite the reader to commit more consciously to the stirring of their soul.

Take for example the concept of immortality, a spiritual idea that suggests that we are all already immortal. Now, indeed, we have an opportunity for immortality but it is not guaranteed; in this we have been sold a lie. The universal soul is infinite but the individual soul is temporary. We can work to become an immortal being but we must apply ourselves. Karam Kriya is an invitation to align our earthly life with the divine DNA by attending to what goes on in between them – the space of effects, the shapes that change through time. But attending with a difference, attending in a way that involves much less of our own imposed ideas and projected fantasies about what we want and more in a way that involves listening.

This arena that is filled with many manifestations of information and energy, through the mediums of time and space, has a lot to tell us. But we are busy trying to tell it what we want instead of listening through it to what the abacus and matrix of all things want to create in and through us. In this space between the heavens and earth, above and below, we create many types of structures that act as vehicles or ships to take us across the ocean of life. The types of external environments we construct, as well as our interior psychological structures, use up the energy of time and kidnap our awareness. Small changes in structure may result in big changes to the quality of life experienced and appropriate structures can carry us towards the moment of our liberation. Thus in the practice of Karam Kriya we negotiate changing the designs of the shapes of our life. While the oriental art of Feng Shui focuses more on the external forms, the outer environment, Karam Kriya turns our attention to the shape of our lived behaviors, habit patterns, and the formation of our mental beliefs that stand behind them.

The intention is to align with primary intelligence rather than to impose our secondary intellect, which is a mere effect. In practice this often means negotiating an expression of the balance between what we personally believe we want to achieve and what we understand the universe wants to achieve. Ultimately these are the same things. However, we rarely feel this until we step into the realm of negotiation where change occurs. This is a realm beyond what we rationally know into the realm of our intuitive sensitivity. Entering into this negotiation is not about giving up our intention but more like letting it go through some alchemic transmutations. These are transmutations out of which our primary self is perpetuated rather than lost. Our primary self comes through in a way that aligns with the primary intent of heaven and earth; in total this means an alignment of the personal with the impersonal. Alignment is a way of being parallel with the universal, side by side as opposed to lost completely, yet paradoxically we sometimes have to get lost to make this possible. The universal intention is within us, manifesting as our personal intent and it is all around us, manifesting in the context given by heaven and earth. This context is always an expression in time and space, the playground for the law of cause and effect to fulfill itself.

Cause and effect means action and reaction, it is a law that governs much of our life. Karam Kriya sets about transforming these patterns of reaction so that instead of repeating them again and again we might be healed and set free. There is a difference between habits that we serve and habits that serve us; in other words, habits that imprison and life structures that are vehicles to carry us through and beyond the game of life. It is known as the difference between karma and dharma. Our habit patterns are set up by many factors ranging from the internal and constitutional to the external and environmental. So, for example, they are partly brought with us into this life with our personality that is reincarnated and partly formed through childhood social education and our reactions to that experience. Further influences can be attributed to subtle forces such as the planets and the vibrations of the calendar numbers of our date of birth, which also have a dynamic impact. When we are young these various structures serve as a means of self-preservation, helping us to survive our environment, while later in life they may be felt as restrictive and inhibiting.

Though there are many diverse and distinct types of action/reaction patterns, which have been classified in various ways by the social and psychological sciences, the basic ingredients of these are consistently the same. Karam Kriya identifies these building blocks of our behavioral patterns and belief systems through reference to the essential properties of numbers. Different combinations of the same ingredients are seen to produce different outcomes. The practice of Karam Kriya is helped by several methods but the principal instrument in every case is language and essentially the language of numbers.

The practice of Karam Kriya cannot be taught systematically nor can it easily be learnt from a book. Living it in the dynamics of human interaction best illuminates the subject, but a book such as this may serve as a reference point from which the reader may begin to apply a more intuitive presence and awareness of Soul. The material in this book can be considered as part of the tools and principles from which to start practicing the negotiating activity of Karam Kriya.

The word "Karam" has two different but associated meanings. The first is in relation to the law of karma, which governs the way our actions return to us and which has an effect on our future capacity to exist in the world. "Karam" is also kindness or mercy, which is the principal quality of the law of karma. The law of returning action is not to punish but rather it is given as an act of kindness to awaken the soul. This gradual awareness of the law of cause and effect makes it possible for us to renegotiate the way we shape our lives.

It is the negotiation that relates to the term "Kriya" and implies the metamorphic action that changes our patterns of reaction. There is an illusory line, like an imaginary glass screen, that separates one person from another. When this line is crossed we enter into the negotiating ground that has transformative and transmutational implications for everyone involved in the interaction and the only safe way to enter this territory is when an attitude of kindness is both felt and given. "Kriya" also means to exhaust, to take the action to its ultimate completion, to finish what has been started. All our patterns were initiated for some basic and primal purpose rooted in our integrity. However, the system of building pattern over pattern creates such a complex construction that we lose the contact with that initial intent.

In the return journey each structure must be brought to its completion so that we are free to conclude other parts of life's pilgrimage.

Karam Kriya is an approach to understanding the influence of the law of karma in our life, reflected in inherited parental attitudes and our reaction to them. Not only must we seek to negotiate the transparency of our history but also immediately consider changes to the structure of our lives, which has been formed by that history. Once we have transparency of our past we can introduce changes in our actions and beliefs so that we may begin to travel the distance that will bring us to our destiny. Karam Kriya is the science and art of using the time and energy before it uses us. It is about changing the shape of our lives in order to create opportunities and to seize them. To change the shape of our understanding and to live in this way is to use the tension of the passing time so that we create possibilities and moments of destiny in which lies our full potential.

We are constantly negotiating change in our lives, deciding what to keep and what to transform. Sometimes we have little choice and change is forced upon us, yet we still try to negotiate the inevitable; perhaps to slow it down or to get something in return for the sacrifice even before we make it. Karam Kriya is a conscious engagement with the negotiating dynamic and is done with a firm gentleness that respects the difficulties we have in making these changes. It is practiced through grace, dignity, and humble courage. It is not about filling the emptiness or a problem we may be experiencing in ourselves or another from the outside, but a way of listening and drawing out a new, positive shape from within the negative tension itself. The parallel point of reference that makes listening complete is numbers. This book has told how numbers are the backbone of all teachings, not just in the appliance of Karam Kriya. Here we have simply acknowledged, the multi-dimensional matrix of primary information that they are. When we learn not just to read but also to walk it then we become conscious of our own nature and the inherent bliss. Numbers are guiding points, steps on a ladder of consciousness, specific dimensional states, the essence of all structural entities, provocateurs of consciousness, and our ultimate spiritual ground. We take them for granted but as they serve us we also serve them. It is a mutual interaction and consciousness of this that leads us to the simple awareness of our full participation in the unity of the cosmos down to the finest detail.

Well, that is it for now. All that remains is to give a final summary of Karam Kriya in action and to wish you well in your exploration of the magic that is our shared essence.

Summary

The ingredients for a Karam Kriya consultation could be described as:

1 The essential magic of a global basis for the common elements of the world and the people in it; numbers provide such foundation.

2 The medicine of a compassionate instinct for the dynamics of any relationship between two people, where everything is assessed, reassessed, bargained, and processed, where exchange takes place and change is possible.

3 Access to and understanding of a scientific diagnostic tool such as the interpretation of the date of birth and the appropriate respect in applying such a tool, which comes from a clear psychological insight into the workings of the ego-mind and its tendency towards repetitive and patterned thinking, as well as the creation of sub-personalities.

4 An informed intuition on the basis of the above three points. This means an educated and inspired trust in the process and an artistic sensitivity to that which is distinctively human, along with the committed readiness to take full responsibility for the consequences.

5 Linguistic capability through which we can hear the presence of the five universal voices in all conversation, coupled with the on-going sacrifice of all that we know and so remaining in the movement of the moment, otherwise described as the perpetual state of learning to learn.

... I teach you today a lesson in communication. First talk apathy, then talk sympathy, then speak truth. Poke, provoke, comfort, elevate. You know what I mean? First your job is to merge with another person. Make him feel that you realize somebody's pain. And then make him feel that his pain or

her pain is not in vain. Then become a beam and then assure the person
you can tame as a team that person's pain.　　　　(Yogi Bhajan)

Now I have not tried to validate this book by reference to academic research, scientific documents, specialized texts, or any other kind of known measure of knowledge that is considered to have a status by which all else may be compared and judged. The fascination of reasoned proof is a phantom, which overrides the reality of our experience and thus becomes an entertainment, which exists for its own sake. In this way it fails to draw our attention to that which pervades in the spaces and gaps of our knowledge, between the lines of these words and in the absence of our seeing.

　　The poem from the Sri Guru Granth Sahib that follows gives some feeling of what it is to go beyond the state of subservience to the five mighty and stubborn forces of time and to enjoy the divine marriage. The personal soul is in the position of the bride while the impersonal soul is the groom.

> *without eyes see*
> *without ears listen*
> *without feet walk*
> *without hands work*
> *without tongue speak*
> *in this way live yet die*
> *Naanak the poet says*
> *understand the divine will*
> *and meet the spouse*

　　　　　　　　　　(Guru Angad, Sri Guru Granth Sahib)

To accomplish this is the beginning of Karam Kriya – a negotiated and transformational interaction with another person.

For up to date information on Karam Kriya training see:
www.karamkriya.co.uk or telephone +44 (0) 20 7272 5811

Appendix

Chapter 33

The trigrams of
the I Ching

The trigrams of the I Ching are symbolic or coded characterizations of hidden messages. The essence of their message is the same message as that of the numbers. In many publications on the I Ching or Feng Shui some kind of correspondence between the trigrams and the numbers is given. This relation between trigrams and numbers, however, is never fully discussed and there is no evidence that the properties inherent in the numbers have been deeply considered. In other words it is not clear why a particular number relates to a particular trigram. To answer this question we need to be familiar with the quality of the number by itself before linking it to any particular system. This chapter presents a clear case for linking the trigrams with the pairs of numbers. It also gives a method of interpreting the numbers in a person's date of birth through the trigrams. The result of this study is to identify the hexagrams that are influencing a person's life and that bear special messages for the person.

If the symbol of the trigram (including also its symbolic name) is not the message itself then it is necessary to decode the symbol to get the numerical, originating essence behind it. A sharp intuition and honest confrontation with the unknown is needed for this inner movement of decodifying symbols in the world. The trigrams are not an essential element in the practice of Karam Kriya and applied numerology but just one of many mediums through which to explore the manifestation of the numbers as well as to apply the insights given through the study of applied numerology. Only some individuals might decide to specialize in this kind of study. Our emphasis here is on the numbers as the principle reference in all cases.

Let's take another look at the distinct time cycles that are represented in the calendar structure and our personal date of birth. We will give a further description of the elements associated with each cycle along with the corresponding base numbers. Then, from this natural approach it will be clear that there are pairs of numbers that belong to each cycle. After identifying the trigrams that symbolize each pair of numbers and their corresponding time cycle we will be able to find the hexagrams that offer a message to us through our date of birth.

Year of birth

The EARTH ELEMENT. As a planet, the earth represents a gift to humanity. It was already here with its fruits before we began to exist. Each of us is born into a given situation with the Physical Body and all its potentialities as the essential gift. Like the egg in which we are conceived, this gift was already present in our mother's mother and her mother and so on infinitely back to a time when there was no time. We cannot know the beginning of the earth's time but we can know our own beginning, both of this lifetime and at the original conception of our soul. The moment when this gift of birth is given is unique to every individual, but the experience of its arising is common to all beings.

This gift can be used or abused. It exists in us as a primal instinctive consciousness that is mainly concerned with survival. The gift is our resource of practical and spiritual common sense and is something that we can usually rely upon for our survival or self-perpetuation. Like the earth, our gift has an abundance of provision when rightly cultivated. Disrespect or misuse, on the other hand, can produce either a desert or excessive overgrowth, both rendering the gift useless or even self-destructive. As a substance, earth is the dust from which all things are made and the final quality to which all things return. To reduce something to dust is to violate it but the dust itself can be reduced no further – it is beyond violation and, therefore, sacred by its own nature rather than because it was dictated by someone of authority.

The base numbers 1 and 9 are related to the year of birth, the earth element, and the sense of smell. They are the first and last numbers and so relate to the quality with which we start and finish things in life, or more deeply the qualities that have to be present before we can start and complete. The number 1 suggests a journey, but still in its potential stage, while the 9 is the completion of the journey; just as one seed completes its multiplication in the production of many seeds. Number 1 is the essential number for all other numbers to exist and, therefore, there is a quality of essence and essential substance in relation to 1 and 9; they are the numbers of generation and regeneration.

The trigrams of KAN and KUN symbolize further qualities of our life experience through the yearly cycle. Kan, related to the number 1, bears the message of primal life, impulsive and provocative. It is also suggestive of the narrow passage through which we enter into life and the valley path that brings life into sharp focus. Other issues are gravity, contraction, and frustration. Kun, related to the number 9, is a trigram representing the dust (as essence) and the multiplicity of life. It has a quality like the collective consciousness that can absorb all things or like an endless string with all events and beings strung on as beads on the universal necklace. This is an impersonal trigram indicating the continuation of life beyond that of a personal individual and the drive to perfection, though without pressure, through the dispersion of individual life and endless multiplying.

The day of birth

The WATER ELEMENT is indicative of the rivers of life, which have been traveling through the ages. Even though it is a feminine element it carries the sperm of the father winding its way down or up stream to find the egg of earth to which it will bring power and moisture. The water element bears the essence of our past experiences into the present moment. When we can learn the lessons of history we can be free of our past. Through the process of evaporating and distilling our past we draw out the purified essence. It is by this essence of our experience, which is unique to each individual, that we know we exist. The water element will, therefore, indicate an aspect of the process of spiritual purification.

Water is also related to the emotions of sorrow, loss, and yearning. Our emotional undercurrents will, therefore, influence our experience of time flowing by. When this flow is interrupted, stagnation is the result. When the flow is too strong, when the future confronts the past quicker than we can cope with, there will be an emotional overflow. The balanced experience of passing time allows us to exist more fully in the dynamic, ever-present moment of now. Water is a conductor and so acts as a link between two worlds – for example, the mountain source and the ocean or the soul in finite existence to its infinite possibility. Water can divide and be divided and so empowers our sense of discrimination and discernment.

Water is also a flow of energy and relates to our sense of vitality and our sense of movement or flow. It will be the disruption of movement rather than its continuity that will be brought to our attention. The sense of power and vitality is brought about by virtue of the flow of fluids; prana and chi are often described in ways similar to the properties of water. It is experienced in our sexuality, our deep hunger, and our endless thirst that brings our dreams to life.

2 and 8 are the base numbers for the day of the month in which you are born. The duality of number 2 gives rise to all our hungers, sorrows, and passions. To exist in a process of time is to be in the middle of all the tensions resulting from multiple polarizations. This tension is usually approached as a problem to solve but could also be considered as a charge of energy available for us to use. The number 2 is not substantial in itself but it is the necessary energetic quality that both separates and also holds two things or people in relationship. There is, otherwise, just one individual and another individual; to think of two individuals is to hold these people in a certain kind of separation yet togetherness. Number 8 expresses the infinite nature of our polarity when given in basic terms of our existence in a particular time and space in the immeasurable tension of a relationship to eternal time and unlimited space. 8 is also the abundance of energy which is created in this infinite tension and which also holds it together. Issues include the inevitable tension relating to death, as well as concerns about power and authority.

The trigrams CHIEN and CHEN relate to the numbers 2 and 8 and symbolize some aspects of the daily cycle. Chien is a trigram of force and pure energy. It is old, as is the passing of time without any content. It is full but full of nothing other than itself. This is a kind of emptiness also and presents many problems in life. The emptiness of time is like a big black hole into which many things disappear. In this respect it is an expression of the number 2. Therefore, this trigram is often considered as presenting obstacles but it should be clear that the obstacle is time itself prior to the secondary obstacles with which we fill the empty time. Chen (also know as Ren or Jen) is another expression of energy and vitality but more in relation to the imagination. It does, though, also indicate a kind of waterfall, fountain, or life-spring out of which pour wealth and health. It is the energy that waters the seed in the earth so that it can begin to realize itself. This trigram is also suggestive of a united duality, like the number 8, linking two worlds and bringing a flow to and from each other.

The month of birth

The FIRE ELEMENT is the flame of self-identity. It is the self, which shines by burning up some matter and consuming the air. This is not the essential self but the visual self, the self that burns up the substance reducing it to ashes and earth, and also the heat which gives form and shape. This is the element that gives you a personality and a character to portray in life. Fire is the heat of the moment that can act as an activator, a catalyst for action. It compels movement and presents coded signals about our motivations and purpose in life. Since action produces reaction it is by the actions catalyzed by the fire element that we create or resolve our karma.

The base numbers for the month of birth are 3 and 7. The number 3 governs our behavior while the number 7 governs the beliefs behind our behavior. Both our actions and our thoughts tend to fall into habitual structures and patterns that then get reinforced by repetition. This repetition creates an illusion of permanence and a magnetic field (self-image) by which we can attract attention to ourselves. 3 is the created vehicle while 7 is the driver who has the controls (but don't forget it is the passenger that must be the master).

Symbolizing some aspects of the monthly cycle are the trigrams GEN (ken) and TUI (dui) which belong with the numbers 3 and 7.

Gen is the trigram that represents the pragmatic, problem-solving approach to life. It is about helpfulness and tends to indicate expansion into three-dimensional space, something we only do if we feel life is enjoyable. It also suggests reliability, which may only mean predictability and repetitiveness. There is protectiveness in the regularity of the static patterns governed by this trigram. However, such habitualness can also result in resistance to change. All these are qualities of the number 3. The trigram of Tui is a bit like the control tower but does not indicate the real master, rather the deputy or lookout, who keeps watch. The guardianship of this trigram may manifest as imprisonment and punishment or it may be protective, supporting, and encouraging. There may be the manipulation and control of a prison watchtower or simply a lighthouse helping us through the fog and mist. The tower is usually decorated to indicate status – this decoration will be colorful, tempting, and seductive and many people compete to get into the tower. Other issues include mental gain, relative security, acquisition/accumulation (of knowledge and control), temptation, and fascination. These are all qualities of the number 7.

The full year of birth

The AIR/METAL ELEMENT. Air is associated with the number 4 while metal is associated with the number 6 as the sword which cuts through the air or the stormy wind that can cut to the bone. The air element is like our future, hard to grasp; it slips through our fingers, past before we know it. The breath we breathe now is nothing more than our destiny, which was written into the earth since before the beginning of time. It is the aspirations and inspirations of our life, which we are forever trying to realize. It is our ability to turn a thought into a living experience and to make this moment a dynamic movement of forever going beyond. The air element also indicates the relationship with our children or the nature of our projects in life, the arrows we fire into the future, our loves and our fears, and our relationship to the community. Like the sense of touch the wind can be either penetrating or embracing in its approach to us.

4 and 6 are the base numbers for the total year of birth. Inner feel-

ings of intuition and sensitivity are linked to the number 4, which is also a number of choice and being at the crossroads of life. Being able to trust our sensations is a result of developing the quality of number 4; prior to that we find this number expressed as a kind of numbness or paralysis. 6 is a number of fear or faith and indicates our capacity to meet the unexpected in life. Future orientation, sense of destiny, and the fighting spirit are also given by the number 6.

The relevant trigrams are SUN and LI, which correspond to the numbers 4 and 6. In the oriental tradition these express the cycle of dynasties while in the modern western calendar they symbolize the century cycle. Sun is the trigram of injury and wounding and, therefore, our capacity to feel pain. It requires gentleness and so knows how to give gentleness. This trigram represents the soft, inviting and enveloping aspect of the wind; however, it can be so faint as to be quite elusive. The wind is never very predictable but its presence makes all the difference and so it is considered as a decisive influence; this is the number 4. The trigram Li is the wind that blows behind the sword of justice and gives that sword the decisive swing. It could be the luck of the wind that tips the scales to one side or another, bringing grace to one and crisis to another. It is a mysterious trigram bringing the sharp touch of the unknown from which some feel fear and others experience pleasant surprise. Both ways it is stunning and shocking and only an intuitive awareness can meet it with harmony. It is the number 6 that catches us as if by ambush and confronts us to respond immediately without the delayed reaction of the interfering mind.

The total date of birth

The ETHER/WOOD ELEMENT exists within each of the other four elements and, therefore, also contains them. It is the total number of the date of birth, day, month, and full year.

Ether is both a background shade as well as a tinted veil. It is because of ether that the other elements are seen as they are. More accurately it is the sound that lies beyond all sound, the peak of the pyramid from which creation emerges and returns. Ether indicates the road upon which we are always in the middle, never sure if we are being pulled or pushed. Like the earth, it is another part of our ever-present experience that we do not notice because it has always been there like a continuous humming vibration.

5 and 10 are the base numbers relating to the total date of birth and represent the holistic and dynamic harmony which is regulated by 5 and held as one whole by 10, the unity which is more than all the parts together. All the trigrams of the I Ching have a relation to the number 5, which is in the center and the number 10, which is the periphery.

Summary

Last two digits of the year
Area of talent

· Element - Earth
roots, standpoint, grounding, basicness, womb and tomb, beginning and end, life/death/rebirth, being at home, homelessness, the journey and the traveler.
· Senses - smell, intent, direction
· Base numbers - 1/9
Start and finish, first and last, the essential substance, one seed to many seeds.
· Trigrams - Kan, Kun

The whole date of birth

· Element - Ether/wood
movement, growth, change, flexible - stiff, co-ordination or lack of, relationship
· Sense - sound, wholeness, balance
· Base numbers - 5/10
In the center is the area of communication
· Trigrams - all

The day of the month
Area of life and death

· Element - Water
medium of life, conductor of information - a mea to travel, flow, water needs containing to tal shape, drying up - flooding, calls to life the w impulse - waters the seed.
· Senses - taste, instinct, discrimination
· Base numbers - 2/8
Vitality, life-thread. The bonding forc
· Trigrams - Chien, Chen

The month of birth
Area of karma

· Element - Fire
warmth, protective, light rays, colorful, catalyst, lively, active, excitable, joy, success.
· Senses - vision, reason
· Base numbers - 3/7
The chain of action and reaction in the realms of thought patterns and habitual behavior. The structure.
· Trigrams - Gen, Tui

The full year of birth
Area of opportunity

· Element - Air/metal
conductive - conducive to communication, building bridges - possibilities, air can't be grasped - unknown, sensitive medium - touc - pain.
· Senses - touch, intuition
· Base numbers - 4/6
injury, crisis, surprise. The presence.
· Trigrams - Sun, Li

The trigrams that have been identified with each of the time cycles are the impersonal contribution; they are the same for all people. The personal trigrams will be identified through the numbers of our date of birth. The impersonal is above the personal. Therefore, the hexagram is made by placing the impersonal trigram in the upper part of the hexagram and the personal trigram in the lower part of the hexagram.

Example

Keeping in mind the following connection with the numbers and their trigrams we can easily see if there are some specific messages to be appreciated.

1	2	3	4	6	7	8	9
Kan	Chien	Gen	Sun	Li	Tui	Chen	Kun

For someone born on the 14th January 1957 the number arrangement and corresponding hexagrams will be made of the trigrams as follows:

	Year		Day	Month		Full year		Total
	57 = 3		14 = 5	1		1957 = 4		28 = 10
Impersonal	Kan	Kun	Chen	Gen	Tui	Sun	Li	
Personal	Gen	Gen	Chien	Kan	Kan	Sun	Sun	

Since the day of birth for this person is a number 5 (from 14) then there is a relation to all the trigrams. Alternatively we could reflect on the two trigrams made by the interaction of Ren and Chien.

ALTERNATIVE PRESENTATION OF THE SAME EXAMPLE:

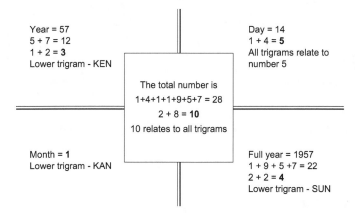

Year = 57
5 + 7 = 12
1 + 2 = **3**
Lower trigram - KEN

Day = 14
1 + 4 = **5**
All trigrams relate to number 5

The total number is
1+4+1+1+9+5+7 = 28
2 + 8 = **10**
10 relates to all trigrams

Month = **1**
Lower trigram - KAN

Full year = 1957
1 + 9 + 5 +7 = 22
2 + 2 = **4**
Lower trigram - SUN

The next step is to place these trigrams below the trigrams that correspond to the base numbers in each quarter.

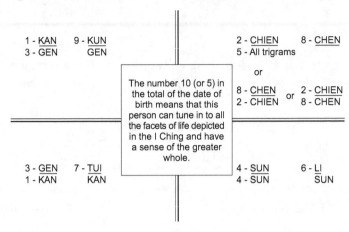

The result is six particular hexagrams, two in each of the first, third, and fourth quarters, whilst the second quarter (the daily cycle) will have a more general influence of sixteen hexagrams, eight with Chien as the upper trigram and eight with Ren as the upper trigram. Alternatively, the second quarter can be interpreted through the hexagram that combines Ren as the upper trigram with Chien as the lower trigram. For further confirmation the six important hexagrams giving symbolic representation of key concerns for this person's life are named below.

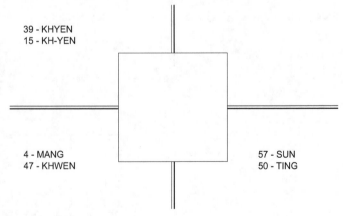

The hexagrams of the first quarter, the annual cycle, will especially relate to the inner ground of a person's life as well as to the ground upon which their home is built. The hexagrams of the second quarter, the daily cycle, will relate to the organic level of a person's inner life and environment, which includes the energy flow. In the third quarter, the monthly cycle, the hexagrams indicate the person's relationship to inner form and structure as well as the culture of their environment and the way it is decorated. The fourth quarter, the full year of birth, holds the hexagrams that relate to a person's opportunities and human possibilities.

Further interpretation of the date of birth and the relevant hexagrams can be done by referring back to earlier sections of this book, complemented by your own intuitive relationship to the person in question. Remember also that any interpretation is most valid in the moment it is offered and that nothing is static and, therefore, the interpretation may change in accordance with the individual's development.

Note: Why do we add the numbers?
There are four basic mathematical operations, namely:
$\times \div + -$
The operation that is most relevant to a diagnostic approach is the one that will give the overall general characteristics. This means the simple sum total of what is given and it is achieved by the operation of addition.

Chapter 34

Going fishing

Here is a miscellaneous example of studying numbers in life rather than studying them separately from life – the example of the fish and the ocean. Notice how the study of particular examples helps to suggest further qualities for each number as well as illuminating the relation that makes the pairs of numbers.

1 The basic existence of the fish: its soul, originating, foundation, basis, a unit, a seed, potential, latent impulse, alone, isolated, unique, still, rigid, stable, concentrated, compact, single point, location, the point.	**9** The fisherman and the ocean bed: the master, the end, enduring, completion, arrival home, perfection, peace, rest, calm, the many, scattering, dispersing, subtle.
2 The vital life force of the fish: living in division, diversity, separation, gap, emptiness, hunger, tension, a pair, bonding, attachment, movement (from 1), time, fluidity, symmetry.	**8** The ocean: mother as medium for life and death, water, reflection, infinite, eternal return, infinite time, healing, cleansing.
3 The type of fish: triangles, closed shapes, patterns, territory, including/excluding, vice, habits, structures, support, trinity of the created universe, 3 primary colors, vision, searching, eyes as third leg.	**7** The bait: seduction, trap, kidnap, imprisoned, 7 colors, chakras, inner vision, fantasy, inner law and structure, knowledge, attainment, crown, administration.
4 The awareness of the fish: flexibility of structure, beyond the structure, double duality, crossroads, choice, consciousness, freedom, square and circle.	**6** The hook: the cube, dice, luck, fortune, grace, the moment, surprise, ambush, crisis, the unknown, fear and destiny.
5 The meeting: half-way, center, balance, threshold, relationship, communicative link, bridge, turning point, reversal, transformation, sacrifice, nature - 5 elements and senses	**10** The one whole, the whole one: wholeness, totality, all-encompassing, gathering, circumference, apartness, more than the whole, transcendent unity, extra, extra-ordinary, standing out, outstanding.

Chapter 35

The heart organ

It has been stated that there is a relation between the numbers and the organs of the body. Therefore, we can take several approaches to go into this a little deeper. Here is the example of exploring the heart organ in relation to the date of birth.

First we can realize that the heart itself is directly linked to the number 7. Then it follows that if there is a number 7 in the date of birth anywhere there will be some numerological influence.

Normally the daily cycle is an expression of the numbers 2 and 8 and governs the kidneys and the bladder. However, if a person is born on the 7th, 16th, or 25th day of any month then the impact of the high or low energy of the kidneys or infections of the bladder will have a stronger influence over the heart energy than might normally be the case. Emotions of sorrow and depression will greatly weaken the heart while compassion and innocence will bring strength and calm. There will be a lighter impact if a person is born on the 17th or 27th day of any month.

The yearly cycle (the last two digits of the year) express the numbers 1 and 9 as well as governing the spleen and stomach. The blood quality produced by the spleen, in conjunction with the bones and lymph glands, gives the directive impulse to the heart. Impatience, frustration, and restlessness will not be helpful, while tolerance and steady patience will keep the heart in regularity. This relation will be more important for a person born in the years 07, 16, 25, 34, 43, 52, 61, 70, 88, and 97 of any century. A lesser, but still significant influence, can be considered for the years 17, 27, 37, and so on.

The full year, including the century cycle, expresses the numbers

4 and 6 and relates to the large intestine and lungs. Whenever the addition of all the numbers of the full year add up to 7 we should consider the relation between the lungs and the heart as being of particular importance. Feelings like fear and grief will have a stronger impact while faith will support the heart.

The monthly cycle expresses the numbers 3 and 7 and affects the small intestines and heart. Normally it would mean that someone born in the seventh month will have a strong heart. However, it also means that the person will be more directly influencing their heart when they allow themselves to be excessively angry. And, of course, laughter will be of much benefit.

The total date of birth expresses the numbers 5 and 10 and is in relation to the liver and gall bladder. So if the addition of all the numbers of a person's date of birth gives a number 7 then we should explore the relation between the liver and the heart. We will find that the heart may be over-reactive to slight imbalances in the person's active and mental life. Regularity and routine will be helpful as well as the frequent use of affirmations and right thinking.

Then, given that the monthly cycle is closely linked to the number 7, we can also explore possible qualities of the heart by looking at the month in the date of birth. These will also be qualities associated with the person's Aura since that is the seventh Spiritual Body.

Month 1, January – a contraction in the heart so you may need to increase the heart rate on a regular basis because it could be too slow.

Month 2, February – there may be a weakness, or the feeling of the heart missing beats.

Month 3, March – an important connection of the heart to the navel rhythm. Feeling like a victim will constrict the heart. Laughter will release it.

Month 4, April – a broken heart that can affect your physical heart. You could be too conscious of your heartbeat.

Month 5, May – nervous energy will have an impact on the heart. Balance and circulation are very important because circulation connects through all the joints, which correspond to number 5.

Month 6, June – trauma-related fear, which will increase the heart rate as will an excessive sense of responsibility.

Month 7, July – very strong but could be too controling and this can be seen in people who are very controling in business. If in excess it could cause a heart attack.

Month 8, August – a lot of power and energy in the heart but excess could overwork it.

Month 9, September – a dispersion rather than a contraction as in its corresponding number, number 1. You would benefit by working the heart through pressure and learning to slow down the heart rate in order to find enough energy to contract and pump the heart. If the blood is not circulating well you may feel cold.

Month 10, October – all or nothing. Everything is in the heart and if that does not work nothing else will.

Month 11, November – the strange concept of a twin heart might make sense to someone born in the eleventh month. Otherwise the 11 will reduce to a number 2 and the qualities of this number will influence the heart.

Month 12, December – in most cases the 12 is expressed through the qualities of the 3 but with a greater intensity and earnestness.

These are just examples and not hard and fast rules. They are the kind of things to look at when you are listening to someone's story and you want to know the condition of the heart. Then you could develop this same approach to investigate any other organ.

Chapter 36

The family

Each of the ten Bodies is like a member of your family and there are five main types of relationships in life.

The family circle

The entire family of relationships that come to assemble in the person are indicated in the diagram below.

Ego-hero King	7	Mother Queen	8	Father Magician	9
Bride Princess	4	Teacher Student	5 10	Bridegroom Prince or Warrior	6
Infant Baby	1	Daughter	2	Son Golden boy	3

Whichever numbers are present in the person's date of birth it may suggest a stronger influence of the corresponding type of relationship. If any number is absent then there may be a need to invest more in developing this role or the relationship to that role, in themselves and in life, in order to improve their experience of the relevant level of their life.

You may wish to look back to the earlier chapters describing the organs and the rooms of the house. Comparisons can be made between these and types of personalities associated with each number. As indicated in the description of each relationship the different aspects of the date of birth will also indicate something about the person's experience of that relationship.

The date of birth also contains information about the nature of the key relationships of your life. There are four basic relationships in life through which we experience and develop the four levels and our own four identities. The fifth relationship is the synthesis of these four. The discussion of these relationships below is brief and only introduces the topic rather than giving a full account. Some generalizations are made and the reader must consider this in identifying these aspects in the specific details of an individual's life. For example, a mother may play the role of father for the developing child and hence the concerns that belong in the discussion that are associated with the relation to the father will be found to manifest in the relation to the mother. In the end it may be true to say that every kind of relationship contains the whole range of possible relationships and, therefore, also the whole range of issues and concerns. It has been found, however, that it helps to identify specific tendencies in specific relationships while at the same time maintaining a whole perspective.

The first relationship in life is to the mother. Being in relationship to the feminine quality will awaken in us the reciprocal qualities of masculinity (and even fatherhood). The first experience, however, is of being a baby and the concerns are survival, nourishment, and validation. By imitation we learn some feminine qualities through the relation to the mother. This relationship will be mostly influenced by the number of the last two digits of the year of birth.

Our second relationship in life is to the father. Being in relation to the masculine we might consider the reciprocating feminine qualities that this awakens in us, in particular the energy of the daughter and the mother. The concerns include the father's absence and issues such as use and abuse of power and authority. By imitation we will learn some masculine qualities through the relation to the father. This relationship is mostly influenced by the qualities of the number that is the day of birth.

Then there is the third relationship, which is to our peers, siblings, or contemporaries, who may come in the form of brothers and sisters, cousins, or as friends in the playground of life. It is in this relationship that the ego is most active. Issues relate to being a friend, rescuing and giving advice, sharing knowledge and know-how, likes and dislikes, competition and so on. This relationship is largely influenced by the qualities of the number that is the month of birth.

The fourth relationship is when we become adults (not parents), in relationship to other children and other human beings as children of the world that is as yet still becoming, and in fact goes on becoming (which is not the same as growing). Children challenge us with matters of truth, trust, and spontaneity as well as inviting us into a less conditioned quality of love. Through this quality of love we develop the game of courtship in preparation for the learning relationship which takes place between lovers. (Note: In some ancient traditions marriages were arranged for people when they were still children.) It is the number of the full year of birth that will have the most influence over this relationship.

The fifth relationship is the learning relationship. You may wonder why the relationship with children is placed before that with a partner. It is suggested that the relationship to the partner is the amalgamation of these four relationships and that we can never be just the partner of another person. We are the partner only through these expressions of mother and infant, father and daughter, supportive friends or egos in competition or responsible adult to child, and finally as a courting couple. The quality that holds these in dynamic balance is the mutual learning conversation. It is when our attention is drawn to the mutual studentship that no one type of relationship can dominate and we move toward something that is greater than the parts. This relationship is expressed through the qualities of the number that results as the total date of birth.

Glossary

Akaal. Undying.

Amrit. Spiritual nectar; the ceremony where vows are taken on becoming a Sikh.

Arcline. The sixth of the ten Spiritual Bodies, the halo of presence manifest in the world as intuition.

Aura. The seventh of the ten Spiritual Bodies, the wider magnetic field for projecting ourselves into space.

Chakra. Energy centers of consciousness located along the spinal cord. Chakra means "wheel" in Sanskrit – there are seven of these spinning vortexes that vibrate at different frequencies, each with a different area of concern.

Destiny. The path you choose in life. It is an attitude you have come to embody and touch the world with.

Dharma. The spiritual path of right understanding, of righteous living. It is an action without reaction or karma.

Duality. Experienced as the basic problem of life, the gap is the infinite abyss of our longing and hunger but also the depth of the relation between the two.

Fate. If you do not choose conscious consciousness, then fate will decide for you.

Golden Temple. Founded by Guru Ram Das, the fourth Sikh Guru, the Harimandir Sahib in Amritsar, India is the most revered and sacred temple in the world.

Gunas. Qualities of energetic states that make up the fundamental forces in nature – Satva, the state of purity or innocence, Raja, the state of dynamic activity, and Tama, the state of inertia.

Gurbani. Word of the Guru, particularly related to the Siri Guru Granth Sahib.

Guru. One who transforms darkness into light (Gu – darkness, Ru – light).

Karam. Meaning "kindness" or "mercy," it governs the way our actions return to us, the action to end all actions, the last judgment.

Karma. The cosmic law of cause and effect, action and reaction.

Khalsa. Literally means "pure one" or "unalloyed."

Kriya. To take the action to its ultimate completion, to finish what has been started and thereby establish a dharmic structure.

Kundalini. Meaning "the curl of the lock of the hair of the beloved," an image that describes the flow of creative energy within us all, waiting to be uncoiled so that we may experience our highest consciousness.

Mantra. "Man" means mind, "tra" means to vibrate and "tara" means to cross – the crossing into consciousness. A mantra is usually made up of a few words, which are constantly repeated or chanted, a process known as Jap.

Maya. Meaning "that which can be measured," what we perceive. It is the outside of our being and although it can bring us happiness, it is only for a while, unlike the eternal flame within us that never dies. Maya is the Mother Nature that feeds us, fattens us, and ultimately eats us unless we can awaken to our spiritual identity; therefore, she is in some way illusion.

Negative Mind. The second of the ten Spiritual Bodies, an organic or vegetative vital system that is in a state of need. It is the sub-conscious in the body that absorbs and stores our patterns and blocks.

Neutral Mind. The fourth of the ten Spiritual Bodies, the possibility of conscious choice in relation to the world.

Physical Body. The fifth of the ten Spiritual Bodies, not only the physical body itself but especially the inter-related expanse of the nervous system.

Positive Mind. The third of the ten Spiritual Bodies, the creature-like body armor that works to fill the gap of the second Body, the Negative Mind.

Prana. The infinite vital force that runs through the meridian channels of the body. Also known as chi and manifesting in the material form as libido or sexual energy.

Pranic Body. The eighth of the ten Spiritual Bodies, the infinite fuél supply sustaining our temporary projection.

Radiant Body. The tenth of the ten Spiritual Bodies. When the whole ecology of our being is in dynamic harmony then not only are we transparently alight but also we become a self-sustaining source of light and thus realize our immortality.

Royal Road. The golden thread that extends from the crown of the head, the seventh chakra, and links us to the Divine. The silver thread is the journey up the spine.

Sat Nam. True Name – in the name of truth.

Siri Guru Granth Sahib. The words and teachings of the ten Gurus combined as the eleventh Guru, the Word itself. These pages of poetry, written as Naad (the sound current, an expression of the Absolute) can raise consciousness and is worshiped as the living Guru of the Sikhs.

Sohung. I am God, God is me.

Soul Body. The first of the ten Spiritual Bodies, the innermost essence of being, a passenger through time and space.

Subtle Body. The ninth of the ten Spiritual Bodies, the home of the soul's emanations.

Tenth Gate. The inner portal to the Divine, said by some to be located at the top of the head (seventh chakra) and by others in the heart.

Third Eye. The center of intuition and insight, the sixth chakra is located between the eyebrows. It is associated with the pituitary gland, the master gland of the endocrine system, and one of the main focal points in meditation.

Turya State. State of reality. The fourth state beyond the three gunas.

Wahe Guru. Wow! God is ecstasy.

Yin Yang. Oppositional forces, the two polarities of the feminine and masculine.